AMERICAN TORTURE

AMERICAN TORTURE

From the Cold War to Abu Ghraib and Beyond

MICHAEL OTTERMAN

Pluto  Press

LONDON • ANN ARBOR, MI

First published 2007 by Melbourne University Press.

This edition first published 2007 by Pluto Press
345 Archway Road, London N6 5AA
and 839 Greene Street, Ann Arbor, MI 48106

www.plutobooks.com

This edition is not for sale in Australia, New Zealand or PNG

British Library Cataloguing in Publication Data
A catalogue record for this book is available from the British Library

Hardback
ISBN-13 978 0 7453 2671 9
ISBN-10 0 7453 2671 4

Paperback
ISBN-13 978 0 7453 2670 2
ISBN-10 0 7453 2670 6

Library of Congress Cataloging in Publication Data applied for

10 9 8 7 6 5 4 3 2 1

Design and typography © Melbourne University Publishing Ltd 2007
Typeset in Bembo 11.75/14 pt by Midland Typesetters, Australia
Printed and bound in the United States of America

For my parents

CONTENTS

LIST OF ACRONYMS

ABC	Australian Broadcasting Company
ACLU	American Civil Liberties Union
APA	American Psychological Association
ASIO	Australian Security and Intelligence Organisation
BSCT	Behavioral Science Consultation Team
CAT	UN Convention Against Torture and Other Cruel, Inhuman or Degrading Treatment or Punishment
CDRB	Canadian Defence Research Board
CI	counterintelligence
CIA	Central Intelligence Agency
CID	Criminal Investigation Division
CITF	Criminal Investigation Task Force
CT	counter-terror
CTC	Counterterrorism Center
DDD	debility, dependency and dread
DHA	Defence Housing Authority
DHS	Defense Human Intelligence Service
DIA	Defense Intelligence Agency
DOD	Department of Defense
DOJ	Department of Justice
EPW	Enemy Prisoner of War
FBI	Federal Bureau of Investigation
FM	Field Manual
FOIA	Freedom of Information Act

GPC	Geneva Convention relative to the Protection of Civilian Persons in Time of War
GPW	Geneva Convention relative to the Treatment of Prisoners of War
GVN	government of Vietnam
ICC	International Criminal Court
ICE	Interrogation Control Element
ICRC	International Committee of the Red Cross
INDUMIL	Industrias Militares
IPA	International Police Academy
ITT	International Telephone and Telegraph Company
IVS	International Voluntary Services
JIG	Joint Interrogation Group
JTF GTMO	Joint Task Force Guantánamo
KLA	Kosovo Liberation Army
KGB	Commmittee for State Security
KSM	Khalid Sheikh Mohammed
LEA	law enforcement agencies
LET	Lashkar e Tayyiba
LSD	lysergic acid diethylamide
LTC	Lieutenant Colonel
MCA	Military Commissions Act of 2006
MI	military intelligence
MP	military police
MRE	Meals Ready to Eat
MTT	Mobile Training Team
NIC	National Interrogation Center
NKVD	People's Commissariat for Internal Affairs
NSC	National Security Council
OLC	Office of Legal Counsel
OPS	Office of Public Safety
PIC	Provincial Interrogation Center
PRU	Provincial Reconnaissance Unit
PUC	Person Under Control
R2I	Resistance to Interrogation
RTL	Resistance Training Laboratory
SAP	Special Access Program
SEAL	US Navy Sea, Air, Land Special Forces
SERE	Survival, Evasion, Resistance and Escape

SOA	School of the Americas
SOP	Standard Operating Procedures
THC	tetrahydrocannabinol
TSD	Technical Services Division
TVPA	Torture Victim Protection Act of 1991
UCMJ	Uniform Code of Military Justice
USAID	US Agency for International Development
USC	US Code
VBI	Vietnamese Bureau of Investigations
VC	Vietcong
VCI	Vietcong civilian infrastructure
WCA	War Crimes Act of 1996

IN THEIR OWN WORDS

Mamdouh Habib is a broken man. As he describes in detail how his clothes were cut from his body, a forced enema administered, and an adult-sized nappy roughly taped to his emaciated frame, he begins to pick away at his right hand. His wife Maha looks at me. She is embarrassed. 'Stop', she tells her husband, as she reaches over and places her small hands atop his. As Habib continues speaking I look down at his right hand. Along the fleshy mound of tissue between the thumb and forefinger there are deep scars etched into the skin. The scars, some still flecked with scabs and dry white skin, follow the contour of his hand along the underside of his forearm. 'He can't help it', Maha pleads. 'He can't stop.'

Habib is Australian, but was born in the Egyptian port city of Alexandria in 1955. After serving two years in the military, Habib left Egypt when he turned eighteen. For a time he worked in Jordan, Lebanon, Iraq, Syria and Tunisia, taking jobs as a waiter, as a deliveryman, or any other work that came his way. In his late twenties, he moved to Europe, and settled for a time in Italy where he toured the country with a circus. Habib trained elephants and horses—he proudly showed me a worn ID card featuring the words 'Horse Training Licence' in black cursive script. 'That's me', he says, referring to the tanned young man pictured on the card in a dark leather coat with dark intense eyes and cascading jet-black hair. Thirty years later, Habib today doesn't look all that different. He wears his hair now in a ponytail and has grown a thin moustache that wraps tightly along his upper lip. His piercing glare remains.

In 1982, he moved to Sydney and married Maha, who had spent her childhood in Lebanon before immigrating to Australia with her parents. Habib and his wife met through family—her sister was married to his brother. Together they raised four children and lived in Sydney's predominantly Muslim south-west. He opened a string of businesses, including a cleaning service, a security company and a café called the Alexandria Family Restaurant.

Over the years, he grew more religious and more sympathetic to Muslim causes around the world. While visiting his sister in New York City, he attended the 1991 trial of El Sayyid Nosair, a man charged with the murder of fundamentalist Rabbi Meir Kahane. 'We went to see how the law works in the US', he said. 'To make sure he had [a] fair trial.' Outside the courthouse, Habib bumped into two friends from Egypt he had grown up with. The men, Ibrahim El-Gabrowny and Mahmud Abouhalima, were raising money for Nosair's legal fund and insisted that he help the cause. Habib agreed. He said he raised about A$400 in Sydney when he returned, and forwarded it to his friends. The fundraising raised the suspicions of ASIO, the Australian Security and Intelligence Organisation. The agency wanted to have an insider in Sydney's Muslim community and was curious about Habib's ties to Nosair. 'They wanted me to work for them', he said. 'I said I'm not interested.'

ASIO's interest in Habib was renewed in 1993 after the World Trade Center bombing in New York. Investigators linked blind Egyptian spiritual leader Sheikh Omar Abdel-Rahman and Habib's two friends to the bombing. From Sydney, Habib again took up their cause, and led a rally in Bankstown to raise funds for the sheikh. 'A magazine article said no one was helping him', he said, adding that the sheikh was a diabetic and the money was for his medicine. In 1995, El-Gabrowny, Abouhalima and Rahman, among others, were convicted of 'seditious conspiracy' to bomb various New York City landmarks. Referring to Rahman, Habib said: 'I can't say he was guilty or not—I was standing up for his human rights.'

The 1993 Rahman rally was a bust. 'More ASIO was there than protesters', said Habib. After the failed event, ASIO stepped up its efforts to recruit Habib. 'They would come to the house, leave their business cards', said Maha. They offered to bring Habib's parents from Egypt to Australia, and promised to send him on trips around the world. He still refused. Other members of the Muslim community were aware of ASIO's repeated contact with Habib and grew suspicious. He was labelled an ASIO informant by some and was ostracised by many of his friends. In the late 1990s, his cleaning business began to fail. A lucrative three-year contract with the Defence Housing Authority (DHA) was suspiciously cancelled, a move in which Habib believes ASIO had a hand. After Habib placed several angry phonecalls to the housing authority, the DHA obtained an Apprehended Violence Order against Habib and his wife. Habib was not legally permitted to enter any DHA property anywhere in New South Wales. His business soon went bankrupt.

At this point, he said, he decided to move his family from Australia. Beginning in 2000, Habib started to search for new opportunities overseas. On 29 July 2001, he left Sydney with a ticket to Pakistan. 'I wanted to see the situation', he said. 'And to find out about religious schools for the kids.' Habib said he was in Pakistan on 11 September 2001. When he found out what happened in New York, he immediately rang his wife. He was shocked by what he saw on television and wanted to touch base with his family. 'Did you see what happened?' he asked. 'No', Maha replied drowsily. It was 11.30 p.m. in Sydney at the time. 'I'm going to bed, let's talk about it later', she said. Before they next spoke, Habib's Sydney home had been raided by ASIO. They took passports, laptops, and mobile phones from the house. Habib told his wife not to worry because there was nothing to hide. The day before he was scheduled to leave Pakistan, he called home again but got the answering machine. 'See you soon', he said. Habib did not see Maha for more than three years.

———

Apart from a love of horses and an Australian passport, David Hicks has little in common with Mamdouh Habib. Born and raised in Adelaide, he held a string of menial jobs in the Northern Territory and rural South Australia before deciding at age twenty-three to seek adventure outside Australia. He said goodbye to his two young children from an earlier broken relationship and took a job training horses in Japan. The job lasted only three months and Hicks returned to Adelaide. He was determined to travel again. Hicks described this early transformation in an interview with the Australian Federal Police:

Well, I realised that life was more than just living the way I was, which was pretty boring, so I wanted to travel. So I looked at the atlas and had a look at the world, basically, and I liked the idea of the Himalayas … You've got, like, Kashmir, Afghanistan. If you can get there, it's like a great big adventure and stuff like this … Like being a horse rider. I was determined I'd ride a horse, basically like the old Silk Route sort of thing.

As Hicks readied for his next adventure, a new idea came his way. According to Hicks:

At that time Kosovo was dominating the media and after watching that I just had something inside that said I had to go and do that, like a spur of the moment sort of thing. I was watching the briefings. I found out there was one group and they were training in northern Albania. They were going into Kosovo and I realised that maybe, at a wild guess, I could go there and try it and I did it. To me that was doing the impossible … I knew the Serbs, Milosevic, was oppressing the Kosovan people and basically the Western world came to help them.

By the time Hicks arrived, the fighting was nearly over. Still, he briefly joined the Kosovo Liberation Army, a NATO-backed militia fighting against Serbian forces. After two months with the KLA, he returned to Australia again with his thoughts still on the Middle East. A travel book on the region discussed Islam at length, and it piqued Hicks' interest. 'I had to learn once and for all what is Islam and speak to a Muslim to find out what is this life he's living, what is his belief and thoughts', Hicks told federal police. Hicks began attending at a local mosque and soon converted. He left Australia, and headed to Pakistan to study his new faith. From Pakistan, Hicks wrote:

Hello, family. How are you? I'm fine. I'll give you a rundown on where I've been, what I've done and learned. Peshawar is three hours from the Afghanistan border but it is not in the mountains. It's a lot bigger than Adelaide. Pakistan produces all the fruits and veggies I've seen in Adelaide plus so many more.

Hicks briefly joined a group called Lashkar e Tayyiba, or LET, a paramilitary organisation closely aligned with the Pakistani Army that conducted military operations against Indian troops along the Kashmir border. In October 2001—nearly a year after Hicks joined the group—the United States designated LET as a terrorist organisation. Hicks trained for three months in a LET camp, and accompanied Pakistani troops on trips along the border. The Australian Broadcasting Company reported that Hicks grew bored with the group and left them to study Arabic. At this stage, Hicks wrote home: 'My time in Pakistan so far has been unbelievable. I have seen so many things and places. I've learned so much. My best adventure yet. Action packed. But what I am doing now is of the most importance, a major obligation to Islam—knowledge.'

In early 2001, a fellow student asked Hicks to come with him to Afghanistan. Hicks agreed and he soon began training with Taliban and al Qaeda forces. After basic training, Hicks took specialised courses in guerrilla tactics and urban warfare. During training, Hicks' faith grew more extreme. In one letter home he bragged about meeting Osama bin Laden. In another, he wrote: 'You once told me that I listen to anything that I hear. But now who's talking? I don't believe everything I hear. I've always looked at the other side of the coin. That's how I got to where I am. Islam is the truth.'

Hicks was in Pakistan on 9/11, and told Australian Federal Police he was disgusted by the attacks. 'It's not Islam, is it? It's like the opposite of what I ... wanted to do. Meant to help the people, stop oppression. And they did the opposite.' Hicks decided to return to Afghanistan to collect his personal belongings from a guesthouse in Kandahar, and then travel back to Australia. But soon after he crossed the border, it sealed behind him. 'I was too afraid ... to try and travel off by myself to the border when it's closed', he told police. The USA invaded on 7 October and Hicks and his friends took up arms. 'Our job was just to watch the tank', he told federal police. 'I didn't see myself as assisting them, the al Qaeda. Basically, I was stuck where I was. There wasn't much I could do about it.' Taliban strongholds were quickly overrun and Hicks was captured by the US-backed Northern Alliance and turned over to the Americans.

Hicks was first taken to a warship, the USS *Peleliu*, stationed in the Arabian Sea. Hicks has alleged that he was taken by helicopter from the boat to a nearby base for ten-hour beatings by US forces. While blindfolded he was spat upon, punched, kicked and called an 'Aussie kangaroo', he said. 'I know their accents, they were definitely American.' Hicks was then transferred to Guantánamo Bay, a naval base in Cuba where America detains and interrogates prisoners deemed 'unlawful enemy combatants'. He spent his first six months in Camp X-Ray, a series of small wire cages hastily built on the base only days before the first detainees arrived. According to an affidavit he lodged at the base:

> I have had my head rammed into asphalt several times (while blindfolded).
> I have been deprived of sleep as a matter of policy.
> I have had medication—the identity of which was unknown to me, despite my requests for information—forced upon me against my will.
> I was told repeatedly that if I cooperated during the course of interrogations, I would be sent home to Australia after the interrogations were concluded. I was told there was an 'easy way' and a 'hard way' to respond to interrogation.
> Interrogators once offered me the services of a prostitute for fifteen minutes if I would spy on other detainees. I refused.

In mid April 2002, Camp X-Ray was shut and replaced by a multi-building complex known as Camp Delta. The harshest wing of Delta is called Camp Echo. According to Hicks: 'At Camp Echo, I have been held in a solitary cell and have been so since arriving … I was not allowed outside of my cell in Camp Echo for exercise in the sunlight, from July 2003 until March 10, 2004.'

The effects of solitary confinement were profound. A letter sent home from the base in late 2004 read:

> Dear Dad, I feel as though I'm teetering on the edge of losing my sanity after such a long ordeal—the last year of it being in isolation. There are a number of things the authorities could do to help to improve my living conditions, but low morale and depression seems to be the order of the day.

Hicks remains at Guantánamo, just one victim of American torture.

———

While travelling to Karachi to catch his flight home, Mamdouh Habib said Pakistani police boarded his bus. Two Germans were singled out and removed. Habib, who had talked to the men during the trip, grew concerned and exited the bus. The police seized Habib and took him to a police station. Crude physical tortures began right away, Habib said. He described a device resembling an oil drum suspended length-wise from the ground by a wire. He said he was forced to hold himself up above the drum by two hooks in the ceiling. If he touched it with his feet, he'd receive an electric shock. They asked him if he was with al Qaeda, if he trained in Afghanistan. 'No', he said over and over, before passing out.

The German government pushed for the release of their two nationals and they were sent home uncharged. Meanwhile torture grew worse for Habib. 'They put electric shocks on me and beat me', he said. After about fifteen days in the Pakistani prison, Habib was hooded, led outside by guards and then driven away. At first he thought he was to be released, but Habib's journey had only begun. He recalled hearing American voices and then he was set upon by a group of men. He felt his clothes cut from his body, something inserted into his rectum, then the nappy put on. He felt them fit a jumpsuit over his body and they then began leading him towards what sounded like a waiting plane. Along the way, a scuffle broke out and for a moment his hood was knocked loose. The men were wearing black T-shirts, grey pants, yellow boots and dark ski masks. One appeared to be filming everything on a small video camera. The men put sticky tape over his eyes and a mask over his face. For a moment, he recalled, he saw a tattoo on the forearm of one of the men. It appeared to be an American flag unfurled from a middle finger.

'During the flight I was not allowed to sleep', Habib said. 'They would wake me up and make noises.' One of the men said to Habib, 'We have the power, no one can stop us.' Hours later the plane landed: he was now in Cairo. When he first arrived, he said, a man he later identified as Omar Solaimon, chief of Egyptian security, came to his cell. Solaimon told him that Egypt receives US$10 million for every confessed terrorist they hand over to the United States. Solaimon offered Habib a deal. 'He said I should admit to be a terrorist, then he would put aside $4 million of the reward and he would keep the $6 million. He would then give me a new identity and give me the money.' Presumably, Solaimon would then hand someone else

over to the Americans. 'You might as well do it', Solaimon told
Habib. 'You're here in our hands, we're not going to let you go.' Habib
refused.

The next five months in Egypt were a blur of pain and fear. In
Egypt 'there was no interrogation, only torture'. Habib reached towards
his collar and pulled it down. Under his collarbone there were four or
five round patches of skin that were hairless and pink. 'This is where
they burned me', he said. 'They threatened me with dogs. They said
the dogs will rape me.' He was also stripped and shocked with a stun
gun. Habib can still hear the 'tick tick tick' sound of the device in his
head, he said. During this time he recalls hearing American voices at
the prison, although Egyptians were in charge of the torture. At one
stage, he recalled, he was drugged and began to hallucinate. Another
time they propped open his eyes with plastic fittings and placed what
he described as a mask with a screen over his face. 'They showed bad
stuff', he said, refusing to elaborate. 'You want to close your eyes, but
you can't.' Habib recalled being chained to the ground, then placed in
a room that slowly filled with water. The water level stopped just
below his nose. He doesn't, to this day, know how they did it, but
Habib recalls seeing his family brought in before him. Habib paused
before he told me: 'I see my family get raped in front of me. I feel it is
true. They use their real names and then kill all of them. After I see my
family gone—I feel like a dead person. I was gone. I become crazy.'

Habib's recollections about his time in Egypt after this point are
fragmentary. He remembers admitting things to interrogators, everything they asked. 'I didn't care', he said. 'At this point I was ready to
die.' But Habib did not die in a prison in Cairo. In May 2002, men in
masks took him from his cell. His clothes were cut off, something
inserted into his body, and he was dressed in a nappy and put onto a
waiting plane. Habib was back in American hands.

He was first taken to Bagram Air Base, a cavernous hangar
abandoned by the Russians when they left Afghanistan in 1989. The
tortures here were different. They were 'American techniques', said
Habib. He was kept in a cage and the rule was 'no talking to anybody'.
There were 'sounds, music, American music'. After about ten days, he
was transferred to a new site at Kandahar. During his time at Bagram
and Kandahar, Habib wasn't interrogated, but he did recall hearing a
variety of accents, including English and Australian. In Kandahar, he
was introduced to a new torture: self-inflicted pain. 'Sit on your knees',

soldiers told him. He was then forced to extend his arms outward for hours at a time. 'They make you lift up your arms in the sun', he said. There were also sexual tortures. 'They put us on top of each other, like you see in Abu Ghraib, and they take photographs. They enjoy to do it, but they were told to do it.'

After several weeks in Kandahar the men in masks visited him again. Same routine: stripped, enema, nappy. This time, though, he said, they placed tape over his eyes and mouth, then wrapped goggles, a breathing mask and sound-dampening earmuffs over his head. After he was dressed, he was placed on another plane. Unlike the earlier flights, the flight lasted not hours, but days. When he landed in Guantánamo Bay, Cuba, he was shuttled 'straight away into isolation', he said.

Habib described isolation as like 'being in a dream'. He believes that he was first put in Camp Echo. Like Hicks, Habib recalled that he was injected with drugs against his will. 'Every two weeks they give injections', he said. When he asked what it was, they said it was a tetanus shot. 'After the drugs I hear stuff and see stuff', said Habib. At one stage he decided to stop eating because he believed that drugs also were put into his food. He began to feel better, he said, but was then force-fed. 'They put a tube in my nose, no anaesthetic. There was a lot of blood', he recalled.

Habib also recalled how guards would use detainees' religion to inflict psychological trauma. The Koran was frequently defiled, he said. 'They would take it and do like this', he said. Habib reached for my notebook and threw it against the wall behind my head. 'They would then open it and flip through the pages.' Habib roughly fingered through the pages of my book, tearing at them. 'This is what they do.' Another time, he said, a female interrogator flicked him with a red liquid—she told him it was menstrual blood.

Interrogations were infrequent and haphazard. In the course of more than three years, Habib said, he was only interviewed about twenty times. Several times, he said, an Australian came to see him. 'They never ask me specific things. They would only ask about what I think about bigger things like: Osama bin Laden and jihad.' 'What do you think about those things?' I asked. 'Osama, after what he did to New York, he is a terrible man', he replied.

In mid 2004, he was transferred to Camp Five, a state-of-the-art maximum security facility. 'It was the worst', he said. His life was even more controlled in Camp Five than in Echo. To create dependency on the interrogators, staff took away all of Habib's 'comfort items'. In Guantánamo this includes bottled water, soap and toilet paper. Habib was forced to drink only 'bad, yellow water', he said. 'I was CI lost', he said—short for 'comfort item lost'. 'If you co-operate', one official told him, 'you get a blanket, clothes, shoes …'. Habib refused, and only told his interrogators about the torture he had endured. At Camp Five he was placed in isolation for more than twenty-three hours per day. Mamdouh has difficulty remembering his time at Camp Five. 'I was out of my head. I was crazy all day.' Next to his cell, he said, military police placed giant fans that roared all day and night. The lights at Camp Five were never switched off.

In late 2004, Habib recalled, a US Navy officer entered his cell and read him a list of charges. 'Mr Habib', the man said as he put his feet up on the desk, 'you are charged with the following crimes'. He listed things like training 9/11 hijackers in martial arts, attending an al Qaeda training camp in Afghanistan, transporting chemical weapons, and communicating with agents from Hezbollah. 'Who is the judge?' Habib asked. 'A Marine', the man answered. 'Who decides?' 'Army, Air Force, and Navy officers', the man said. A fair hearing, said Habib, was impossible. He refused to participate.

Meanwhile, in Sydney, Maha had been fighting for her husband's freedom. Joseph Margulies, a Chicago-based human rights lawyer who had taken on Habib's case, began meeting with him in Cuba. Lawyers were allowed access to the base after the US Supreme Court held in June 2004 that detainees at Guantánamo were entitled to legal counsel. One day, Margulies noticed that Egypt had requested that a man named 'Mamdouh Ahmed' be transferred back to Egyptian custody. 'He called me from Cuba and asked what Mamdouh's middle name was', said Maha. It is Ahmed. Margulies immediately filed a restraining order to keep Habib from being returned. In the court filing, he detailed all of Habib's allegations of torture, starting in Pakistan. After the filing was processed, it became a public document and Margulies slipped it to the *Washington Post* newspaper. The *Post's* Dana Priest wrote a passionate account of Habib's ordeal that appeared on page one. Suddenly, he became a liability for the US government. If Margulies proceeded with the restraining order in court, Habib's allegations would be repeated under oath in open testimony before a judge. Rather than face further public scrutiny, US officials sent him home. Mamdouh Habib landed in Sydney on 28 January 2005—the same day as his youngest daughter's sixth birthday.

———

In *Ashcraft v State of Tennessee* (1944), the United States Supreme Court overturned a murder conviction based on a confession extracted from Ashcraft, a suspect questioned for more than thirty-six hours under the bright glare of an interrogator's lamp. Chief Justice Hugo Black noted that 'as the hours passed [Ashcraft's] eyes became blinded by a powerful electric light, his body became weary, and the strain on his nerves became unbearable'. Black, setting a precedent that effectively banned coercive interrogations in America, held:

> The Constitution of the United States stands as a bar against the conviction of any individual in an American court by means of a coerced confession. There have been, and are now, certain foreign nations with governments dedicated to an opposite policy: governments which convict individuals with testimony obtained by police organizations possessed of an unrestrained power to seize persons suspected of crimes against the state, hold them in secret custody, and wring from them confessions by physical or mental torture. So long as the Constitution remains the basic law of our Republic, America will not have that kind of government.

Tragically, history has proven Black wrong. Soon after the ruling, the US military and the newly minted Central Intelligence Agency (CIA) embarked on a quest to find sharper tools to break down prisoners and extract confessions. The search began in the earliest days of the Cold War, when government officials were convinced that communists had perfected ways to gain complete control over the human mind. Two distinct programs emerged.

The first was the US military's Survival, Evasion, Resistance and Escape (SERE) program, which was ostensibly designed to inoculate soldiers against the stress of torture. Starting as early as 1953, students in SERE were hooded, nearly drowned, positioned into painful and sexually explicit positions, subjected to abuse focusing on their race and religion, and held in solitary confinement for days at a time.

While the US military tortured its own soldiers using methods drawn from communist adversaries, the CIA embarked on a program to discover powerful drugs to control the body and mind. Only after these programs failed did the agency turn to the SERE techniques used by the military. These methods—centred on self-inflicted pain, sensory deprivation and humiliation—render victims delirious, dependent and highly suggestible. According to the CIA's 1963 *KUBARK Counterintelligence Interrogation* training manual, SERE techniques 'succeed even with highly resistant sources [by] inducing regression of the personality to whatever earlier and weaker level is required for the dissolution of resistance …'.

Beginning in the late 1950s, the CIA and US military exported SERE methods of interrogation to American allies in South-East Asia and Latin America via counterinsurgency training programs. By 1971, more than one hundred thousand foreign officers had been trained to use SERE tortures that leave deep psychological wounds but few physical scars. In 1983, the CIA produced a new guidebook, the *Human Resource Exploitation Training Manual*, which made the 1963 version seem tame in comparison. Unlike the earlier edition, this manual advocated the use of physical violence, extreme sensory deprivation and sexual humiliation to break down suspects.

Although the Cold War ended in the late 1980s, SERE programs remained. The Reagan and first Bush administrations kept SERE techniques legal for the CIA and the military by inserting narrow definitions of torture into the UN Convention Against Torture and various domestic statutes. After 9/11, SERE tortures were transmitted to Afghanistan, Iraq and Cuba by interrogators who had passed through these schools themselves, and by health care workers and instructors with SERE backgrounds. SERE techniques have now become so commonplace that interrogators later charged with murdering detainees have successfully defended themselves in court by claiming that their actions were no worse than what American soldiers themselves endure during training. While the military has sworn off SERE techniques in the wake of the Abu Ghraib scandal, the *Military Commissions Act of 2006* essentially legalised these methods of torture for use by the CIA in secret black site prisons. Today, hypothermia, forced standing, sleep deprivation and even simulated drowning are legal tools in the interrogator's toolbox.

The United States now holds more than 14 000 prisoners across a vast network of prisons in Iraq, Afghanistan and Cuba. In Guantánamo, unlawful enemy combatants number about 450, while in Iraq nearly 13 000 'security detainees' held for 'imperative reasons of security' languish. In Bagram, 500 are held without charge. The USA contends that it can hold these prisoners until the war on terror ends—a 'war', according to former Secretary of Defense Donald Rumsfeld, 'that very likely will go on for many years, much like the Cold War went on for many years'. As long as they are in US custody, these prisoners are fodder for American interrogators authorised to use SERE torture.

The experiences of Mamdouh Habib and David Hicks are harrowing, but are not unique. Since 2001, more than 800 allegations of abuse have surfaced and at least thirty-four American-held prisoners have been murdered while in custody. 'Every country has its own way of torturing people', said Rustam Akhmiarov, a Russian detainee who, like Habib, was arrested in Pakistan, sent to Guantánamo, then later released. 'In Russia, they beat you up; they break you straight away. But the Americans had their own way, which is to make you go mad over a period of time. Every day they thought of new ways to make you feel worse.'

George W. Bush calls SERE torture an 'alternative set of procedures', vital tools needed 'to protect the American people and our allies'. But SERE torture—like all forms of torture—radicalises enemies, yields unreliable information, and is ultimately self-defeating. These lessons are discernible from the history of the last sixty years, starting from the febrile days of the early Cold War period. It is here my inquiry into American torture begins.

———

1

A CLIMATE OF FEAR

'**I** am guilty in principle and in detail of most of the accusations made', said the cardinal in a low, stammering voice.

On 27 December 1948, József Cardinal Mindszenty was arrested on charges of treason and attempting to overthrow the Hungarian government. Mindszenty, the first prelate tried on civil charges since the days of Napoleon, was a vocal critic of the newly installed Communist regime. Earlier that year he had called for a general amnesty for all political prisoners and threatened to excommunicate any Catholic who supported government plans to nationalise religious schools. One month before his arrest, the Hungarian Premier branded Mindszenty a 'reactionary'. The 'liquidation of clerical reaction' was imminent, warned another government official.

Mindszenty penned a statement to his supporters prior to his arrest. Any confession he made, it said, would either be 'forged or false'. Two months later, a public trial began. On the first day of the hearings Mindszenty retracted the letter. In a quiet voice the cardinal confessed his guilt and stated that the letter was simply 'outdated'. Days after his confession, the Hungarian court sentenced Mindszenty to life imprisonment.

World reaction was fierce. 'May the mock trial … arouse all Christians, all Americans, all believers in God and human freedom, all civilized men and women, to realize the meaning of the cruel, inhuman and godless creed of Marxian communism and totalitarian despotism', urged New York Bishop William Thomas Manning. A resolution introduced in the US Senate condemned the verdict and the Vatican affirmed that the cardinal was 'morally and civilly innocent'. President Harry Truman weighed in, agreeing that the trial was 'a sickening sham'.

During Mindszenty's trial, *The Tablet*, a Roman Catholic newspaper, published an article written 'by a priest who has been very close to the Cardinal'. It insisted that Hungarians used 'a tablet of the potent nerve-destroying Actedron' to secure the confession. The effects of Actedron were profound:

> It begins with a strong headache and vertigo. Then a steadily increasing sense of uncertainty overcomes him. Then the prisoner begins to feel frightened. Finally he becomes semiconscious. He is paralyzed as though in a hypnotic trance. Neither his judgment nor his memory functions any more. He has the impression of having a deadly paralyzed vacuum in his head. He has the urge blindly to obey the slightest orders and is psychologically incapable of saying no to anything. Victims are led to trial in this condition.

The notion that a simple drug could enslave the mind was alluring in the fevered anti-Communist atmosphere of the postwar era. Today, the Mindszenty episode represents a bizarre but often neglected chapter in Cold War history. The cardinal's trial kick-started fears in the USA that the 'Reds' had mastered the art of mind control—paranoid suspicions that only grew in the years that followed.

In 1949—the same year the Soviets tested their first atomic bomb and Communists seized control in China—the Hungarian government announced the arrest of another 'enemy of the state'. This time it was not a Hungarian, but an American: Robert Vogeler of Jackson Heights, New York. Vogeler, an Assistant Vice President of the International Telephone and Telegraph Company (ITT), was seized on 18 November 1949 en route to Vienna from Budapest. According to the Hungarian government, upon arrest Vogeler 'confessed to having committed sabotage and espionage against the Hungarian people's republic for a considerable time'. Using the arrest as a pretext, four weeks later the Hungarian government nationalised all ITT holdings.

Vogeler's crimes were clearly imagined. According to the Hungarians, Vogeler initiated a plot against the Hungarian government in 1942—a dubious claim given that he joined the company in 1943 and didn't visit Hungary until 1948. But despite the discrepancy, on 19 February 1950 Vogeler appeared in a Hungarian court and testified: 'I used my business activities only as a cover for my espionage work … I am sorry for the detrimental deed I committed against this country and I ask for a mild sentence.' According to the Associated Press, Vogeler spoke 'without a show of emotion or strain'.

It was suggested that Vogeler was not in control of his own mind. 'Mrs Vogeler tells me her husband used phrases in his confession he never employed in his life—the kind of phrases in which Communists express themselves', said Morris Ernst, the family's New York lawyer. The US State Department didn't accept Mr Vogeler's 'so-called confession nor his self-incriminating testimony', adding that 'his behavior was clearly not that of a man free to speak in his own defense'. The *New York Times* labelled the trial a 'diabolical puppet show'. The editorial continued: 'Some terrible thing has taken place behind the scenes of this Budapest spectacle and we are right in feeling horror and loathing when we are confronted by it … It is natural that we should suspect that behind these sinister trappings is some method even more hellish than anything we know.'

The Vogeler trial spurred speculation about communist inter-rogation methods. The State Department suggested that he had been 'subjected to coercion by intimidation, lack of food, drugging, or other forms of mistreatment'. The *New York Times Magazine* featured a five-page spread on the topic, headlined 'Why Do They Confess—A Communist Enigma'. The article suggested three alternatives: 'black psychiatry', drugs, or physical torture. W. H. Lawrence, the author of the piece, was quick to discount the last option. The theory of physical torture 'hardly explains the conduct of men like Mindszenty', he wrote. 'Physical torture, presumably, would only strengthen their will as it had some of the early martyrs. Yet they, too, confessed.' Lawrence gave cre-dence to the possibility of black psychiatry—Communist psychiatrists deliberately weakening the human mind to the point that a victim 'reverses his scale of values and becomes subservient to their will'. The final possibility involved drugs. 'One man who lived to tell of his examination said he thought they gave him morphine', Lawrence wrote. 'Another drug mentioned is mescaline [which is] said to pro-duce a depersonalization effect, giving the subject the feeling of being someone else.'

In 1950, Edward Hunter of the *Miami Daily News* coined the word 'brainwashing' to describe communist mind perversion. 'The intent is to change a mind radically so that its owner becomes a living puppet—a human robot—without the atrocity being visible from the outside', wrote Hunter in *Brainwashing* (1960), one of several books on the subject that he authored. Hunter, later exposed as being on the CIA's payroll, carved out a lucrative career writing about the cruel dangers of the practice—fanning the flames of popular outrage along the way. By the early 1950s, the concept of brainwashing had quickly evolved into a 'lurid mythology', noted psychiatrist Dr Robert Jay Lifton. Brainwashing became 'a rallying point for fear, resentment, urges toward submission, justification for failure, irresponsible accusation, and for a wide gamut of emotional extremism', he said.

In late April 1951, Communist police seized another American—this time in Czechoslovakia. Three Czech agents arrested William Oatis, an Associated Press bureau chief, as he parked his car. Seventy-two hours after he disappeared the government formally charged Oatis with 'hostile activities' and spreading 'secret information'. His arrest and confession followed a similar pattern: taken in April, confessed in July, sentenced to ten years. Harry Martin, President of the American Newspaper Guild, protested the arrest in a letter he hand-delivered to the Czech embassy in Washington, DC. Oatis' statement, wrote Martin, is 'merely one more in a series of phony confessions forced from helpless victims by methods that outdo barbarism even in the historic terrors of the Spanish Inquisition'. The arrest was 'a hoax', said Lincoln White, US State Department spokesperson. 'I hope and trust that the American people will understand the absolute worthlessness of any alleged confession or "revelation" beaten out or otherwise obtained from anyone who is held incommunicado for seventy days or more', added the official. A *New York Times* editorial cautioned: 'Surely we have reached a point where helpless acceptance of barbarity against American citizens is becoming unbearable ... [But] we must be careful not to commit the same type of judicial iniquity of which we accuse the Reds. To descend into their mire would be to lose the ideals for which we strive.'

Discussions at the highest levels of government reached a markedly different conclusion. A secret panel appointed by President Dwight D. Eisenhower, chaired by Lieutenant General Jimmy Doolittle, found that the Cold War represented a new paradigm where 'acceptable

norms of human conduct do not apply'. The panel advised the president to take an aggressive stance against communism on all fronts. It
concluded that:

> It is now clear that we are facing an implacable enemy whose
> avowed objective is world domination by whatever means and at
> whatever costs. There are no rules in such a game ... If the US is
> to survive, longstanding American concepts of 'fair play' must be
> reconsidered. We must develop effective espionage and counter-
> espionage services and must learn to subvert, sabotage and destroy
> our enemies by more clever, more sophisticated means than those
> used against us. It may become necessary that the American
> people be made acquainted with, understand and support this
> fundamentally repugnant philosophy.

To combat the so-called scourge of communist brainwashing, America
looked to her enemies for insight into their methods: first to the Nazis,
then to the Soviet Union and China. Although public outrage against
communist coercion peaked in the early 1950s, select agencies in the
US government had set to work on discovering the key to mind control soon after World War II.

In 1945, the US Naval Technical Mission swept across Europe in
search of useful scientific data from the Third Reich. In addition to
uncovering valuable information about German V2 rockets, the Naval
mission found documentation of Nazi human experimentation. At
the Dachau concentration camp inmates were injected with gasoline,
frozen to death in vats of ice water, and crushed in pressure chambers
in a series of trials designed to test the limits of human endurance. In
addition to the twisted 'aviation medicine' trials, the mission found
evidence documenting interrogation-related research. At Dachau,
thirty inmates were injected with mescaline to see if they would reveal
their innermost thoughts. The results were mixed. While one Nazi
study noted that it was 'impossible to impose one's will on another
person as in hypnosis even when the strongest dose of mescaline had
been given', another report found that interrogators were able to
obtain 'even the most intimate secrets from the [subject] when questions were cleverly put'.

Under Operation Paperclip, the Navy recruited Dr Kurt Plotner, who directly oversaw human experimentation at Dachau, to continue his interrogation research within the USA. Nazi doctors for whom the United States had no use were tried at Nuremburg. For the trials, a new code of ethics was produced, known today as the Nuremburg Code. Among others, Article 1 declares that 'the voluntary consent of the human subject is absolutely essential'; Article 4 states that 'the experiment should be so conducted as to avoid all unnecessary physical and mental suffering and injury'; and Article 9 instructs that 'during the course of the experiment the human subject should be at liberty to bring the experiment to an end if he has reached the physical or mental state where continuation of the experiment seems to him to be impossible'. Sixteen of the doctors charged were found guilty of violating these basic principles. Seven were executed.

Unaffected by the lessons of Nuremburg, the US government pushed ahead with human experimentation in the name of national security. In 1947, the US Navy launched Operation Chatter after receiving reports citing 'amazing results' of Soviet drug research. Under this program, mescaline was tested upon volunteers at the Naval Medical Research Institute in Bethesda, Maryland, and on unwitting subjects in western Europe. Like the Nazis, the Navy doctors sought a fail-safe 'truth drug'. According to Dr Samuel Thompson, Operation Chatter's director, the program was 'unethical' but 'we felt we had to do it for the good of the country'.

The scope of US military mind control research pales in comparison with work undertaken by the CIA. The agency was better suited than the military to conduct unsavoury research given its broad mandate, secret budget and insulation from congressional oversight. Established by an Act of Congress in 1947, the agency, in the words of CIA framer William Donovan, was envisioned as an 'organization which will procure intelligence both by overt and covert methods and will at the same time provide intelligence guidance, determine national intelligence objectives, and correlate the intelligence material collected by all government agencies'. In reality, the CIA's powers are far greater.

In 1947, the National Security Act reorganised the armed forces and established both the National Security Council (NSC) and the CIA. The NSC is an executive body chaired by the president, which coordinates national security issues and directs foreign policy. The

same fears that consumed mainstream media and the general public
during the Red Scare are reflected in NSC reports of the time.
According to one 1950 directive: 'the Soviet Union, unlike previous
aspirants to hegemony, is animated by a new fanatic faith, antithetical
to our own, and seeks to impose its absolute authority over the rest of
the world'. These fears trickled down to CIA agents in the field. Hugh
Cunningham, an early agency official, later recalled: 'What you were
made to feel was that the country was in desperate peril and we had
to do whatever it took to save it.' According to Harry Rositzke,
ex-head of the Soviet Division, agents felt they were 'the first line
of defense in the anticommunist crusade'.

The CIA was granted extra-legal powers in this new 'crusade'.
The 1947 Act contained a small clause granting the CIA the power to
'perform such other functions and duties related to intelligence
affecting the national security as the President or the National Security
Council may direct'. From the agency's inception, this clause has been
used to justify covert action, as directed by the president, outside the
bounds of conventional law. For example, NSC 1/1, the NSC's first
action, ordered covert manipulation of the Italian elections. To achieve
this aim, the CIA transferred millions of dollars to anti-Communist
political parties and produced anonymous pamphlets describing in
lurid detail the sex lives of Communist candidates. On 9 December
1947, the NSC met again to discuss anti-Soviet propaganda efforts.
This time the NSC directed that 'in the interests of world peace and
US national security, the foreign information activities of the US
Government must be supplemented by covert psychological operations'. The need to keep these activities secret, stated the directive,
'renders the Central Intelligence Agency the logical agency to conduct such operations'.

The Central Intelligence Act, passed two years later, exempted the
agency from normal financial controls regulating the expenditure of
public funds. In order to protect the details of its programs, the agency
was not required to disclose to Congress its 'organization, functions,
names, officials, titles, salaries, or numbers of personnel employed'. In
addition to having extra-legal powers, the CIA was to operate under a
veil of secrecy.

Given its unique status, the CIA was the primary agency charged
with mind control research during the Cold War. Although two congressional inquests—the Rockefeller Commission and the Church

Committee—revealed many vital clues, the bulk of what is known today about the CIA's quest for mind control stems from a 1975 Freedom of Information Act (FOIA) request by American journalist John Marks for documents relating to agency-sponsored human experimentation. After nearly three years of delays, the CIA delivered to Marks more than 16 000 pages of documents concerning various top secret CIA behavioural control programs. Today, these files are on view at the National Security Archive in Washington, DC.

Dozens of the documents make direct reference to the trial of Cardinal Mindszenty. Following the trial, one CIA memorandum declared that 'some unknown force' had controlled the cardinal. Agents dubbed this the 'Mindszenty Effect'. As the chief of the CIA medical staff wrote in 1952:

> There is ample evidence in the reports of innumerable interrogations that the Communists were utilizing drugs, physical duress, electric shock, and possibly hypnosis against their enemies. With such evidence it is difficult not to keep from becoming rabid about our apparent laxity. We are forced by this mounting evidence to assume a more aggressive role in the development of these techniques, but must be cautious to maintain strict inviolable control because of the havoc that could be wrought by such techniques in unscrupulous hands.

The CIA initiated research into mind control four months after Mindszenty's trial. At first, agents worked with the Navy's Chatter team with drugs and hypnosis. Then, on 20 April 1950, CIA Director Roscoe Hillenkoetter launched Project Bluebird. The program's official objectives were:

A. Discovering means of conditioning personnel to prevent unauthorized extraction of information from them by known means.
B. Investigating the possibility of control of an individual by application of special interrogation techniques.
C. Memory enhancement.
D. Establishing defensive means for preventing hostile control of Agency personnel.

Bluebird agents reopened Nazi studies of interrogation techniques into drugs and studied the results of the deadly survival tests. According to one researcher who reviewed the Nazi records, the information was of little help to the CIA: 'There were some experiments on pain, but they were so mixed up with sadism as not to be useful … [But] how the victim coped was very interesting.'

Drug testing was central to Bluebird. In addition to mescaline, Bluebird researchers performed extensive tests with LSD (lysergic acid diethylamide) for use during interrogations. LSD is more than a thousand times more potent than mescaline and more than a million times stronger than tetrahydrocannabinol (THC), the active ingredient in marijuana. The drug's bizarre effects were first discovered in 1943 when Swiss chemist Albert Hofmann mishandled the drug, resulting in accidental absorption into his skin. He experienced 'a peculiar sensation' in which 'fantastic pictures of extraordinary plasticity and intensive color seemed to surge towards me'. LSD's potential applications in psychological warfare and mind control intrigued US officials, and reports of communist interest in the drug added a sense of immediacy to the research. According to one agent: 'It is awfully hard in this day and age to reproduce how frightening all of this was to us at the time, particularly after the drug scene has become as widespread and as knowledgeable in this country as it did. But we were literally terrified, because this was the one material that we had ever been able to locate that really had potential fantastic possibilities if used wrongly.'

Under Bluebird, agents first dosed twelve US soldiers with the potent hallucinogen. According to CIA documents, the subjects were mostly black and 'of not too high mentality'. Although they were assured that 'nothing serious or dangerous would happen to them', the profound effects of LSD were well known at the time. Clinical reports about the drug first appeared in 1947 and attested to side effects like uncontrollable paranoia and temporary schizophrenia. Bluebird researchers soon expanded the trials to more than 7000 unwitting soldiers at Maryland's Edgewood Chemical Arsenal. Years later, it was discovered that nearly 1000 of these soldiers developed serious psychological complications such as depression and epilepsy. Scores attempted suicide. A CIA agent involved with these early LSD trials later recalled: 'We thought about the possibility of putting some in a city water supply and having the citizens wander around in a more or less happy state, not terribly interested in defending themselves.'

According to a report by the CIA's Inspector General, testing on subjects without their full knowledge was deemed necessary because 'testing of materials under accepted scientific procedures fails to disclose the full pattern of reactions and attributions that may occur in operational situations'.

In addition to unwitting soldiers, subjects used in these trials included 'individuals of dubious loyalty, suspected agents or plants, [and] subjects having known reason for deception', according to one agency document. Another lists 'potential agents, defectors, refugees, [and] POWs' as ideal 'research material'. Morse Allen, head of the Bluebird program, called trials with these types 'terminal experiments'— terminal in the sense that they would end at the discretion of the experimenter, not the subject.

In August 1951, Bluebird was officially re-dubbed Project Artichoke. The aim of this operation was to further explore interrogation through 'the application of tested psychiatric and psychological techniques including the use of hypnosis in connection with drugs'. One document stressed goals like 'controlling an individual to the point where he will do our bidding against his will and even against such fundamental laws of nature as self-preservation'. Chemical and biological agents were studied in order 'to perfect techniques … for the abstraction of information from individuals whether willing or not'. Under Project Artichoke, overseas interrogations featured combinations of sodium pentothal and hypnosis. At home, the CIA expanded its trials using LSD. Notably, the agency funded a project at the Addiction Research Center in Lexington, Kentucky. The subjects there were 'volunteers' who, after signing a general consent form, were administered high doses of LSD. As a reward for participation, the addicts were provided with any illicit drugs of their choice. One subject was given 'double, triple, and quadruple doses' of the drug, while another was kept on LSD for seventy-five days straight.

In addition to LSD, agents experimented with a host of other drugs including marijuana, cocaine, PCP, ether, mescaline and heroin. Of these drugs, heroin was deemed to hold the most potential. CIA officials determined that highly addictive opiates such as heroin 'can be useful in reverse because of the stresses produced when they are withdrawn from those who are addicted to their use'. The rationale was simple: an addict will do anything to get his next hit.

By 1953, the growing array of behavioural testing was reorganised under a new operational banner. On 13 April 1953, CIA Director Allen Dulles approved Project MKULTRA (pronounced M-K-Ultra) with an initial budget of US$300 000—6 per cent of the CIA's total research budget for the year. The proposal for MKULTRA called for

> the development of a chemical material which causes a reversible non-toxic aberrant mental state, the specific nature of which can be reasonably well predicted for each individual. This material could potentially aid in discrediting individuals, eliciting information, and implanting suggestions and other forms of mental control.

For the next decade, taxpayer funding to MKULTRA totalled more than US$25 million. During this time, the operation supervised 149 projects and thirty-three more subprojects focused on controlling the human mind. A small unit within the CIA called the Technical Services Division (TSD) was charged with running the top secret program. Like Bluebird and Artichoke, MKULTRA's existence was known only to a select few—Congress was kept completely in the dark.

Most of the research for MKULTRA was conducted at mainstream institutions. Between 1953 and 1963, the CIA funded human experiments by 185 non-governmental researchers at eighty institutions, including forty-four universities and twelve hospitals. This included work at prestigious universities like Princeton, Harvard, Yale, Columbia and Stanford and at centres like the Georgetown University Hospital in Washington, DC, the Boston Psychopathic Hospital and the Mt Sinai Hospital in New York.

One project, code-named QK-Hilltop, was based at Cornell University under the direction of Dr Harold Wolff. At Cornell, Wolff was an early pioneer of human ecology, an interdisciplinary field incorporating psychology, medicine and sociology. When the project began, Dr Wolff asked the CIA to provide him with all its information regarding 'threats, coercion, imprisonment, deprivation, humiliation, torture, "brainwashing", "black psychiatry", hypnosis and combinations of these, with or without chemical agents'. According to Wolff, the Cornell team will assemble, collate, analyze and assimilate this information and will then undertake experimental investigations designed to develop new techniques of offensive/defensive intelligence use … Potentially useful secret drugs (and various brain damaging procedures) will be similarly tested in order to ascertain the fundamental effect upon human brain function and upon the subject's mood … Where any of the studies involve potential harm to the subject, we expect the Agency to make available suitable subjects and a proper place for the performance of necessary experiments.

Remarkably, Wolff was considered a top expert at the time. As John Marks notes in *The Search for the 'Manchurian Candidate'* (1979), Wolff served as editor-in-chief of the American Medical Association's *Archives of Neurology and Psychiatry*, had been the President of the New York Neurological Association and in 1960 became President of the American Neurological Association.

Doctors like Wolff were funded by the CIA via organisations like the Ford and Rockefeller foundations and through dummy institutes set up by the agency. Scientists and doctors involved in these trials published topical results of their research in journals and reported the bulk of their detailed findings directly to the CIA. According to one CIA Inspector General Report, this secrecy was essential because:

A. Research in the manipulation of human behavior is considered by many authorities in medicine and related fields to be professionally unethical, therefore the reputation of professional participants in the MKULTRA program are on occasion in jeopardy. B. Some MKULTRA activities raise questions of legality implicit in the original charter. C. A final phase of the testing of MKULTRA products places the rights and interests of US citizens in jeopardy. D. Public disclosure of some aspects of MKULTRA activity could induce serious adverse reaction in US public opinion, as well as stimulate offensive and defensive action in this field on the part of foreign intelligence services.

LSD was used extensively in early MKULTRA research. In addition to the drug being tested on voluntary subjects at universities and hospitals across the USA, under MKULTRA countless numbers of unsuspecting civilians were dosed as well. MKULTRA's subjects included 'informers or members of suspect criminal elements' as well as 'individuals at all social levels, high and low, native American and foreign'.

One such victim was Dr Frank Olson, a CIA researcher at Fort Detrick, Maryland, who specialised in biological weapons. On 19 November 1953, top CIA officials met with Detrick researchers at the Deep Creek Lodge in rural Maryland to discuss their projects. During the meeting, Sid Gottlieb, MKULTRA's chief scientist, slipped LSD into Olson's drink, hoping to observe changes in his colleague's behaviour. By most accounts, Olson suffered a 'bad trip'. He grew disoriented, panicky and paranoid. Although the drug ran its course after about twelve hours, Olson remained depressed and on edge. Days later he was flown to New York for psychological treatment by a doctor on the CIA payroll who had experience with LSD. While in New York, Olson jumped or fell to his death from the tenth floor at the Statler Hotel. While the CIA initially labelled it a suicide, twenty-two years later the Rockefeller Commission—appointed to investigate allegations of illegal CIA wire-tapping—revealed the circumstances surrounding his death. In turn, the Olson family received a personal apology from President Gerald Ford and a congressional payment of US$750 000. According to Sid Gottlieb, who received only a mild reprimand for his actions, Olson's death was just 'one of the risks running with scientific experimentation'.

Agency employees, alongside undercover officers of the Bureau of Narcotics, also conducted LSD testing. In 1953, Gottlieb contacted George Hunter White, a narcotics officer for the bureau—today known as the Drug Enforcement Agency—who had conducted small-scale drug research during World War II. During the war, White was a lieutenant with the Office of Strategic Services, the military predecessor to the CIA. In August 1943, White rented a room at the Belmont Plaza Hotel in New York and distributed THC-laced cigarettes to seven military officers, and, according to White, to a 'well-known New York hoodlum'. The purpose of these trials was to ascertain whether THC could be used as a truth serum. The 'guinea pig' tests were unsuccessful, White later wrote. Rather than loosening lips, the effect of THC is that 'the sense of humor is accentuated to the point where any statement or situation can become extremely funny to the subject'. Generally, the trials revealed, 'the reaction will be one of great loquacity and hilarity'.

Although the 1943 tests failed, Gottlieb wanted White to try again—this time with LSD. Using CIA funds, White set up a safe house in Greenwich Village, New York, where agents lured subjects, served them LSD-laced cocktails and observed their behaviour. In 1955, White moved the operation to San Francisco but added a twist: he hired prostitutes to pick up men in bars and bring them back to the safe house. The 'Johns' were served laced drinks while CIA officers observed from behind two-way mirrors. White dubbed the San Francisco project 'Operation Midnight Climax'.

White's LSD program continued uninterrupted until 1963 when an internal audit discovered the illegal nature of the program. After a damning report by the CIA's Inspector General, major funding for MKULTRA was halted. Although limited drug trials continued, the halcyon days of CIA drug research had come to an end. Over the years the CIA had doled out more than 25 000 doses of LSD to university students, professors and the general public—accelerating the drug's popularity in American counter-culture.

Fearing a congressional inquest, Gottlieb destroyed dozens of boxes of MKULTRA files in 1973. The destruction had 'nothing to do with covering up illegal activities', he later testified, but was done because the 'material was sensitive and capable of being misunderstood'. A secret 1957 Inspector General Report provides a more candid explanation:

> Precautions must be taken not only to protect operations from exposure to enemy forces but also to conceal these activities from the American public in general. The knowledge that the Agency is engaging in unethical and illicit activities would have serious repercussions in political and diplomatic circles and would be detrimental to the accomplishment of its mission.

2

STRESS INOCULATION

As CIA-sponsored interrogation research spiralled into LSD lunacy, the US military took a more pragmatic approach to the so-called problem of brainwashing. Rather than sink millions of dollars into interrogation research involving illicit drugs, the Pentagon developed physical and psychological techniques ostensibly to enable soldiers to resist communist coercion.

In May 1953, a special US Air Force 'prison camp school' was opened in the mountains outside Chinhae, South Korea, twenty-two miles west of Pusan. The school was likely the brainchild of the Air Force's Psychological Warfare Division, a secretive office charged with covert operations. Prominent sociologist Dr Albert Biderman, psychiatrist Dr Robert Jay Lifton, neurologist Dr Lawrence Hinkle Jr and human ecologist Dr Harold Wolff, who also worked with the CIA, were all associated with this top-secret group. The operating theory behind the Chinhae school was 'stress inoculation', a psychological exercise used today by therapists to treat patients suffering from anxiety and anger. According to psychologist Dr Clayton Tucker-Ladd, under normal circumstances:

> [S]tress inoculation involves gaining awareness of why we get upset. Then we learn ways to control our emotions, e.g. through self-instructions and rational thinking and by changing our attitudes and expectations. Finally, by imagining being in the stressful situation over and over, we can practice calming ourselves down with these self-help methods. Later, we use these same self-instructions and techniques to stay calm in the real situation.

At Chinhae, the Air Force pushed this concept one step further. Rather than having students imagine they were being tortured, instructors actually tortured them. According to Captain Keith D. Young, head of the school, the program taught students about 'the psychosis of prisoner-of-war life, the abrupt transition from American life to Commie prisoner life'.

The three main elements of the torture resistance training involved self-inflicted pain, sleep deprivation and isolation. According to the *New York Times*:

> When the students arrive for their six-day training session they are herded into a small, barbed-wire compound with an army squad tent for barracks and told, 'as of this minute you are prisoners of war.' Cigarettes are taken away. For food, the students get rice with leftovers, sometimes including fish heads. Periodically they are ordered out and made to do close-order drill, or march endlessly around the tent with their hands above their heads. 'Enemy' guards, specially selected for the job, show the prisoner no respect … At nightfall, the students' ordeal grows even worse. One by one, they are roughly ordered out by guards and marched with their hands above their heads to an old concrete ammunition bunker … [for] remorseless interrogation by instructors acting as 'commissars', and even a stretch in 'the hole', a dark, dirty solitary confinement cell.

The harsh routine at Chinhae was crafted from methods used in the Soviet Union and Communist China. Although largely ignored by the Central Intelligence Agency and propagandists like Edward Hunter, accurate reports of communist interrogation methods were widely available by 1953. Novelist Arthur Koestler, for instance, revealed the mechanics behind communist coercion in his 1940 work, *Darkness at Noon*. Set during the Moscow show trials of the late 1930s, the book recounts the slow capitulation of a once-famed revolutionary named Rubashov. Gletkin, Rubashov's interrogator, relied only on bright light and exhaustion to force the confession. Koestler wrote:

> [Rubashov] could only remember separate fragments of his dialogue with Gletkin, which extended over several days and

nights, with short intervals of an hour or two. He could not even say exactly how many days and nights it had been; they must have spread over a week ... After forty-eight hours, Rubashov had lost the sense of day and night. When, after an hour's sleep, the giant shook him awake, he was no longer able to decide whether the grey light at the window was that of dawn or evening ... Now temptation accompanied him through the indistinguishable days and nights, on his swaying walk through the corridor, in the white light of Gletkin's lamp; the temptation, which consisted of the single word written on the cemetery of the defeated: Sleep.

Although it is a work of fiction, *Darkness at Noon* presented a composite picture of life in a Soviet prison based on the actual experiences of Koestler's close friends. George Orwell's dystopian classic, *Nineteen Eighty-Four* (1949), was also based on real-life accounts. When protagonist Winston Smith is arrested, he is taken to a small, windowless cell flooded with white light. At first his isolation is punctuated only by beatings at the hands of violent inquisitors but over time the 'ruffians in black' are replaced by men in spectacles. According to Orwell:

These other questioners saw to it that he was in constant slight pain, but it was not chiefly pain they relied on. They slapped his face, wrung his ears, pulled his hair, made him stand on one leg, refused him leave to urinate, shone glaring lights in his face until his eyes ran with water; but the aim of this was simply to humiliate him and destroy his power of arguing and reasoning.

Mainstream newspapers also revealed the 'secret' behind communist coercion. For instance, in March 1950—one month before the CIA launched Project Bluebird—the *New York Times* published a firsthand account of torture penned by Michael Shipkov, a US Embassy employee who was brutalised for weeks by the Bulgarian police. The story was headlined 'How Reds Get Confessions Revealed to US by Victim'. According to Shipkov:

I was ordered to stand facing the wall upright at a distance which allowed me to touch the wall with two fingers of my outstretched arms. Then to step back some twelve inches, keep my heels

touching the floor, and maintain my balance only with the
contact of one finger on each hand. And while standing so,
the interrogation continued—nor was I allowed to collect my
thoughts. This posture does not appear unduly painful, nor did it
particularly impress me in the beginning. And yet, combined
with the mental strain, with the continuous pressure to talk, with
the utter hopelessness and the longing to go through the thing
and be sent down into silence and peace—it is a very effective
manner of breaking down all resistance.

Sleep deprivation and isolation, in addition to forced standing,
were also powerful presssures used by the Soviets. In 1948, Joseph E.
Evans, the *Wall Street Journal*'s Berlin correspondent, discussed the use
of these tortures in Bulgaria:

> [A powerful technique] for securing information or cooperation
> is to stand a man in water up to his waist and leave him there for
> twenty-four or more hours. More subtle psychological tortures
> include simulating terrifying sounds outside an already exhausted
> man's cell in the middle of the night, and the endless interroga-
> tions themselves—calling the victim in from his cell at any hour
> of the day or night, repeatedly, day after day, never allowing him
> to get enough sleep to think clearly or finally, to care. It is this
> sort of thing which reduces human beings to dithering idiots,
> which produces those amazing confessions ...

Americans released from Soviet prisons also attested to the use of
these tortures. For instance, in 1951 Robert Vogeler, the American
ITT official, was released from Hungarian prison after serving seventeen months of his fifteen-year sentence. According to Vogeler, his
initial interrogation lasted seventy-eight hours without sleep or food.
After sixty hours Vogeler hallucinated. 'I thought I was home again—
the picture of my wife kept flashing before me', he said. At the seven-
tieth hour, he collapsed and was moved to a small cell with glaring
lights. Sleep then was limited to one and a half hours per night and
interrogations lasted up to eighteen hours per day. 'I lost twenty pounds
and was maliciously subjected to hours of shouting and screaming or
alternately isolated in utter, dead maddening silence', Vogeler said. At
one stage, he recalled, he was taken to an underground cell, about five

square metres in size, where he was stripped and examined. 'The walls perspired, the floor was wet and the cold unbearable. For the next ten days I was not allowed to wash and my menu consisted of black bread and water three times a day', he said. After days underground, he was taken back to his interrogators. 'I had lost contact with all reality and had been worn down physically and mentally.' In this state, Vogeler signed the confession and agreed to plead guilty at a public trial.

Journalist William Oatis, originally arrested in 1951, spoke of similar tortures. On 15 May 1953, Oatis was granted a pardon from the Czech government after serving two years. Oatis revealed that the Communists used a combination of physical and mental coercion to break him down. He signed a confession stating that he shared military information after being kept awake for forty-two hours. 'I was desperate for sleep. So I signed', he said. He was then kept in strict isolation for sixty-nine days in a two- by three-metre cell to ensure his co-operation during the trial. 'In the early weeks of my imprisonment, I walked the floor like a caged animal, with my head whirling and my stomach turning over, and I felt that I would die if I did not get out of there', Oatis said.

The CIA's deadly foray into drug-based interrogation research appears in hindsight all the more reckless considering what was known about communist coercion by 1953. The 'Mindszenty Effect' wasn't caused by mysterious drugs like Actedron, but by simple physical and psychological tortures designed to wear down the body and mind gradually. Some CIA agents did doubt that the Communists used esoteric methods to extract confessions. For instance, one document dated 14 January 1953 read: 'Apparently [the Communists'] major emphasis is on the development of specially-trained teams for obtaining information without the use of narcotics, hypnosis, or special mechanical devices.' Another memo, issued the next day by the Ad Hoc Medical Study Group, declared that 'the present state of knowledge indicates little, if any, threat to National Security through "special interrogation" techniques or agents'. However, the prevalent position was that drugs were central to interrogation techniques, and the sceptics' opinions were marginalised.

In 1953, the agency launched MKULTRA while the Pentagon cancelled its own mind control program, Operation Chatter, and opened the Chinhae school. In July 1953—two months after the Korean school opened—the Defense Department expanded stress inoculation training. A new school was founded at Camp Mackall, North Carolina, where both Navy and Army soldiers were forced to endure isolation, sleep deprivation and self-inflicted pain. At first, these resistance programs were limited in scope—open to select personnel sent behind enemy lines. This changed in 1955 amid greater calls for brainwashing protection.

On 26 January 1954, twenty-one American POWs held an impromptu press conference in the Korean neutral zone at Panmunjom. One by one the Americans said that it was impossible for them to return to the United States. 'Anyone who breathes the word "peace" in America now becomes at once a "Communist" and UN outlaw', said Richard Corden of Providence, Rhode Island. Each pledged to remain in Communist-held North Korea. Two days after the press conference, the *New York Times* devoted an entire editorial to the 'Red GIs'. According to the editors:

> For men who were born and grew up in this country to say things like 'There is no freedom of speech in the United States' suggests that those making such statements have had their life memories wiped out and delusions put in their place ... The tragedy they represent warns us to prepare better defenses against similar brainwashing should our troops ever again come into similar danger of becoming Communist prisoners.

Calls for resistance training grew louder as the extent of American POWs' co-operation with their Communist captors was revealed. One survey found that 70 per cent of the 7190 US POWs had co-operated with the North Koreans and Chinese. In particular, 39 per cent of the 3323 Army prisoners signed propaganda petitions, 22 per cent made voice recordings, 11 per cent wrote pro-Communist articles, 5 per cent wrote petitions, and another 5 per cent helped to circulate the petitions.

One flier who co-operated was Colonel Frank Schwable, chief of staff of the First Marine Aircraft Wing. On 8 July 1942, Schwable was shot down over North Korean territory. Nearly eight months later, China's Radio Peiping broadcast a four-hour, 6000-word statement attributed to Schwable. According to Peiping, Schwable asserted that the Air Force, the Marine Aircraft Wing, and the Navy were secretly ordered to establish a 'biological contamination belt' to slice the Korean peninsula from the Chinese mainland. The USA was to drop first cholera, then yellow fever, then typhus bombs, said the broadcast. Schwable had allegedly told the Koreans that 'absolutely nothing could appear in writing on the subject and the word "bacteria" was not to be mentioned', and that all orders were relayed 'personally and verbally for security reasons'. According to the *New York Times*, the deposition sounded natural and was written 'in excellent English without the usual mistakes noted in the enemy's propaganda'.

'It's all a damn lie, and I would like to go up to the UN and tell them so under oath,' responded General Clayton C. Jerome, former commander of the First Marine Aircraft Wing in Korea. General Mark W. Clark, the UN Commander-in-Chief in Korea, branded the confessions 'fantastic and utterly false'. Clark doubted that the deposition was penned by the flier, but 'too familiar are the mind-annihilating methods of the Communists in extorting whatever words they want for there to be any mystery as to how they were fabricated'.

Schwable was released on 5 September 1953 following a prisoner-swap dubbed Operation Big Switch. Although he immediately repudiated his confession, four months later the Marine Corps launched an inquiry into the lieutenant colonel's behaviour while a POW. Under the Uniform Code of Military Justice (UCMJ), enacted in 1950, 'cowardly conduct' before an enemy is an offence punishable by death. The inquiry was to recommend whether Schwable should face a court martial or be excused due to the torture he endured.

During the inquiry, Schwable testified that he was 'morally broken' by communist methods of coercion and that he existed in 'a world of fancy that is beyond the power of description'. According to Schwable, he confessed after months of non-stop torture. 'It wasn't a method of physical torture so much as mental torture over a long, drawn-out period of time', he said. Perhaps physical torture would have been preferable, he said, because 'people can understand physical torture better'. Almost every hour, a guard would enter the cell and shine lights into his eyes, depriving him of sleep. The prisoners were always in solitary confinement, he said, and during interrogations, he was forced to stand at attention for six hours at a time. When it came time to write out the germ warfare confession, he was forced to sit at a table in frigid temperatures without moving. Months of torture had reduced him to the status of a 'beast in a cage wallowing in filth'.

He added that he could have held out longer if he had been better prepared for such treatment.

Psychiatrist Dr Joost Meerloo, a lecturer at Columbia University and ex-chief of the Netherlands Army Psychological Department, testified that Schwable suffered from 'menticide'. For Meerloo, this term referred to the destruction of a person's mind via 'psychological attack in the form of perverted mass propaganda and individual mental torture'. No man alive could withstand communist brainwashing, he said. Dr Winfred Overholser, superintendent of St Elizabeth's Mental Hospital in Washington, DC, also testified in Schwable's defence. Overholser—who personally directed the Office of Strategic Services' failed THC truth drug trials in 1943—recommended that the military do more to 'condition our people' to resist communist brainwashing. 'There is no indestructible man', he added.

After four weeks of testimony, the Marine court issued a verdict. The panel found that 'the communists have developed, and perfected, a diabolical method of torture which combines degradation, deprivation and mental harassment, and which is aimed at the destruction of the individual's will to resist'. The panel determined that 'this method can be applied to an individual continuously over such a long period of time by a skillful, ruthless and determined enemy that one of three events inevitably takes place: A. The victim's will to resist is broken, and he responds as the enemy desires. B. The victim becomes insane. C. The victim dies'. The inquiry concluded that since 'Colonel Schwable resisted this torture to the limit of his ability to resist … no disciplinary action [should] be taken'.

Two months after Colonel Frank Schwable was exonerated and given a desk job at the Pentagon, the Marine Corps awarded him the Legion of Merit. Schwable was fortunate—of the 564 other servicemen questioned by Air Force, Army, Navy, and Marine panels, 192 were charged with 'serious offenses against comrades or the United States'.

———

In September 1954, Secretary of Defense Charles E. Wilson set up a committee to investigate the issue of communist collaboration. 'We need to study the techniques of physical and mental persuasion which we can expect our potential enemies to employ', he said, 'in order that we may develop a uniform program of information, indoctrination and training which will serve more effectively the best interests of the Armed Forces as well as the citizenry at large.' Almost one year later, the Pentagon issued a definitive Code of Conduct for POWs. The code grants compassion for soldiers that yield under torture, but demands that POWs resist brainwashing at all costs and at most reveal only name, rank, service number and date of birth. The Code of Conduct directive stated that while a POW 'may be subjected to extreme coercion beyond his ability to resist', a prisoner must attempt to escape at all costs and if tortured 'stand on the final line to the end—no disclosure of vital information and above all no disloyalty in word or deed to his country, his service or his comrades'. When Wilson issued the code, he directed that the armed forces 'give specialized training in evasion, escape, resistance, prison organization and survival'.

To comply with the order, stress inoculation courses were revamped and expanded to all branches of the military. By September 1955, for instance, the Marines had launched a survival program at the Glenview Naval Air Station in Illinois. According to Colonel Robert B. Moore, information officer at the base, the purpose of the 'escape and evasion exercise' was to give pilots 'an idea of what to expect if captured in wartime'. Although the specific techniques used at the school remain secret, Moore insisted that 'it was probably less tough than some college fraternity initiations'.

Resistance training also spread overseas. Six months after the Pentagon POW code was issued, Sir Walter Monckton, Minister of Defence in the United Kingdom, announced that British troops would face similar trials. The aim of the training, he said, was to boost military qualities that 'support a fighting man in the stresses of combat conditions and sustain him if he becomes a prisoner of war'. In the UK, the program was dubbed 'R2I': 'resistance to interrogation'.

By far the most extensive, and brutal, torture course of the 1950s was conducted by the US Air Force. Following enactment of the POW Code of Conduct, the Chinhae course was phased out and replaced by a program at Stead Air Force Base, Nevada. Although small-scale survival training had been conducted at the base since 1950, by 1955 the Stead school was considered the toughest 'torture school' in the armed forces. The school adopted the nickname SERE, an acronym for Survival, Evasion, Resistance and Escape.

The first portion of SERE forced cadets to live off the land. After several days of practical lectures, students were left for ten days in the Sierra Nevada mountains to create shelters and procure their own food. They were only given two and a half days' rations and had to do whatever was necessary to keep from starving, including killing and eating rats, snakes and porcupines. Towards the end of the ten-day stint, the Air Force dispatched squads of 'aggressor' forces. If students were captured by mock enemy forces, they were led in a stockade to the POW camp, where they were subjected to a barrage of physical and psychological trials.

According to an air intelligence officer at Stead: 'First we teach them not to talk. Then we teach them how to talk in the event they are tortured into it.' The interrogation phase of the Stead SERE course lasted thirty-six hours. *Newsweek*'s Peter Wyden dramatically recounted what he saw on a visit in August 1955:

> The lieutenant was young and frail. There had been a time when he had eaten, washed, and slept, but that had been in some other life many nightmares ago. Stripped to his shorts, he stood on the crude wooden floor with his knees slightly bent. It did not look like an uncomfortable position, but the pain in his legs became worse and worse. He began trembling. It was difficult to estimate the temperature in the windowless wooden shack. It might have been 110 degrees [Fahrenheit]. It might have been 130. The lieutenant couldn't see his surroundings because three powerful spotlights flooded his grimy face from three feet away. He kept staring at his arms. They were stretched forward with a thin, naked wire looped around each forefinger. Whenever somebody behind the lights felt like it, the wires pumped an electric shock through the lieutenant's body ...

Electric shocks and forced standing were just the beginning. If students survived this ordeal, they were made to kneel on a broomstick while holding up heavy rocks. Four painful isolation-based tortures were also used at Stead. The first was an upright wooden box, about 40 centimetres wide and deep, that was too short to let a man stand upright. 'After hours of confinement in this device', said Wyden, 'men tumbled out like footballs, muscles temporarily paralysed'. Others were stuffed into 'the coffin' and made to lie flat on its gravel bottom. There was the

steel 'sweat box': a sealed container made even more unbearable by
the clamour of rifle butts incessantly banged against the side. Finally,
some students were forced into 'the hole', a covered pit three metres
underground, filled with shoulder-deep water—a torture reminiscent
of the old Bulgarian technique outlined by the *Wall Street Journal*
in 1948.

At Stead, teams of doctors and psychologists worked closely with
interrogators both before and after torture sessions. The medical teams
would supervise tortures and 'brief their victim on his errors and
most dangerous weaknesses' after the ordeal. Under the watchful eyes
of medical professionals, students at Stead were also subjected to a
lengthy course of humiliating treatment tailored to their individual
vulnerabilities. According to Wyden, 'Lies and insults about a captive's
personality, race, national origin and religion are routine starters.
(Catholics have it extra rough …)'. Tortures were also sexual in scope.
'Men who are shy about undressing may not keep their shorts on',
noted Wyden. During questioning, thirsty students who asked for
water 'get it thrown in the face' while 'anyone asking to go to the
latrine is sure to be questioned longer than scheduled'. The abuse at
Stead didn't end there. According to Wyden:

> To break resistance, interrogators try almost anything to make
> men angry … When a trainee's wallet yields a picture of an
> attractive wife or girl friend, her looks take a verbal beating. A
> major who let slip that he only had an eighth grade education,
> and a lieutenant whose membership card to Alcoholics
> Anonymous laid him open to ridicule about his weakness for
> alcohol, were hammered until they talked just to end their
> humiliation. A bachelor lieutenant, badgered until he became
> convinced he could not find a girl because his face had been
> deformed in a childhood accident, finally broke up in tears.

Failure to complete the course could affect an officer's career,
noted Colonel Burton E. McKenzie, then the commanding officer at
the base. 'We've had some who quit and their commander, naturally,
would not want somebody like that on their crews [who would]
endanger the lives of others by breaking under pressure', he said. Still,
the Air Force claimed that by September 1955 more than 29 000 men
had passed through the Stead SERE school. According to school

officials, none of the airmen who took the course needed any 'extended' medical or mental treatment after the ordeal.

Disclosure of the program by *Newsweek* ignited debate within the USA. 'My own sons are not involved yet. By the time they are, surely the military heads will have discovered that the effects are bad enough to offset the small benefits that they might bring, and will have discontinued it', wrote Edith L. Arthur in a letter to *Newsweek* editors. Another reader countered: 'I have been trying to determine what kind of people are these that have objected to the Air Force's survival training ... Perhaps these people have not yet "gotten the word." How about passing it along to them? War is hell ladies and gentlemen. They put real bullets in those guns and everyone plays for keeps.'

Remarkably, the SERE school survived its exposure. Although it was temporarily suspended in December 1955, the course reopened months later after the controversy abated. During this time, Air Force officials vehemently defended the school. Air Force Secretary Donald Quaries said that based on the advice of Air Force psychologists—most likely the men from the Psychological Warfare Division—he recognised the 'value and need' of the course. Stead officials agreed. Colonel McKenzie believed he was 'running a good school'. According to McKenzie, 'We don't torture or degrade the students. Any man can quit when he wants to but the men take pride in getting through the course.' Major John Oliphant, training director of the school, said most of the students looked at the seventeen-day course as a 'vacation—sort of like playing cops and robbers'. Oliphant denied that the frail lieutenant featured in the *Newsweek* story 'collapsed and cried' after being electrocuted and forced to stand. According to Oliphant, the officer was merely 'laughing triumphantly after having come through the ordeal without cracking'.

While the resistance schools were designed to inoculate students against torture, by the late 1950s US Army Special Forces had co-opted coursework from SERE for more sinister purposes. Army Special Forces are elite fighting units sent behind enemy lines to pre-empt attacks, rescue hostages, destroy infrastructure, and train local forces. Unlike other military outfits, Special Forces soldiers are well versed in guerrilla techniques. According to the 1951 edition of Army Field Manual (FM) 31-21, *Organization and Conduct of Guerrilla Warfare*, guerrilla operations include 'organized and directed passive resistance, espionage, assassination, sabotage and propaganda, and, in some cases, ordinary combat'. Trained in the deadly arts, the Special Forces have the motto 'Anything, Any Time, Any Place, Any How'.

Sergeant Donald Duncan joined the Special Forces in 1959. At the time, Special Forces resistance training was held at Camp Mackall and was supplemented by classroom training at the Army's nearby Special Warfare School at Fort Bragg, North Carolina. Duncan became an interrogation instructor at Fort Bragg after completing the course. According to Duncan, rather than learning how to resist communist torture, students at Fort Bragg learned how to use it to extract information.

In testimony to the 1967 International War Crimes Tribunal, a commission investigating American war crimes in Indo-China, headed by British philosopher Bertrand Russell, Donald Duncan recalled that methods of mental and physical torture were taught in a course named 'Countermeasures to Hostile Interrogation'. According to Duncan, 'The specific thing was always suggested that you do not mark a person. In other words, don't leave physical evidence on his body. Use those types of interrogation where if somebody were to see the prisoner immediately afterwards you couldn't tell that he had been abused.'

Duncan said that in class a translation of an alleged Soviet inter-rogation manual was given to students. According to Duncan, the manual discussed:

> interrogation techniques used in such Communist countries as Hungary ... the isolation, the hot-and-cold treatment, the con-fusing of the man's mind, making it impossible for him to relate time, for instance when is night and when is day ... and how you break the person down. We were encouraged to read these things, and as a matter of fact, we were, in a way, interrogated or tested on these subjects.

Harsh physical tortures, said Duncan, were to be used only 'in times and conditions when it will be impossible to conduct psycho-logical methods of interrogation'. The physical tortures included:

> squashing of the male genitals, putting buckets over people's heads and beating them ... suspending a man from a chain or a rope with a wide belt around the waist and spinning him around

... the use of electricity, [and] field expedient methods such as using the double E-A telephone, just a standard Army field set—battery operated—attaching the lead wires to the genitals, or genital areas, for shock, and so on.

Torture lessons at Fort Bragg were held under tight security with guards posted at the doors. The material itself, Duncan said, conformed to a general policy of plausible deniability: euphemisms were used to shield precise intent. According to Duncan, the material in the class 'was presented in such a way that it left no doubt in anybody's mind that, if you need the information, these are other methods and you certainly can use them'. Added Duncan, 'For the official record, if somebody said: "You're teaching methods of torture," they say, "No, no, no, no, all we're teaching is what the enemy does." Again, it's for the official record.'

In his memoirs, *The New Legions* (1967), Duncan, who was honourably discharged from the Army in 1966, recounted the confusion of one naïve student. After the instructor, Sergeant Lacey, explains some variations to the physical torture methods, the student asks:

Sergeant Lacey, the name of this class is 'Countermeasures to Hostile Interrogation', but you have spent most of the period telling us there are no countermeasures. If this is true, then the only reason for teaching them, it seems to me, is so that we'll know how to use them. Are you suggesting we use these methods?

The class laughs, and Lacey looks down at the floor creating a dramatic pause. When he raises his head, his face is solemn but his deep-set eyes are dancing. 'We can't tell you that, Sergeant Harrison. The Mothers of America wouldn't approve.' The class bursts into laughter at the sarcastic cynicism. 'Furthermore,' a conspiratorial wink, 'we will deny that any such thing is taught or intended.'

———

3

CODIFYING CRUELTY

As American soldiers in the 1950s suffered through stress inoculation schools across the USA, another program was under way
that took students to the limits of extreme deprivation. This wasn't
happening at a survival school, but at McGill University in Montreal,
Canada. At McGill, Dr Donald O. Hebb, then head of the psychology
department, was experimenting on university student volunteers with
a sophisticated isolation box he had built. The results were astounding.
As Hebb later concluded, 'Without physical pain, without drugs, the
personality can be badly deformed simply by modifying the perceptual environment'.

Between 1951 and 1954, Dr Hebb received about US$10000
per year under 'Contract X-38' from the Canadian Defence Research
Board (CDRB) to conduct 'radical isolation' research. Funding began
after American, Canadian and British defence officials met on 5 June
1951 in Montreal to discuss the threat posed by Soviet brainwashing.
Hebb, then chair of the Human Relations and Research Committee
of the CDRB, was present at the conference and volunteered to investigate the effects of sensory deprivation on physiological function—a
subject he had long found fascinating. His 1936 PhD at Harvard, for
example, looked at the effects of visual deprivation in rats. With
government backing, Hebb shifted his focus to humans.

According to Hebb, he performed the isolation research 'with the
hope that some possibilities for protection against brainwashing might
turn up'. Hebb paid students at McGill twice the average salary of
the time, US$20 per day, to lie in a specially designed isolation box

for as long as possible. Hebb had planned to observe changes in his volunteers' behaviour over a period of six weeks. No one stayed in the box longer than six days.

Before entering the box, students were fitted with goggles that diffused light and prevented patterned vision. Gloves and cardboard cuffs limited perception by touch while hearing was cut off by way of a U-shaped foam-rubber pillow placed around the subject's head. Fans and air-conditioners were then turned on to diffuse sound further. Once they were wearing the isolation suit, students were asked to lie comfortably on a bed inside the box. The box remained lit twenty-four hours a day and communications were conducted via tiny speakers embedded in the foam pillow. Writing materials were provided for the express purpose of testing the subjects' penmanship at regular inter-vals. They were only allowed to leave the box to go to the toilet and for meals.

The effects of the isolation were dramatic. At first, many subjects fell asleep. Upon awakening, they would attempt to amuse themselves by whistling, humming, or tapping the cardboard cuffs together. Soon subjects would grow restless, displaying seemingly random movement. Students who tried to mentally review school work found it difficult to focus. Math problems presented to the subjects were left unsolved and penmanship deteriorated. Eventually, subjects reported that it was too difficult to focus on one thing and that they experienced 'blank periods'. Then, most subjects reported having 'dreams while awake'. These hallucinations often started with simple images before becoming more complex. One subject reported seeing dots, then lines, then simple patterns, then recognisable figures, then finally integrated scenes. Another reported seeing dinosaurs stomping through a jungle and one saw 'a procession of squirrels with sacks over their shoulders marching "purposefully" across a snow field'. Some subjects were able to see objects suggested by the experimenters. For instance, a subject instructed to visualise a pen 'first saw an inkblot, then a pencil, a green horse, and then a pen'. The imagery persisted during physical exercise and even when subjects spoke to the experimenters and vice versa.

In addition to intense visual hallucinations, researchers found that isolated subjects were susceptible to 'preposterous nonsense'. After they had spent long periods in the box, Hebb played recorded talks discussing the existence of ghosts and poltergeists. Weeks after the experiment finished, high numbers of subjects admitted that now they were afraid of ghosts. Subjects also said that they heard and felt things while in isolation. One student heard a choir singing in 'full stereophonic sound' while another said he felt as if he was getting hit in the arm by pellets launched by a miniature rocket ship. Finally, some subjects reported out of body experiences: 'My mind seemed to be a ball of cotton wool floating above my body', one recalled. Overall, some students enjoyed the experience. To others, it was a living nightmare.

Hebb reported these finding to the Defence Research Board in 1952 and two years later portions of his research appeared in the *Canadian Journal of Psychology*. When the Canadian Parliament found out that Hebb was paying students to lie around in an air-conditioned cube, his funding was abruptly cancelled. According to Hebb, all his research was then 'snatched immediately to some organization in the States'.

The CIA learned of Hebb's research in September 1954 at the American Psychological Association's annual convention at the Statler in New York—the same hotel where Dr Frank Olson had fallen to his death less than one year earlier. Although by 1954 the agency was pumping millions of dollars into esoteric drug research, agents in the Technical Services Division remained on the lookout for any new scientific breakthroughs relevant to MKULTRA. A TSD official covertly assigned to the convention realised the applicability of Hebb's isolation research. His report to CIA headquarters, uncovered by Alfred W. McCoy in *A Question of Torture* (2006), noted that Hebb's 'experiment gets at some of the psychological factors found in prisoner-of-war treatment where the individual is completely isolated in solitary confinement'. Hebb's volunteers 'were blindfolded and their ears covered with foam rubber and their feet and hands were covered with large mitts and they were placed in soundproof rooms'. The subjects 'tended to lose their sense of time' and some became 'very irritable'.

By 1955, MKULTRA researchers began exploring the potential use of isolation in interrogation. One CIA memo, dated 16 March 1955, discussed the results of isolation trials on six volunteers, all members of the US military. According to the memo, this 'form of psychological harassment' was an 'operational tool of potential'. The effects of isolation intrigued Morse Allen, former head of Project Bluebird. On 21 March 1955, he wrote a memo to the Director of Security that discussed 'total isolation' as a promising 'interrogation aid'. Allen also presented an isolation research proposal to Dr Maitland Baldwin, a neurosurgeon at the National Institutes of Health known for his bizarre research with monkeys. Once he attempted to control a chimpanzee's behaviour by shooting high-frequency radio waves at its brain; another time he cut the head off an ape and transplanted it onto the headless body of another. Morse Allen wanted know about the long-term effects of isolation: so far no had one lasted longer than six days in the box. Baldwin agreed to conduct 'terminal type' isolation experiments on humans provided that the CIA would supply funding, subjects, and a plausible cover for the research. But before the project got off the ground, an agency medical officer cancelled the project, branding it 'immoral and inhuman'. Instead of humans, Baldwin used monkeys. His results remain classified.

Two years later, Baldwin came across the work of Dr Ewan Cameron, then Director of the Allen Memorial Institute in Montreal and a former member of the Nuremburg Tribunal. In the early 1950s, Cameron had pioneered a treatment known as 'psychic driving' that he believed could cure psychological ailments such as depression, paranoia, and schizophrenia. The treatment called for a progression of electro-shock treatments and drug-induced comas, ostensibly to obliterate a patient's memories, followed by hours of looped pre-recorded messages intended to reintroduce new behaviours.

In 1957, Baldwin met with Cameron in Montreal to investigate psychic driving and share his findings into sensory deprivation. Following the meeting, Cameron added an isolation component to his psychic driving model and applied for a grant from the CIA. In Cameron, Baldwin saw a doctor willing to perform terminal isolation experiments, with access to an unlimited number of human guinea pigs. For Cameron, the CIA was an ideal donor—an organisation lacking strict ethics that was willing to provide generous funding for controversial research. Cameron sent his grant application to 'The Society for the Investigation of Human Ecology', a CIA front headed by Cornell's Harold Wolff. The proposal, titled 'The Effects Upon Human Behavior of the Repetition of Verbal Signals', described four steps to a successful 'conversion':

1. The breaking down of ongoing patterns of the patient's behavior by means of particularly intensive electroshocks (depatterning).

2. The intensive repetition (16 hours a day for 6–7 days) of the prearranged verbal signal (driving).
3. During this period of intensive repetition the patient is kept in partial sensory isolation.
4. Repression of the driving period is carried out by putting the patient, after the conclusion of the period, into continuous sleep for 7–10 days.

The application was quickly approved and was designated 'MKULTRA Subproject 68'.

According to ex-patients and staff at Allen Memorial, Cameron often went above and beyond the limits of the proposal. Cameron gave patients electro-shock treatment ('depatterning') up to three times a day for thirty days at a time and slipped others into drug-induced comas for up to eighty-eight days. 'Driving' was performed by playing recorded statements via little speakers implanted in blacked-out football helmets bound to the patients' heads. The isolation phase took place in a deprivation box Cameron built on the hospital grounds. One 52-year-old patient, 'Mary C.', was admitted to Allen Memorial suffering from anxiety and hypochondria. Blacked-out goggles were placed over her eyes, her ears were covered with earmuffs, and her hands were padded to limit physical sensation. Cameron then placed her in the box for more than a month. According to Cameron, 'Although the patient was prepared by both prolonged sensory isolation (35 days) and by repeated depatterning, and although she received 101 days of positive driving, no favorable results were obtained'.

During his time as Director, Cameron took hundreds of patients to extreme limits of sensory deprivation without their full voluntary consent. Cameron's assistant, Leonard Rubenstein, later explained to the *New York Times* that the CIA-funded work at Allen Memorial 'was directly related to brainwashing'. According to Rubenstein, 'They had investigated brainwashing among soldiers who had been in Korea. We in Montreal started to use some [of these] techniques, brainwashing patients instead of using drugs'.

When Cameron left Allen Memorial in 1964, he penned a letter to 'The Society for the Investigation of Human Ecology', thanking them for their 'invaluable' support and sharing his 'considerable sense of indebtedness' for the nearly US$60 000 in funding they provided over the years. Cameron's successor, Dr Robert A. Cleghorn, immediately halted the psychic driving trials after Cameron's exit. A follow-up study found that 60 per cent of Cameron's patients who reached the isolation stage suffered from persistent amnesia and 23 per cent developed physical complications like epilepsy. Although litigation was initially hampered by Cameron's untimely death in 1967 from a heart attack, to date, seventy-eight former Allen Memorial patients have received compensation—Can$100 000 each—for the 'treatment' they received at the hospital.

It pained Dr Hebb to see his initial sensory deprivation work so perverted by Cameron and the CIA. Hebb later reflected:

> Cameron was irresponsible—criminally stupid, in that there was no reason to expect that he would get any results from the experiments. Anyone with any appreciation of the complexity of the human mind would not expect that you could erase an adult mind and then add things back with this stupid psychic driving. He wanted to make a name for himself—so he threw his cap over the windmill ...

While the CIA probed the mysteries of sensory deprivation, attention was also given to other interrogation methods used by Communists abroad and at SERE schools in the USA. In 1956, CIA Director Allen Dulles commissioned Cornell's Harold Wolff and colleague Lawrence Hinkle Jr to determine why communist techniques worked so well time and time again. Hinkle and Wolff delivered the study 'Communist Control Techniques' to the CIA's Technical Services Division on 2 April 1956. The 118-page report lucidly explained the effects of physical and psychological torture on the bodies and minds of its victims. Isolation, they discovered, was only one part of the puzzle.

Hinkle and Wolff found that the basis of the communist interrogation system lay in emotional exploitation framed by anxiety, fear and brutality. In parts, their report reads like Koestler's *Darkness at Noon* or Orwell's *Nineteen Eighty-Four*. Hinkle and Wolff recount in meticulous detail how in communist states a sudden abduction at night marked the start of a long and gruelling interrogation process. Often seized without explanation, the prisoners were then left alone in solitary confinement for weeks in a cell measuring no more than two by three metres. Captives were placed under constant surveillance by a rotation of armed guards. All contact with the outside world was shut off—no books, magazines or newspapers were permitted. Suspects were also not allowed to talk to the guards or any of the other prisoners. The silence of captivity was punctuated only by orders from the guards. At night, prisoners were ordered to sleep with the lights on and with their hands above the sheets. If someone moved the slightest bit while asleep, the guards woke him up. Often, the guards would mock and humiliate prisoners or manipulate the temperature of the cells, making it unbearably hot or uncomfortably cold. Both extremes produced fatigue. Exhaustion was induced by withholding food for indefinite amounts of time and sometimes by waking suspects every time they shut their eyes to rest.

The stress of captivity was compounded by the prisoners' own anxiety, the study found. They worried about how long they were to be confined and with what they were to be charged, knowing full well that punishment could be life in prison or the death penalty. A prisoner's uncertainty was also augmented by not knowing what would happen to friends, family and colleagues whose guilt the KGB often assumed by association. Left alone to ponder these questions, prisoners gradually lost touch with reality. Wrote Hinkle and Wolff:

> When food is presented to him, he eats it all, but he no longer bothers with the nicety of eating. He may mix it up into a mush and stuff it into his mouth like an animal ... He may soil himself. He weeps; he mutters, and he prays aloud in his cell ... God may appear to such a prisoner and tell him to cooperate with his interrogator. He may see his wife standing beside him, or a servant bringing him a large meal ... He follows the orders of the guard with the docility of a trained animal.

Interrogation would begin when the prisoner reached this stage. By then, the prisoner is starved for human contact and the KGB interrogator fulfils this need. 'If he is given an opportunity to talk, he may say anything which seems to be appropriate, or to be desired by his listener ... The mere opportunity to talk to someone is intensely gratifying.' Compliant prisoners were rewarded with better treatment while disobedience was punished. Some captives, the study found, were forced to stand for up to twenty-four hours at a time. Forced standing, 'like other features of the KGB procedure, is a form of physical torture, in spite of the fact that the prisoners and the KGB officers alike do not ordinarily perceive it as such', they noted. Standing for more than eighteen hours causes 'excruciating pain':

> the ankles and feet of the prisoner swell to twice their normal circumference ... The skin becomes tense and intensely painful. Large blisters develop, which break and exude watery serum. The accumulation of the body fluid in the legs produces impairment of the circulation. The heart rate increases, and fainting may occur. Eventually there is a renal shutdown and urine production ceases ... Ultimately [victims] usually develop a delirious state, characterized by disorientation, fear, delusions and visual hallucinations.

Hinkle and Wolff also discovered a cruel psychological aspect of forced standing. At first prisoners attempt to 'stick it out' and assume a feeling of moral superiority against their captor. Over time, 'there develops a conflict within the individual between his moral determination and his desire to collapse and discontinue the pain'. According to Hinkle and Wolff, 'It is this extra internal conflict that tends to make this method of torture so effective in the breakdown of the individual'.

Prisoners eventually learned that the more they revealed—whether true or imagined—the closer they were to ending the ordeal. Slowly, a list of crimes was compiled and a confession signed. The same detention regime continued until trial. The promise that tortures would worsen if the victim recanted in the courtroom was a threat 'as poignant as a cocked pistol'. According to one former KGB officer interviewed in the study, more than 99 per cent of all Soviet prisoners eventually signed a confession and co-operated in court.

Hinkle and Wolff found that the KGB's methods of interrogation were inherited from Russia's czarist past. Since the reign of Ivan the Terrible, Russia had one of the strongest and most feared secret police systems in Europe. Over the years, the methods used for interrogation were refined through experience—not through the aid of psychiatrists or psychologists. After the Communists swept to power in 1917, the same repressive security apparatus was adopted by the People's Commissariat for Internal Affairs (NKVD) under Stalin, then later by the Commmittee for State Security (the KGB). In turn, the KGB taught these methods to the Chinese in 1949.

The Chinese added a few variations to the Soviet system. The Chinese 'require men in total isolation to sit rigidly on their bunks at all times when they are not eating, sleeping, or exercising. This greatly adds to their discomfort'. They also added public humiliation. Like instructors at the Stead SERE school, Chinese interrogators limited prisoners' use of the toilet. When they were allowed to go, these trips were dreadful affairs. According to Hinkle and Wolff:

> It is a Chinese custom to allow defecation and urination only at one or two specified times each day—usually in the morning after breakfast. The prisoner is hustled from his cell by a guard, double-timed down a long corridor, and given approximately two minutes to squat over an open Chinese latrine and attend to all his wants. The haste and public scrutiny are especially difficult for women to tolerate. If the prisoners cannot complete their action in about two minutes, they are abruptly dragged away and back to their cells ... Many [prisoners] think of it as one of the most fiendish tortures devised by the Chinese Communists ...

Taken together, Soviet and Chinese torture represented a total assault on the senses. Forced standing, isolation, humiliation and starvation 'lead to serious disturbances of many bodily processes'. These methods, note Hinkle and Wolff, 'constitute torture and physical coercion'.

The Hinkle–Wolff report opened a window of understanding into the effects of communist torture. Four months after it was delivered to the CIA, Hinkle and Wolff published a declassified version of their work in the *Archives of Neurology and Psychiatry*. Dozens of subsequent studies into communist coercion—and CIA interrogation manuals—cite the findings of Hinkle and Wolff.

In December 1957, a study expanding on their work, funded by the US Air Force, was published in *Sociometry*. This paper gave a theoretical label to the state of mind that communist interrogators induced in their victims. The authors, Dr I. E. Farber, Dr Harry Harlow and Dr Louis Joylen West, dubbed this the 'debility, dependency and dread state'.

Debility, dependency and dread, or DDD, is crucial to the psychological breakdown of prisoners. In the DDD state, victims 'have reduced viability, are helplessly dependent on their captors for the satisfaction of many of their basic needs, and experience the emotional and motivational reactions of intense fear and anxiety'. Debility, the authors found, was induced via starvation, isolation, chronic physical pain, and a lack of facilities for personal hygiene. These combined factors led to 'inaction and a sense of terrible weariness and weakness'. As inmates grew debilitated, they became increasingly dependent on their captors. Brief respites, the authors found, reminded prisoners that the captors have total control.

Debility and dependence are accentuated by perpetual fear. According to the study:

> Fear of death, fear of pain, fear of non-repatriation, fear of deformity or permanent disability through neglect or inadequate medical treatment, fear of Communist violence against loved ones at home, and even fear of one's own ability to satisfy the demands of insatiable interrogators ... constituted the final component of the DDD syndrome.

The power of DDD rests in the fact that the system can be easily manipulated to foster compliance. According to the authors, 'As soon as resistance appears, the intensity of DDD can be increased, thus at one and the same time punishing resistance and increasing the influence of the reward when relief occurs'. Overall, the DDD state in its full-blown form 'constituted a state of discomfort that was well-nigh intolerable'.

The discovery of DDD shifted the CIA away from its early fascination with drugs. In 1961, for example, the agency's classified in-house journal, *Studies in Intelligence,* sombrely conceded that 'no such magic brew as the popular notion of truth serum exists'. Another study from this period further downplayed the importance of drugs in interrogation. Drugs 'may make the prisoner feel that the interrogator is more powerful or more prescient than he really is', the report said, but they 'have no effect in producing truth'. This report concluded that the dreaded Actedron implicated in Mindszenty's confession was a benzedrine derivative similar to caffeine, and other so-called 'truth drugs' were merely barbiturates like sodium amytal or sodium pentothal. 'Under some circumstances, individuals intoxicated by these drugs become loose in talk', said the report, but 'persons under their influence can resist their action to the same extent that they can resist the action of alcohol'. These findings reflected a growing consensus. According to CIA psychologist Dr John Gittinger, 'By 1962 and 1963, the general idea we were able to come up with is that brainwashing was largely a process of isolating a human being, keeping him out of contact, putting him under long stress in relationship to interviewing and interrogation … without having to resort to any esoteric means'.

The communist methods described by Gittinger began to surface in CIA literature as early as 1958. An article that year in *Studies in Intelligence*, 'The Interrogation of Suspects Under Arrest', outlined a variety of these DDD techniques. Today, this article can be read as an early blueprint for the interrogation system employed by the CIA and armed forces in the war on terror—a regime engineered to elicit debility, dependence and dread.

According to 'Don Compos' (a pseudonym used by a frequent contributor to the journal), the 'recalcitrant subject of an intelligence interrogation must be "broken" but broken for use like a riding horse, not smashed in the search for a single golden egg'. Interrogators, he wrote, should avoid brute physical torture because 'maltreating the subject is from a strictly practical point of view as short-sighted as whipping a horse to its knees before a thirty-mile ride'. Instead, slight physical and psychological pressures should be applied to foster dependence and produce 'a continuing flow of information'.

The 'softening-up process', said Compos, begins at the time of arrest. According to Compos:

> The arrest should take the subject by surprise and should impose on him the greatest possible degree of mental discomfort, in order to catch him off balance and deprive him of the initiative. It should take place at a moment when he least expects it and when his mental and physical resistance is at its lowest. The ideal time which meets these conditions is in the early hours before dawn, when an abrupt transition from sleep to alert mental activity is most difficult.

After subjects are apprehended, they should be isolated from inter-rogators and other prisoners. 'A prisoner left in solitary confinement for a long period with no one, not even his custodian, speaking a word to him may be thoroughly unnerved by the experience', wrote Compos, clearly drawing on Hinkle and Wolff's research. 'When this course is chosen', he added, 'it is important to deprive the prisoner of all his personal possessions, especially of things like snapshots and keepsakes, symbols of his old life which might be a source of moral strength to him'.

During interrogation, CIA interrogators 'should attempt to control the psychological factors in every aspect of the subject's life from the earliest possible stage'. According to Compos, 'Everything possible must be done to impress upon the subject the unassailable superiority of those in whose hands he finds himself and therefore the futility of his position'. During the interview, for example, interrogators should sit with their backs to a strong lamp 'in order to obscure their faces, veil their expressions, and place a strain on the prisoner ... The subject can be placed under further strain by providing him an uncomfortable chair, say one with a polished seat and shortened front legs so that he tends to slide off it, or one with wobbly legs'. It is also important for interrogators to record the interrogation because '[c]onsciousness of a recording going on in full view may be unnerving'. Plus, playing back the recording may 'make a psychological breach in his defenses'.

Compos stressed the importance of constantly changing the methods used to break down prisoners because familiar pressures lose their effect over time. To this end, he recommended 'drastic variation of cell conditions and abrupt alternation of different types of interrogators'. According to Compos:

> A sample device in the regulation of cell conditions for unsophisticated prisoners is the manipulation of time: a clock in a windowless cell can be rigged to move rapidly at times and very slowly at others; breakfast can be brought in when it is time for lunch or in the middle of the night's sleep; the interval between lunch and dinner can be lengthened to twelve or fifteen hours or shortened to two.

A successful interrogation is no easy task, but an agent can master the 'interrogation art' by examining these principles. Compos then adds a curious but revealing aside. Foreshadowing the implementation of military tribunals at Guantánamo Bay, Cuba, Compos notes that an intelligence interrogation is usually incompatible with one intended to produce legal evidence for a court conviction, since statements by the accused may be barred as court evidence on the ground that they were made under duress, during prolonged detention without charge, or in some other violation of legal procedure.

Five years after Compos' seminal treatise on interrogation appeared, the CIA unveiled its first comprehensive interrogation manual incorporating the DDD paradigm. The 128-page *KUBARK Counterintelligence Interrogation* handbook is an expanded version of the Compos piece, reflecting a collage of Soviet and Chinese techniques and more than a decade of behavioural science research. (The cryptonym KUBARK was an early codename for the CIA itself.) The manual was published in 1963—the same year MKULTRA's funding was slashed following a scathing report by the CIA's Inspector General. The guide was declassified in 1997 following a Freedom of Information Act request by the *Baltimore Sun* newspaper.

The KUBARK manual's 'fundamental hypothesis' is that coercive techniques 'can succeed even with highly resistant sources ... [and] are in essence methods of inducing regression of the personality to whatever earlier and weaker level is required for the dissolution of resistance and the inculcation of dependence'. Twenty-two pages of the manual are devoted to 'The Coercive Counterintelligence Interrogation of Resistant Sources'. Citing a study by Lawrence Hinkle Jr—just one of the dozens of CIA- and military-funded researchers whose names appear in the appendix—the handbook states that small degrees of pain, sleep loss and anxiety may affect a person's ability to 'meet new, challenging, and complex situations, to deal with trying interpersonal relations, and cope with repeated frustrations'. As a result, 'most people who are exposed to coercive procedures will talk and usually reveal some information that they might not have revealed otherwise'. After all, the manual assures, 'the use of coercive techniques will rarely or never confuse an interrogatee so completely that he does not know whether his own confession is true or false'.

In some areas, the KUBARK manual goes beyond the confines of the Compos article and touches upon the types of tortures used in the military survival schools. For instance, the manual states that prior headquarters approval must be obtained in three cases: '1) If bodily harm is to be inflicted; 2) If medical, chemical, or electrical methods

or materials are to be used to induce acquiescence; or 3) [Redacted]'
(deleted by the CIA prior to declassification). The manual adds that
before an interrogation takes place 'the electric current should be
known in advance, so that transformers or other modifying devices
will be on hand if needed'. This is a clear reference to the application
of electric shocks.

Apart from these tortures, the manual sticks closely to the methods
discussed by Hinkle, Wolff and Compos. For example, the manual
explains the importance of inflicting maximum psychological discomfort on the detainee at all times. This begins with a surprise arrest
and continues during isolated detention. The manual draws four
conclusions about isolation:

1. The more completely the place of confinement eliminates
   sensory stimuli, the more rapidly and deeply will the interrogatee be affected. Results produced only after a few weeks
   or months of imprisonment can be duplicated in hours or
   days in a cell which has no light (or weak artificial light
   which never varies), which is sound-proofed, in which
   odors are eliminated, etc. An environment still more subject
   to control, such as water-tank or iron lung, is even more
   effective.
2. An early effect of such an environment is anxiety ...
3. The interrogator can benefit from the subject's anxiety. As the
   interrogator becomes linked in the subject's mind with
   the reward of lessened anxiety, human contact, and meaningful activity, and thus with relief for growing discomfort,
   the questioner assumes a benevolent role.
4. The deprivation of stimuli induces regression by depriving
   the subject's mind of contact with an outer world and thus
   forcing it upon itself. At the same time, the calculated provision of stimuli during interrogation tends to make the
   regressed subject view the interrogator as a father-figure.
   The result, normally, is a strengthening of the subject's tendencies towards compliance.

The four findings above correspond precisely to the DDD paradigm. Item 1 relates to debility, item 2 relates to dread, and items 3 and
4 relate to dependency.

To augment effects of DDD during isolation, the manual recommends that interrogators determine a prisoner's 'diet, sleep pattern, and other fundamentals'. According to the manual, 'manipulating these into irregularities, so that the subject becomes disoriented, is very likely to create feelings of fear and helplessness'. Furthermore, during detention, circumstances should be arranged 'to enhance within the subject his feelings of being cut off from the known and the reassuring, and of being plunged into the strange'. To disrupt a subject's sense of time and space, '[t]he subject may be left alone for days; and he may be returned to his cell, allowed to sleep for five minutes, and brought back to an interrogation which is conducted as though eight hours had intervened'.

Dread is crucial to the interrogation process because 'sustained long enough, a strong fear of anything vague or unknown induces regression'. In fact, the manual states, 'the threat to inflict pain ... can trigger fears more damaging the immediate sensation of pain'. If pain is to be administered, the manual suggests forced standing. A subject's 'resistance is likelier to be sapped by pain which he seems to inflict upon himself'. Quoting a US Air Force-funded study by Dr Albert Biderman, the manual recounts that:

> In the simple torture situation the contest is between the individual and his tormentor ... [but] when the individual is told to stand at attention for long periods, an intervening factor is introduced. The immediate source of pain is not the interrogator but the victim himself. The motivational strength of the individual is likely to exhaust itself in this internal encounter ...

Although the KUBARK manual frequently cites Biderman and many other government-funded researchers, the manual criticises the limitations of their work. The Hinkle–Wolff report, for example, 'may be useful to any KUBARK interrogator charged with questioning a former member of an Orbit intelligence or security service but does not deal with interrogation conducted without police powers'. Biderman's work is also singled out. While Biderman's research does 'merit reading by KUBARK personnel concerned with interrogation', his studies employ 'practically no valid experimentation ... conducted under interrogation conditions'. The CIA moved quickly to resolve this problem.

One year after *KUBARK Counterintelligence Interrogation* was published, the CIA found an ideal guinea pig to test and fine-tune the manual's DDD techniques. Yuri Nosenko was a KGB colonel who defected to the United States on 14 February 1964. To prove he was a bona fide defector, Nosenko divulged sensitive information to agency officials about covert KGB operations. Nosenko disclosed the names of more than twenty Soviet sleeper agents in the West and revealed that the KGB had bugged the American embassy in Moscow. Nosenko also claimed that he had personally inspected the KGB file on Lee Harvey Oswald. According to the file, he said, the KGB was not involved in JFK's assassination. Rather, the file suggested that Oswald was a hired assassin for a group of right-wing American millionaires who wanted to silence the liberal president permanently. This remarkable charge caused widespread consternation in the agency. The CIA was divided. Was Nosenko telling the truth or was he a Soviet double agent sent by Moscow to infiltrate the CIA?

On 16 March 1964, Richard Helms, then CIA Assistant Deputy Director for Plans, ordered Nosenko interrogated using the Soviet system of the new KUBARK manual. Nosenko was taken to a safe house in Maryland, where he was kept in strict isolation in a cell-like room in the basement. Occasionally, he was taken to a second room where he was subjected to polygraph tests by agency psychiatrists. Time after time, the tests proved inconclusive. After three months, Helms decided to increase the psychological pressure. The Russian was taken to a new cell where CIA officers watched over him day and night, never letting him out of their sight. This cell was stripped bare save for a light bulb that burned twenty-four hours a day. He was not allowed to communicate with the outside world and all reading material was banned. One day, Nosenko fashioned a chess set out of lint in his cell but the guards immediately swept up the little diversion.

After 500 days Nosenko hadn't confessed. He was then sent to a specially built bank vault that measured 3.6 by 3.6 metres and cost US$8500 to make. In the steel vault, Nosenko suffered a nervous breakdown. He experienced terrifying hallucinations and wept uncontrollably. Still, he would not confess to being a double agent.

On his 700th day of captivity Helms ordered still harsher methods. The CIA, in the belief that physical weakness would elicit further regression, starved Nosenko. He was forced to stand and guards beat on the steel cell for hours at a time. At one point, earphones were strapped to his head and a barrage of sounds played for twenty-three hours—a method pioneered by Dr Cameron in Montreal. Helms, out of desperation, ordered the use of LSD and other mind-altering substances. Despite the physical and psychological torture, Nosenko still insisted he was a genuine defector.

Finally, on 21 September 1967, Helms, who by this time had become Director of the CIA, yielded to increasing pressure in the agency and reluctantly authorised Nosenko's release. Nosenko received several weeks of rehabilitation, a US$150 000 stipend for his ordeal and a new identity. In all, Nosenko spent 1277 days in illegal captivity. Helms later testified to Congress that the 'fact that [Nosenko] may have been held too long was … deplorable, but nevertheless we were doing our best'.

Nosenko's exit left the CIA without a subject to use for testing DDD methods and training novice agents. This problem was, again, short-lived. By the late 1960s, the CIA had created a DDD interrogation school at 'The Farm', a 3753-hectare training site in rural Virginia. According to former CIA interrogator Bill Wagner, the program at The Farm was the agency's 'premiere course'. In order to obtain a spot, students first had to agree to play the role of the prisoner. Wagner attended the three-week program in 1970. In an interview with journalist Mark Bowden, he recounted that students were

> deprived of sleep, kept doused with water in cold rooms, forced to sit or stand in uncomfortable positions for long periods, isolated from sunlight and social contacts, given food deliberately made unappetizing (over-salted, for instance, or tainted with a green dye), and subjected to mock executions.

Roughly 10 per cent of all students dropped out, he said. 'To say you had been through it was a real feather in your cap.' Many, though, refused to assume the role of the interrogator after playing the prisoner. 'They lost their stomach for it', he added.

4

THE PHOENIX FACTOR

By the 1960s, CIA interrogators and Army Special Forces soldiers had adopted communist-style DDD torture. In Vietnam, both organisations worked closely together in the Phoenix Program—an American initiative designed to capture, interrogate and kill Vietnamese civilians sympathetic to the communist Vietcong (VC). Tens of thousands of men, women and children were swept up in Phoenix operations. For American interrogators and their Vietnamese counterparts, Phoenix prisoners were fodder for deadly DDD interrogation sessions.

America's involvement in Vietnam was rooted in the Cold War ethos of the time. The policy laid out in the 1947 Truman Doctrine— to provide financial and military support to states under communist threat—had expanded in the years since the Korean War. Vietnam was viewed as a democratic keystone in South-East Asia. As succinctly summarised by General Edward Lansdale: 'If Free Vietnam is won by the Communists, the remainder of South-east Asia will be easy pickings for our enemy, because the toughest local force on our side will be gone.'

On 20 July 1954, the Geneva Conference put a formal end to France's war in Vietnam two months after the French defeat at Dien Bien Phu. The United States declined to sign the settlement, as it precluded any further military aid to defeat the communist Vietminh. Within weeks, a joint CIA–Special Forces paramilitary force led by Lansdale arrived in South Vietnam. The team drew up plans for the 'pacification' of Vietcong and dissident areas, initiated guerrilla training, and smuggled in large quantities of arms and military equipment to support the government of Vietnam based in Saigon (GVN).

While Army Special Forces, also known as Green Berets, worked closely with the Vietnamese military, the CIA trained the police force. The police were deemed to be key players in the growing counter-insurgency against North Vietnamese guerrillas. At the time, notes political scientist Thomas Lobe, counterinsurgency theorists believed that police were 'the suppressive force that can best react to subversive behavior'. According to Sir Robert Thompson, a British military planner hired by the State Department's Office of Research and Intelligence to advise the USA and GVN, police were well-suited for counterinsurgency work because the police force was an organisation 'reaching out into every corner of the country and will have had long experience of close contact with the population'.

Beginning in 1955, Michigan State University initiated a lucrative police and security assistance program with the GVN. The university received US$15 million over a seven-year period to reorganise the police force and train officers in methods of crowd control, surveillance and interrogation. The Sûreté, the government body charged with customs, immigration and the handling of investigations, was renamed the Vietnamese Bureau of Investigations (VBI) and assigned to the Ministry of Interior. While most Michigan State advisers were ex-cops or detectives, the CIA was responsible for training the VBI.

In 1959, the State Department put the CIA's VBI adviser program under the auspices of the Office of Public Safety (OPS), a division of US Agency for International Development (USAID). CIA officer Byron Engle led the OPS, which was founded in 1954 to support police training to Third World countries considered to be at risk of communist takeover. Under Engle's direction, the OPS was staffed with CIA officers who had previously worked with foreign police. Between 1961 and 1971, the GVN received more than US$85 million through the Office of Public Safety—30 per cent of the OPS's total worldwide spending for the period. By 1971, the OPS assistance programs had trained more than one million police officers in forty-nine different countries, including 80 000 South Vietnamese alone.

According to historian Douglas Valentine, in Vietnam 'the VBI was the most powerful security force and received the lion's share of American "technical" aid. While other services got rusty weapons, the VBI got riot guns, bulletproof vests, gas masks, lie detectors, a high-command school, a modern crime lab, and modern interrogation centers'. In addition to receiving superior facilities and equipment, many VBI agents were sent to Washington, DC, to train under CIA and Federal Bureau of Investigation (FBI) officers at the OPS's International Police Academy (IPA). While course manuals remain sealed, some clues into what was taught at the IPA come from students' exams. In one paper, Nguyen Van Thieu thanked the free world, 'the US most of all', for making interrogation more effective with 'technical and equipment aid'. Le Van An defended torture: 'Despite the fact that brutal interrogation is strongly criticized by moralists, its importance must not be denied if we want to have order and security in daily life.' Luu Van Huu, also a South Vietnamese police officer, summarised the lessons he learned from the CIA: 'We have 4 sorts of torture: use of force as such; threats; physical suffering, imposed directly; and mental or psychological torture.'

While the IPA was significant, the biggest channel for American torture training came via the Phoenix Program. Phoenix was a CIA operation aimed at eliminating the Vietcong civilian infrastructure (VCI). The CIA defined the VCI as the 'political and administrative organization through which the communists control or seek to control the people of South Vietnam'. In 1970, the agency estimated that the VCI consisted of at least 63 000 people. Unlike standard military operations, Phoenix targeted civilians, not soldiers. Phoenix was launched in 1965—the same year the USA announced it would abide by the Geneva Conventions in Vietnam. The Geneva Conventions provide broad guarantees against inhumane treatment of civilians and combatants during times of war. Under the *Geneva Convention relative to the Protection of Civilian Persons in Time of War* (GPC), captured civilians are protected from 'acts of violence or threats', 'physical or moral coercion', and 'murder, torture, corporal punishment, mutilation and medical or scientific experiments not necessitated by the medical treatment'. GPC covers all non-combatants 'who, at a given moment and in any manner whatsoever, find themselves, in case of a conflict or occupation, in the hands of a Party to the conflict or Occupying Power of which they are not nationals'. Even those 'suspected of or engaged in activities hostile to the security of the State' are still afforded basic rights. These persons 'shall nevertheless be treated with humanity, and in case of trial, shall not be deprived of the rights of fair and regular trial ...'. Given that Phoenix targeted only non-combatants, from its inception the program violated the GPC.

There were two main components to the Phoenix Program: Provincial Reconnaissance Units (PRUs) and regional interrogation centres. The PRUs would kill VCI members, terrorise civilians and capture those deemed to have knowledge about VCI structure. At the interrogation centres, CIA interrogators, alongside their Vietnamese counterparts, would torture VCI prisoners in an effort to learn the identity of VCI members in each province. The information obtained in the centres was then shared with the US and GVN military and was filtered back to the PRUs, who, in turn, would capture, kill or detain new VCI targets.

The interrogation centres and the PRUs were developed in tandem, starting in 1964 under the direction of Peer DeSilva, the CIA's Saigon station chief at the time. The operating theory behind the PRUs was the notion of counter-terror, or CT. Proponents of CT believe terror is a legitimate tactic in unconventional warfare, namely in guerrilla and counterinsurgency operations. The importance of terror was discussed in the 1962 edition of FM 33-5, *Psychological Operations*. Noting that unconventional warfare was 'inherently psychological', it instructed that terror was useful when dealing with 'enemy civilians'. According to the manual:

> Civilians in the operational area may be supporting their own government or collaborating with an enemy occupation force. An isolation program designed to instill doubt and fear may be carried out, and a positive political action program designed to elicit active support of the guerrillas also may be effected. If these programs fail, it may become necessary to take more aggressive action in the form of harsh treatment or even abductions. The abduction and harsh treatment of key enemy civilians can weaken the collaborators' belief in the strength and power of their military forces.

DeSilva was a fond supporter of counter-terror. The idea behind Phoenix, he said, was 'to bring danger and death to the Vietcong functionaries themselves, especially in the areas where they felt secure'. According to Wayne Cooper, a former Foreign Service officer who spent eighteen months as a Phoenix adviser, the project initially

> was a unilateral American program, never recognized by the South Vietnamese government. CIA representatives recruited,

organized, supplied and directly paid CT teams, whose function was to use Viet Cong techniques of terror—assassination, abuses, kidnappings and intimidation—against the Viet Cong leadership.

Chalmers Roberts, a reporter for the *Washington Post*, wrote that 'one form of psychological pressure on the guerrillas which the Americans do not advertise is the PRU. The PRU work on the theory of giving back what the Viet Cong deals out—assassination and butchery. Accordingly, a Viet Cong unit on occasion will find the disemboweled remains of its fellows along a well-trod canal bank path, an effective message to guerrillas and to non-committed Vietnamese that two can play the same bloody game'.

PRUs were financed by the CIA, composed of Vietnamese fighters, and led on missions by members of the Navy SEALs or Green Berets. Elton Manzione is a former SEAL who worked in the Phoenix Program. According to Manzione, PRU squads included a 'combination of ARVN [Army of North Vietnam] deserters, VC turncoats, and bad motherfucker criminals the South Vietnamese couldn't deal with in prison'. Many of these criminals were released with an incentive plan. 'If they killed X number of Commies, they got X number of years off their prison terms', said Manzione.

According to Jim Ward, a CIA officer stationed in Vietnam from 1967 to 1969, 'The PRU started off as a counterterror program, [but] their basic mission was as an armed intelligence collection unit—to capture prisoners and bring back documents'. PRUs often blurred the line between counter-terror and intelligence gathering. Manzione recalled:

We wrapped det [detonator] cord around [prisoners'] necks and wired them to the detonator box. And basically what it did was blow their heads off. The interrogator would tell the translator, usually a South Vietnamese intelligence officer, 'Ask him this.' He'd ask him, 'Who gave you the gun?' And the guy would start to answer, or maybe he wouldn't—maybe he'd resist—but the general idea was to waste the first two. They planned the snatches that way. Pick up this guy because we're pretty sure he's VC cadre—these other two guys just run errands for him. Or maybe they're nobody; Tran, the farmer, and his brother Nguyen. But bring in two. Put them in a row. By the time you get to your man, he's talking so fast you got to pop the weasel just to shut him up. I guess you could say that we wrote the book on terror.

Prisoners who survived encounters with PRUs were taken in for further interrogation at either the National Interrogation Center (NIC) in Saigon or at a Provincial Interrogation Center (PIC). Interrogations at these centres were conducted by the CIA, Special Forces, and members of the Vietnamese Special Branch police.

The Special Branch was formed from a section of the Vietnamese Bureau of Investigations in 1964. Special Branch interrogators were trained at the NIC in Saigon by American advisers. John Patrick Muldoon was a CIA officer who advised Vietnamese interrogators at the NIC. Previously Muldoon worked CIA interrogation operations in South Korea. Muldoon was one of two CIA advisers at the centre; three others were from the US Air Force. According to Muldoon, Special Branch interrogators were already well versed in 'the old French methods' of interrogation—namely water torture and use of electricity. 'All this had to be stopped by the agency. They had to be retaught with more sophisticated techniques', he said. According to Douglas Valentine, Special Branch interrogators were trained by 'experts from the CIA's Support Services Branch, most of whom had worked on Russian defectors'. Given the period of time during which the training took place, these 'experts' were likely the men who worked on Nosenko in Maryland and graduated from the CIA's interrogation school at The Farm.

When PRUs captured someone considered to be extremely valuable, the prisoner was sent to the NIC for interrogation. Based on the accounts of a Vietnamese prisoner, Nguyen Van Tai, and his CIA interrogator, Frank Snepp, it appears that both the techniques of the 1963 KUBARK manual and 'old French methods' were used at the NIC. Tai, the most senior North Vietnamese officer captured during the Vietnam War, was apprehended while en route to a political meeting south of Saigon in the Mekong Delta. At first, Tai insisted he was a low-level North Vietnamese military intelligence agent. South Vietnamese interrogators believed he was hiding something and he was sent to the NIC.

The Special Branch in Saigon was charged with discovering Tai's true identity. According to an account of Tai's biography featured in *Studies in Intelligence*, the South Vietnamese interrogators:

administered electric shock, beat him with clubs, poured water down his nose while his mouth was gagged, applied 'Chinese water torture' (dripping water slowly, drop by drop, on the bridge of his nose for days on end), and kept him tied to a stool for days at a time without food or water while questioning him around the clock.

Despite the torture, Tai remained silent. Vietnamese detectives soon discovered his true identity by showing his picture to other prisoners and defectors in custody. In 1968, it was revealed he had engineered an attack on the US Embassy in Saigon and had been responsible for several successful assassinations. Once his cover was blown, Tai admitted his true identity as a colonel in the National Liberation Front of South Vietnam. His co-operation didn't end the torture. According to the account in *Studies*, he was then 'kept sitting on a chair for weeks at a time with no rest; he was beaten; he was starved; he was given no water for days; and he was hung from the rafters for hours by his arms, almost ripping them from his sockets'.

Tai probably would have died from such treatment, but in the autumn of 1971 the government of North Vietnam requested that he be exchanged for a US State Department official held since 1966. Tai suddenly became a valuable pawn for American hostage negotiators. After the request, the CIA took over Tai's interrogation from the Special Branch. The agency then carefully followed the advice of the 1963 KUBARK manual. According to Tai's primary CIA interrogator, Frank Snepp:

With American help the South Vietnamese had built him his own prison cell and interrogation room, both totally white, totally bare except for a table, a chair, an open hole for a toilet and ubiquitous hidden television cameras and microphones to record his every waking and sleeping moment. His jailers had soon discovered one essential psychic-physical flaw in him. Like many Vietnamese, he believed his blood vessels contracted when he was exposed to frigid air. His quarters and interrogation room had thus been outfitted with heavy-duty air conditioners and been kept thoroughly chilled.

Tai lived in this windowless nine- by nine-metre 'snow white cell' for three years, never knowing where he was. During this time CIA interrogators struggled fruitlessly with Tai. In an attempt to foster dependence, the CIA offered him better medical treatment, new clothes and better food. Tai declined all three. When he did talk to his interrogators he would only reveal 'secrets' already disclosed by other prisoners. Other times he would pretend not to understand the interrogator employed by the CIA. In the end, Tai beat the methods of KUBARK by staying physically and mentally active. He would wake automatically at 6 a.m. every day. He would then silently recite the North Vietnamese national anthem, perform calisthenics, compose poems and songs in his head, and salute a star he had scratched on his wall to represent the North Vietnamese flag. He would repeat this routine throughout the day, then at ten o'clock every night he would put himself to bed.

On 27 January 1973, the Paris Peace Agreement was signed, freeing all prisoners held by North and South Vietnamese forces. On 3 February 1973, said Snepp, he informed Tai of the news. According to Snepp: 'He sat for a moment, trembling in the draft of the air conditioning. "If what you tell me is true," he said in French, "then this is the happiest day of my life."' Although he was kept in prison until 1975, Tai survived the ordeal.

It was innocent civilians and low-level VC and VCI personnel who suffered the worst treatment at the hands of American interrogators and their South Vietnamese counterparts under the Phoenix Program. More often than not, these prisoners would not survive.

The most violent Phoenix interrogations were conducted at the Provincial Interrogation Centers. The concrete centres were built between 1964 and 1966 under the direction of CIA interrogator John Patrick Muldoon and Tucker Gougleman, chief of Special Branch field operations. After each centre was built, the CIA would 'donate' the facility to the National Police, who in turn would place it under the direction of the Special Branch. Interrogations were directed by American advisers and conducted by Special Branch interrogators. By 1966, forty-four centres had been built—one in every South Vietnamese province.

Like Tai's 'snow white cell', the PICs were designed along the guidelines laid out in the KUBARK manual. According to Muldoon, PICs consisted of rows of interrogation rooms and 'twenty to sixty solitary confinement cells the size of closets'. The prisoners, he said, 'were completely isolated. They didn't get time to go out and walk around the yard. They sat in their cells when they weren't being interrogated'. A system of rewards and punishments was also instituted. 'There were little things you could give them and take away from them, not a lot, but every little bit they got they were grateful for.' At night, prisoners slept on concrete slabs. 'Depending on how cooperative they were, you'd give them a straw mat or a blanket. It could get very cold at night in the highlands', he said.

Although the prisons were set up for DDD, which relies more on discomfort and psychological pressure than on beatings, brute physical torture was commonplace. Muldoon blames the prevalence of brutality on two main factors. First, he said, ex-Special Forces ran many of the PICs. 'Advisors who wanted to do a good job ran the PICs themselves', said Muldoon, 'while the others hired assistants—former cops or Green Berets—who were paid by the CIA but worked for themselves'. As discussed in Chapter 2, Donald Duncan alleged that Green Berets had been trained in various physical and psychological tortures since the late 1950s. These soldiers, in turn, likely taught Vietnamese interrogators methods from Fort Bragg. According to Duncan:

> The specific purpose for teaching this [at Fort Bragg] is so the student in turn, once he is put in another country, can teach these methods to what we refer to as an 'indigenous counterpart', somebody indigenous to the country. And he in turn then would become the interrogator … In Vietnam, of course, that would be the Vietnamese.

Muldoon also noted that most of the advisers assigned to the PICs had little or no experience with interrogation and 'were not trained interrogators'. This also added to the abuses, he said. According to Muldoon, 'Some had been in the military; some had just graduated college. They put them through a six-month course as either intelligence or paramilitary officers and then sent them over. They were just learning and it was a hell of a place for their baptism of fire.'

A popular saying of the CIA-trained interrogators was *Khong, danh cho co*—'If they are innocent, beat them until they become guilty'. According to emergency laws formulated with the help of the CIA in Saigon, prisoners could be held for up to forty-six days at the PIC without charge. US Representative to Congress Paul McCloskey, who spoke to a PIC adviser while investigating Phoenix abuses, later recounted, 'When I asked an American pacification officer if the 46-day period of interrogation was not reasonable, he replied, "We've never had to interrogate anyone for 46 days—they've all broken and confessed in 30 days"'.

According to a member of the International Voluntary Services (IVS), an interrogation at a PIC

> begins with a beating. The prisoner is not tied or blind-folded but he in no way must defend himself, a question is asked and before he can answer he is kicked in the chest or stomach or hit in the face—again a question and again no answer is allowed. By noontime the Americans involved are soaking their sore fists and having the interpreter do the work ...

If prisoners remained unco-operative, interrogators resorted to more imaginative tortures. According to the same IVS official:

> I have seen blind-folded men, their hands tied behind them, thrown out of helicopters—the helicopter was only three feet off the ground, but the blind-folded men couldn't know that. They would collapse in shivering heaps when they hit the ground, and often would have to be dragged away from the helicopter so it could land. I have watched while these same men, still blind-folded and tied, were made to run down a steep hill, at the bottom of which were three rows of concertina barbed wire. The first row would hit them across the knees and they would plunge head first into the second and third rows of wire. They lie there until they are dragged out and sent skidding down another hill, at the bottom of which there is not barbed wire—their only defense is to collapse into a shivering heap on the ground—but that is sure to earn a few kicks and orders, given in English, to stand up if they want the kicks to stop.

As noted by Muldoon, Americans didn't introduce electrical torture to the Vietnamese: the French first imported the technique during the French Vietnam War. Americans simply advised the Vietnamese on how to make the torture more painful and effective. Under American

supervision, Vietnamese interrogators often combined electrical torture with sexual abuse. According to a US Senate inquiry, one woman,
Ms Nguyen Thi Nhan, was given electric shocks under the supervision
of three CIA officers. One of the men directed a Vietnamese interrogator to ram needles under her fingernails. Another ordered the
insertion of an iron rod into her vagina to exacerbate the damage
caused by the electricity.

Medical staff with the American Friends Service Committee, a
Quaker organisation, treated many victims of this form of torture.
According to Dr Jane Barton, a woman named Nguyen Thi Lang was
'given electric shocks under her fingernails. She often blanked out and
once when she awoke, she found blood coming from her vagina'.
Another victim of electric torture was a victim known only as 'Young
boy, 17 years old'. Barton reported: 'The boy had not gone to the
bathroom for four days (urinated) and was in extreme pain … Later,
we were told that the young boy prisoner had been tortured with
electricity attached to his penis.'

In addition to these forms of torture, the CIA used Phoenix
prisoners as live human subjects for experimentation. The Phoenix
Program produced tens of thousands of prisoners completely under
the control of the CIA—a situation Richard Helms had privately
wished for back in 1963 when he was Assistant Deputy Director
for Plans. Several months after MKULTRA was cancelled, Helms
penned the following note to a colleague about the future of CIA
mind control experimentation:

> We have attempted several times in the past ten years to establish
> a testing program in an overseas setting, using indigenous subjects.
> In every case the necessity of making foreign nationals aware of
> our role in this very sensitive activity has made such options
> undesirable on security grounds … While I share your uneasiness
> for any program which intrudes on an individual's private and
> legal prerogatives, I believe it is necessary that the Agency maintain
> a central role in this activity, keep current on enemy capabilities
> in the manipulation of human behavior, and maintain an offensive
> capability.

Prisoners caught up in Phoenix's web became unwilling subjects
in deadly terminal experiments. As Gordon Thomas uncovered in

Journey Into Madness (1989), in the summer of 1966 the CIA conducted a host of terminal electro-shock experiments on VC prisoners. Two agency doctors and one private physician went to Vietnam in order to see whether a person's ideological views can be transformed via painful shocks—a hypothesis seemingly inspired by the work of Dr Cameron. For several weeks they experimented extensively on VC prisoners housed in a high-walled and heavily guarded area of the Bien Hoa Hospital in Saigon. According to Dr Lloyd Cotter, one of the CIA doctors present, Vietcong prisoners were selected because they were 'typical cases of communist indoctrination'. The trials consisted of massive quantities of electro-shocks. One VC soldier was strapped to a table and shocked six times every twelve hours. After seven days of this treatment, the man died. Later, Dr Cotter recalled that he administered more than 'several thousand shock treatments' during his time at the hospital. After three weeks, all of the VC prisoners were dead and the Americans flew home.

About a year later, another CIA team was sent to Bien Hoa Hospital for more radical human experimentation. It appears that this time the doctors were sent to investigate the strange simian-related work of Dr Maitland Baldwin. Instead of a Page-Russell electro-shock device, this time the team brought with them instruments for neuro-surgery. Upon the team's arrival at the hospital, the National Police produced three men for them to work on. After each man was given anaesthesia, a neurosurgeon peeled back his scalp and hinged open a small section of the skull. The surgeon then placed tiny electrodes into various parts of each victim's brains. Once the men regained consciousness, the team of scientists experimented with various frequencies to activate the electrodes. One frequency caused the men to vomit uncontrollably. Another caused the men to defecate. At one stage, the three men were given knives and the doctors broadcast frequencies they believed could trigger violent responses. After a week of unsuccessfully trying to get the victims to attack each other, the team flew back to Washington. While the medical team was still in the air, Green Berets killed the subjects, as previously arranged, and burned their bodies on the hospital grounds.

In late 1968, the CIA began withdrawing direct support for the Phoenix Program, due, according to one internal agency document, to 'poor press image, highlighted by charges that it was a program of assassination, etc.'. In 1970, the GVN assumed control and the National

Police took a leading role in running Phoenix. By 1972, arrests by the National Police force, which numbered 120 000 strong, occurred at a rate of 14 000 per month. These arrests were wildly indiscriminate. According to the *New York Times*, it was

> impossible to tell how many of those arrested really have communist connections and how many are simply opposed to the government of President Thieu, because the police seem to make little distinction. There is a third category of prisoners as well—people who were apparently seized at random and who committed no crime. They just happened to be at the wrong place.

Some experts believed that up to 80 per cent of those detained were innocent of any crime. Compounding the problem were the monthly quotas imposed on all forty-four regional PICs. In 1968, for example, Phoenix officials in Saigon demanded that operatives 'neutralize' (kill) 1200 VCIs per month. In 1969, the number jumped to 1800 per month, in 1970, 1800 per month, and in 1971, it was reduced to 1200 per month. According to a CIA report on the program, quotas were used 'for their incentive effect upon lower officials'. Also exacerbating the problem was a reward system that applied to Phoenix operatives. Agents were given cash for successful 'neutralizations'. According to the same 1970 CIA report, 'Rewards have been authorized in the past ... a new effort is being made in this area'.

In 1971, the US House Operations Subcommittee launched an investigation into claims of widespread Phoenix-sponsored torture in Vietnam. CIA officer William Colby, who directed Phoenix during the late 1960s, testified at the hearing that the program had 'neutralized' 20 587 VCIs during the period between early 1968 and May 1971. The *New York Times* placed the death count closer to 60 000. During the hearing, a member of Congress asked: 'Are you certain that we know a member of the VCI from a loyal member of the South Vietnamese citizenry?' Colby replied: 'No, Congressman. I am not.' To Colby, who in 1973 was appointed Director of the CIA, the 'collateral damage' was justified. Phoenix, he said, was 'an essential part of the war effort' that was 'designed to protect the Vietnamese people from terrorism'.

Also at the hearings, Kenneth Barton Osborn, an Army military intelligence (MI) officer who worked with Phoenix in 1967–68, described the horrors he observed at the PICs. He described 'the use of electronic gear such as sealed telephones attached to the genitals' of both men and women '[to] shock them into submission'. Osborn added that he observed the murders of two suspected VCI members. He recalled

> the insertion of the 6-inch dowel into the 6-inch ear canal of one of my detainee's ears and the tapping through the brain until he dies. The starving to death of a Vietnamese woman who was suspected of being part of the local [VC] political education cadre in one of the local villages. They simply starved her to death in a cage that they kept in one of the hooches at that very counterintelligence team headquarters.

Osborn testified that not a *single* VC suspect survived an interrogation under his supervision during his eighteen months in Phoenix. For Osborn, Phoenix was a 'categorically inhuman ... murder program'.

In Vietnam, torture became standard procedure during the interrogation of all VC suspects. In 1975, Amnesty International astutely concluded that in South Vietnam

> victims are tortured to discover innocence or guilt, and then to extract information, not simply to extract information after guilt has been established. Moreover ... there can be no doubt that torture is now widely used in the areas controlled by the Saigon government not only as an instrument of intimidation but as an end in itself.

———

5

IN AMERICA'S BACKYARD

The most notorious Office of Public Safety adviser of the 1960s and 1970s did not work in South-East Asia, but in Latin America. While Phoenix interrogators shocked, bludgeoned, and starved their way through tens of thousands of Vietnamese civilians ostensibly protected by the Geneva Conventions, the United States also spent more than US\$51 million on police training in 'America's backyard'. The standard Cold War rationale applied: 'The structural weaknesses, social cleavages, and growing pains of less developed countries constitute particular points of vulnerability which the Communists seek to exploit so that they may divert the desire for reform and development for their own ends', said Secretary of State Dean Rusk in 1962. According to Colonel John D. Weber, who oversaw counterinsurgency training in Guatemala, 'The communists are using everything they have including terror. And it must be met'.

Dan Mitrione was a Johnny Appleseed of American DDD torture. Mitrione grew up in Richmond, Indiana, a small town about a hundred kilometres east of Indianapolis. He was known in Richmond as good-natured, hard-working, and always eager to please. After high school he served in the Navy and joined the Richmond Police Department. In 1956, he became Richmond's chief of police and by the late 1950s worked for the FBI. He accepted a spot in the Office of Public Safety's adviser program in 1960 and was sent to Brazil to oversee police training in Belo Horizonte and Rio de Janeiro. In *Hidden Terrors* (1978), former *New York Times* Saigon bureau chief A. J. Langguth wrote about Mitrione's time in Latin America. It was here, said Langguth, that the 'straightforward police chief from the heartland of America had been corrupted like Mr Kurtz in "Heart of Darkness"'.

By 1967, the Office of Public Safety had spent US$5.9 million in Brazil and trained nearly 100 000 police officers—one-sixth of the country's total police force. Dan Mitrione personally trained hundreds of these Brazilian officers. Manuel Hevia Cosculluela was a Cuban intelligence agent who infiltrated the CIA during the Cold War and worked closely with Mitrione in Latin America. According to Cosculluela, Mitrione introduced new sophisticated methods of torture to police and held training sessions on unwilling human guinea pigs. 'Mitrione was a perfectionist', he said. 'He was coldly efficient, he insisted on economy of effort. His motto was: "The right pain in the right place at the right time". A premature death, he would say, meant that the technique had failed.'

Prior to his arrival, Brazilian interrogators brutally beat suspects until they neared death, at which point they either talked or were killed. Under the guidance of Mitrione, Brazilian police learned the refined techniques drawn from the KUBARK manual.

Cosculluela recounted a conversation where Mitrione outlined his philosophy on interrogation: 'He said that he considered interrogation to be a complex art. First you have to soften up the detainee with blows and the usual abuse. The objective was to humiliate the victim, separating him from reality, making him feel defenseless. No questions, just blows and insults. Then just silent blows.'

Fernando Gabeira, a former member of a revolutionary group in Brazil, was arrested by police in Sao Paulo in January 1970. According to Gabeira, who today is noted Brazilian politician, the torture he endured reflected 'psychological and technical expertise'. In 1974, he recounted:

> when we enter a prison they force us to remain kneeling on the floor, looking at the cells where those who have been tortured are thrown half-dead and they also keep us awake for a long time. This is a procedure which is supposed to break our resistance ... Nowadays they employ highly sophisticated sound equipment and cells where the temperature can be changed abruptly ... There are also cells where we were kept so as to completely lose any sense of time, cells where one loses any sense of day and

night, and where sound equipment produces dreadful noises all night, all in fact, part of the pre-torture process.

In Rio de Janeiro, where Mitrione spent the bulk of his time while in Brazil, these tortures were combined in a torture device known as 'the fridge'. In the fridge, said Gabeira, 'the temperature can be changed in such a way that one feels cold for a long time'.

Fred Morris, then an American missionary with the United Methodist Church, lived in Brazil for eleven years before being arrested, tortured, then expelled as a result of his close ties with Archbishop Dom Helder Camara, a vocal opponent of the military dictatorship. According to Morris, police in São Paulo also used 'the fridge', a square cube measuring about a metre and a half equipped with a heating and cooling unit, speakers and strobe lights. Morris recalled that prisoners were locked inside and exposed to a series of ordered stimulations. In the first series, strobe lights would blink, the temperature would drop, and the sound of jet-engine noise would blast from the speakers. Then, a different series would begin. The box may heat up to 115 degrees Fahrenheit (46 degrees Celsius), the lights would turn off and there would be silence. 'When they get a pattern established, which apparently three to four cycles will do', Morris said, 'then they reverse it. Suddenly there is loud noise accompanied by heat, strobe lights instead of darkness.' Extended exposure to the random stimulations, he added, resulted in nervous breakdown.

Under Mitrione, the Office of Public Safety also introduced painful new electrical tortures to the Brazilians to augment the effects of the fridge. According to Langguth, Mitrione informed police about the levels of electric current a body could withstand using frayed wires from military field telephones. Victim Fernando Gabeira stated: 'From personal experience, I know that real torture only begins when they start applying electric shocks.' Another victim, Paulo Schilling, described the effects of electrical torture in his memoir, *Brasil: Seis Años de Dictadura y Torturas* (Brazil: Six Years of Dictatorship and Torture) (1970). According to Shilling:

> the electrical discharge causes a sensation which is difficult to describe: a physical and psychological commotion … The tortured victim shouts with all his might, grasping for a footing, somewhere to stand in the midst of that chaos of convulsions,

shaking and sparks. He cannot lose himself or turn his attention away from that desperate sensation. For him in that moment any other form of combined torture—paddling, for example—would be a relief for it would allow him to divert his attention, touch ground and his own body which feels like it is escaping his grasp. Pain saves him, beating comes to the rescue.

Under Mitrione, Brazilian police pioneered a new method of torture combining electricity, sensory deprivation and forced standing. First the Brazilians would cut open a couple of sardine tins and force the hooded captive to stand on the sharp edges. They would then give the prisoner something very heavy to hold and force him to raise it above his head. When the prisoner began to collapse from exhaustion, jolts of electricity were delivered, making his feet stick to the sardine tins and forcing him to stand up straight. Some called this technique the 'Statue of Liberty'. Others dubbed it the 'Vietnam'.

In 1967, Mitrione was sent to Washington to teach at the International Police Academy and was then transferred to Montevideo in 1969. CIA agent William Cantrell, then the Assistant Director of OPS, briefed Cosculluela on Mitrione's new assignment. 'Cantrell called me to Montevideo and told me that a new public safety director would be bringing instructions on new courses of interrogation', Cosculluela recalled. 'Cantrell said that the new man, Mitrione, was not part of "our program"—he never referred directly to the CIA—but had worked very closely with "our program" in Brazil.'

Upon arrival in Uruguay, Cosculluela said, Mitrione held a torture training course for police. The session took place in a specially designed soundproofed room in the cellar of Mitrione's Montevideo home. 'The special horror of the course was its academic, almost clinical atmosphere', he said. According to Cosculluela:

> As subjects for the first testing they took beggars, known in Uruguay as *bichicomes*, from the outskirts of Montevideo, as well as a woman apparently from the frontier area with Brazil. There was no interrogation, only a demonstration of the effects of different voltages on different parts of a human body, as well as demonstrating the use of a drug which induces vomiting— I don't know why or what for—and another chemical substance. The four of them died.

Mitrione's expertise was used by Uruguayan police to put down a growing guerrilla movement led by the Tupamaros. During the 1960s, the Tupamaros were known for their populist antics and Robin Hood-like flair. They raided corporate offices to expose graft and kidnapped high-ranking politicians suspected of corruption and tried them in 'People's Courts'. One Christmas, members of the group commandeered a food truck destined for a wealthy suburb and 'redistributed' turkeys in impoverished neighbourhoods. The group's motto, 'Either everyone dances or no one dances', earned them many supporters from Montevideo's poorest slums.

Before Mitrione arrived, Uruguayan police tactics were brutal but rudimentary. Uruguayans did employ electrical torture but used an old Argentinean stun device commonly used in abattoirs. Mitrione arranged for the police to get electrified needles of varying thickness made by the CIA's Technical Service Division. The engineers at TSD—likely the same inventors who produced Brazil's dreaded fridge—designed needles small enough to be slipped between teeth to deliver an electrical charge directly to the gums.

In addition to electrical torture, Mitrione also taught police how to use sexual humiliation and forced standing to break victims down. According to Langguth, Mitrione gave the following instructions to an officer on how treat one reluctant trade union official: 'Undress him completely and force him to stand facing the wall. Then have one of the youngest policemen goose him. Afterward, put him into a cell and hold him for three days with nothing to drink. On the third day, pass through to him a pot of water mixed with urine.' To goose, according to the *American Heritage Dictionary,* means to 'poke, prod, or pinch [a person] between or on the buttocks'.

Mitrione also stressed the importance of doctors in the process of interrogation. Langguth discovered that in Uruguay:

> One of the truly disheartening things for so many of the torture victims was having a doctor come into the room where they were being tortured and thinking, 'Well now he'll put a stop to it. He's from the medical profession.' And instead, the doctor was just there to monitor life signs and be sure they weren't torturing to death. And Mitrione bragged about that kind of thing.

Cosculluela also recalled Mitrione's beliefs about the role of doctors during torture sessions. Over drinks at his Montevideo home, Mitrione told him: 'When you receive a subject, the first thing to do is determine his physical state, his degree of resistance, through a medical examination. A premature death means a failure by the technician.'

On 31 July 1970, the Tupamaros kidnapped Mitrione. The group first photocopied his Indiana FBI card and sent it to the press, then demanded the release of 150 Tupamaros prisoners in exchange for Mitrione. Uruguayan officials, upon the insistence of the US government, refused to negotiate. On 10 August 1970, Mitrione's body was found on the back seat of a Buick convertible. He was shot twice in the head.

In America, Mitrione was portrayed as an innocent 'technical co-operation expert' who died at the hands of heartless communists. 'Dan exemplified the highest principles of the police profession, that of social service,' said White House spokesman Ron Ziegler. He added:

> There are a quarter of a billion people in Latin America and in many of these countries the Communist terrorists are trying to tear the fabric of democracy apart. Some of these countries, Uruguay among them, realize that the best protection against this is the development of a democratic police, and asked the United States to help. And this is what Dan was doing in Uruguay.

On 29 August 1970, Frank Sinatra and Jerry Lewis staged a benefit concert in Richmond, Indiana, for the Mitrione family. 'I never met Dan Mitrione, yet he was my brother just as you, Jerry and I are brothers', said Sinatra to a tearful crowd of 4200. He added: 'What do you say in the wake of a sacrifice such as Dan Mitrione's? Abe Lincoln sort of said it all when he said, "It is for us, the living, to dedicate ourselves to that unfinished task for what they gave their last full measure of devotion."'

Mitrione's death was treated differently outside the USA. French historian Alain Labrousse later wrote that in Uruguay Mitrione 'was an example, both in his character and in his job, of the most blatant interference by the United States into the workings of a foreign state'. The former Uruguayan Chief of Police Intelligence, Alejandro Otero, spoke out against Mitrione only days after his murder. In a candid interview published in *Jornal do Brasil*, a leading Brazilian newspaper, Otero said that Mitrione had instituted torture as a routine measure during the interrogation of suspects. According to Otero, 'The advisors advocated psychological torture to create despair. In the next room, they would play tapes of women and children screaming and tell the prisoner that it was his family being tortured'. Otero stated that he disagreed with Mitrione's 'scientific methods of torture'. The Tupamaros, he said, targeted Mitrione because 'he had turned to violent methods of repression and torture with the support of the government'. According to Otero, 'The violent methods which were beginning to be employed caused an escalation in Tupamaro activity. Before then their attitude showed that they would use violence only as a last resort'.

After Mitrione's death, Uruguayan President Jorge Pacheco Areco declared martial law and assumed dictatorial powers. The Tupamaros were eventually wiped out—but at tremendous cost. A Uruguayan Senate investigation later concluded that torture, specifically psychological torture and electric shocks, was a 'normal, frequent and habitual occurrence' in Uruguay's jails and police stations. In 1974, dozens of victims of American-sponsored torture testified at the Russell Tribunal on Repression in Brazil, Chile and Latin America. Uruguayan Senator Zelmar Michelini, who two years later was kidnapped, tortured and murdered in Argentina, testified that the number of Uruguayans tortured was 'more than 5000 while over 40 000 people had been held as political prisoners'. The comparable figures for the USA in proportion to population, he pointed out, would be about 3 200 000 political prisoners and 400 000 torture victims.

In 1975—the same year the Rockefeller Commission introduced the American public to the horrors of MKULTRA—Congress cancelled OPS's funding. During its lifetime, OPS advisers trained more than ten thousand students at the IPA and more than one million police in the developing world, and had shipped more than US$150 million worth of technical equipment abroad. The correlation between the use of torture in Vietnam, Brazil and Uruguay and OPS funding in those countries is in no way unique. Torture was commonplace in twenty-four of the forty-nine countries that had hosted the program.

USAID's Office of Public Safety wasn't the only arm of the US government to export DDD torture to allies in Latin America and across the globe. Beginning in the mid 1960s, the US military also trained Latin officers in American torture techniques. Almost every state in Central and South America received technical advice from the US Army during the Cold War. Describing the nature of this assistance, a retired Army colonel told the *Washington Post*: 'Latin American militaries had no role in the defense of their country. The only real role they had was internal defense. So how do you help them? You can't help them get big airplanes to shoot each other. You can't help them get big tanks. You can help them with information.'

The roots of Latin American military torture training can be traced back to the CIA's deadly Phoenix Program. In 1966, instructors at the US Army Intelligence School, then located at Fort Holabird, Maryland, taught a course about the Phoenix Program to overseas students. While the contents of this particular course remain secret, a 'special Phoenix course' later taught at Fort Bragg included lessons on intelligence collection, interrogation and detention procedures. While Phoenix training was under way at Holabird, the Army launched 'Project X'. According to the Department of Defense, 'Project X was a program to develop an exportable foreign intelligence training package to provide counterinsurgency techniques learned in Vietnam to Latin American countries.' According to Linda Matthews, then a counterintelligence (CI) officer at the Pentagon, between 1967 and 1968, Phoenix advisers prepared some of the Project X training material. 'Some offending material from the Phoenix Program may have found its way into the Project X materials at that time', she told Pentagon investigators.

In 1992, all Project X material was ordered destroyed by an intelligence oversight official who determined that the materials are 'outdated and do not represent US government policy'. According to Major Thomas Husband, the Army's Assistant Deputy Director for Counterintelligence Support who investigated the material, the manuals 'provided training regarding the use of sodiopentathol [truth serum] compound in interrogation, abduction of adversary family members to influence adversary, prioritization of adversary personalities for abduction, exile, physical beatings and execution'. In addition to teaching students about violence and so-called truth drugs, the Project X material laid out a complete system of repression. One 1968 manual, titled *Employee Procurement and Utilization*, recommended that military intelligence officers infiltrate political parties, student groups, trade unions and religious organisations. 'Mass organizations ... villages from which crops are being diverted, and groups of underprivileged people are all potential insurgent targets', notes the manual. Another handbook alerted students to the 'dangers' of the electoral process. Insurgents, it said, 'can resort to subversion of the government by means of elections ... Insurgent leaders participate in political contests as candidates for government office'.

The Project X material above was approved for export by the Army Deputy Chief of Staff for intelligence and was disseminated along several broad channels including the Army's Foreign Officer Course, Special Forces Mobile Training Teams (MTTs), and the Army's School of the Americas (SOA). Since 1948, the SOA, then located in Panama, has taught Latin American military officers skills in combat, intelligence gathering, and counterinsurgency. Today the school, since renamed the Western Hemisphere Institute for Security and relocated to Fort Benning, Georgia, has trained more than 60 000 Latin American officers. Beginning in 1966, the school used Project X material to train officers from dozens of Central and South American countries. In 1976, a congressional panel investigating coursework at SOA discovered the material. According to the Pentagon, the Project X courses were then 'halted by [the] Carter Administration for fear the training would contribute to Human Rights violations in other countries'.

The hiatus lasted until Ronald Reagan took office. According to Thomas O. Enders, then Assistant Secretary of State for Inter-American Affairs:

> Whereas human rights violations had been the single most important focus of the previous administration's policy in Latin America, the Reagan administration had broader interests. It believed that the most effective way to overcome civil conflicts and human rights violations was to promote democratically elected governments ...

Under Reagan, human rights concerns took a back seat to supporting militant anti-Communist regimes. By 9 March 1981, Reagan had signed a secret executive directive known as a 'presidential finding' that expanded covert operations to 'provide all forms of training, equipment, and related assistance to cooperating governments throughout Central America in order to counter foreign-sponsored subversion and terrorism'. Wide-scale torture training using Project X material and the principles of KUBARK resumed soon after.

In 1982, the Pentagon ordered the US Army Intelligence School, which had relocated from Holabird to Fort Huachuca, Arizona, a decade earlier, to supply new CI lesson plans to the School of the Americas. According to an investigation led by Congressman Joseph P. Kennedy, 'The [Pentagon] working group decided to use Project X material because it had previously been cleared for foreign disclosure'.

The officer in charge of CI training at SOA, Major Vic Tise, travelled to Fort Huachuca to obtain the Project X documents. During his research, Tise noticed that information from Project X had by this time been adopted 'word-for-word' into FM 30-18, a classified Army field manual on intelligence tactics. While this manual remains classified, an example of the spread of Project X material can also be found in FM 34-52, *Intelligence Interrogation*. According to the 1987 edition:

> The interrogator should appear to be the one who controls all aspects of the interrogation to include the lighting, heating, and configuration of the interrogation room, as well as the food, shelter, and clothing given to the source. The interrogator must always be in control, he must act quickly and firmly.

Tise used DDD-themed Project X manuals at Huachuca as source material for new SOA coursework and developed 382 hours of lessons for his Latin American students. Richard L. Montgomery and J. W. Taylor of Huachuca's Department of Human Intelligence approved the material. Major Montgomery was a veteran of the Phoenix Program. The material was then sent to Washington for Pentagon clearance. The material was returned stamped 'approved' and 'unchanged'.

While Tise's lesson plans remain sealed, in 1987 the same SOA material was used to create seven Spanish-language manuals by US Army military intelligence officers in Panama. These manuals, totalling more than 1100 pages, recommended torture, extortion, execution and the arrest of witnesses' relatives. One manual, *Manejo de Fuentes* (Handling of Sources), teaches students that threats should be used to initiate a relationship with an informant (an 'employee'). Once an 'employee' is no longer needed, an agent should compromise the source's security and threaten 'serious consequences for the employee and his family'. Another manual, *Interrogación* (Interrogation), gives questionable advice, teaching officers to gag, bind and blindfold suspects and to manipulate a subject's fear to 'induce cooperation' when 'demand necessitates that information be made quickly available'. Although this manual advises against outright violence, it instructs that a prisoner should be 'crushed emotionally' and be 'convinced that something very horrible is going to happen to him' in order to elicit information.

Like the original Project X material, the Spanish manuals equate normal functions of a democracy with the tactics of insurgents. 'It is important to note that many terrorists are very well trained in subversion of the democratic process and use the system to advance their causes', one manual states. 'Discontent that can become political violence can have as its cause political, social, and economic activities of terrorists operating within the democratic system', it adds. Another manual, *Guerra Revolucionaria, Guerri e Ideología Comunista* (Revolutionary War, Guerrillas and Communist Ideology), elevates the threat of communism to near comical heights. It describes communism not as an alternative ideology, but as a

> pseudo-religion, given that it has a founder, a mythology, a sacred book, a clergy, a place of pilgrimage and an inquisition. The founder is Marx; the mythology is communist theory; the sacred book is *Das Kapital*; the clergy are members of the Communist Party; the place of pilgrimage is Moscow; and the inquisition [by] the state (KGB) and others. Truly, as Marx said, communism is 'the spectre surrounding Europe'. Today this spectre is surrounding the whole world.

In 1989, the new manuals were introduced at SOA. According to a Pentagon investigation, between 1989 and 1991 'as many as a thousand copies of these manuals' were distributed at SOA and by Mobile Training Teams throughout Latin America. Students from Colombia, Ecuador, El Salvador, Guatemala, Peru, Bolivia, Costa Rica, Dominican Republic, Honduras, Mexico and Venezuela were given the 'offensive and objectionable material', the report said.

Torture training of Latin American students wasn't limited to the US Army. While the closure of OPS and revelations of the Rockefeller Commission and Church Committee put the CIA under closer scrutiny, the Reagan administration's lenient policy on violent CI training brought the agency back into the fold. In early 1983, an anonymous CIA officer penned a new interrogation handbook called the *Human Resource Exploitation Training Manual*. Unlike the KUBARK handbook, the new guide was written specifically to train foreign intelligence officers. Administrative details set out in the beginning of the manual call for 'two weeks of lectures in the classroom' followed by 'one or two weeks of practical work with prisoners …'. The 1983 manual also has a darker and less nuanced tone than the 1963 edition. It advises against outright torture, but recommends 'coercive "questioning"'. According to the manual, 'While we do not stress the use of coercive techniques, we do want to make you aware of them and the proper way to use them'.

Debility, dependency and dread are 'the three major principles involved in the successful application of coercive techniques'. These forces combine to 'induce psychological regression in the subject by bringing a superior outside force to bear on his will to resist'. Regression begins during arrest, when the subject is 'rudely awakened and immediately blindfolded and handcuffed'. During transport to the detention centre, 'isolation, both physical and psychological must be maintained'. In fact, 'any time the subject is moved for any reason he should be blindfolded and handcuffed'. Humiliation, the handbook implies, further speeds regression. After being fingerprinted and photographed, 'the subject is completely stripped and told to take a shower. Blindfold remains in place while showering and guard watches throughout'. After the shower, 'all body cavities' are inspected, then prisoners are 'provided with ill-fitting clothing (familiar clothing reinforces identity and thus the capacity for resistance.)' They are then taken to their cell, where 'total isolation should be maintained until after the first "questioning" session'.

The 1983 handbook is very particular about the design of the cell. Evoking images of Nguyen Van Tai's 'snow white cell' in Saigon, it states that windows should be adjustable to block out all light ('This allows the "questioner" to be able to disrupt the subject's sense of time, day and night') and bedding should be minimal ('The idea is to prevent the subject from relaxing and recovering from shock'). It also directs that 'heat, air and light should be externally controlled'.

While the exploitation training manual draws heavily from the lessons of KUBARK, some of its advice is strikingly similar to that of the violent SOA *Manejo de Fuentes* (Handling of Sources) manual written four years later. For instance, the 1983 CIA manual states that a 'threat is basically a means for establishing a bargaining position by inducing fear in the subject ... If a subject refuses to comply once a threat has been made, it must be carried out. If it is not carried out, then subsequent threats will also prove ineffective'. Similarly, *Manejo de Fuentes* advises: 'Threats should not be made unless they can be carried out and the employee realizes that such threats could be carried out.' The CIA manual lists the following authorised threats (and by extension, authorised punishments): '(1) Turn him over to local authorities for legal action; (2) Return him to his organization after compromising him; (3) Public exposure; (4) Deprivations; (5) Deportation; (6) Confiscation of property; (7) Physical violence'. The Army manual recommends similar actions, suggesting that the 'agent could cause the arrest of the employee's parents, imprison the employee or give him a beating ...'. Finally, the CIA manual states that the methods listed above to induce co-operation are mere suggestions and 'the number of variations in techniques is limited only by the experience and imagination of the "questioner"'. Likewise, the Army manual states: 'Many other techniques could be used which are only limited by the agent's imagination.'

Similarities aside, the exploitation manual follows the principles of DDD much more closely than the Army SOA manuals. Under the heading of 'Debility (Physical Weakness)', the CIA manual states that 'Meals and sleep should be granted irregularly, in more than abundance or less then adequacy, on no discernible time pattern. This will disorient the subject and ... destroy his capacity to resist'. Under 'Dependency', the manual advises that subjects should be 'helplessly dependent upon the "questioner" for the satisfaction of all basic needs'. In addition to food, clothing, and human interaction, the manual recommends that even the need to use the toilet should be tightly controlled. In the spirit of the Chinese detention routine outlined by Hinkle and Wolff, the manual recommends that the 'subject should have to ask to relieve himself then he should either be given a bucket or escorted by a guard to the latrine. The guard stays at his side the entire time he is in the latrine'. Under the heading: 'Dread (Intense Fear & Anxiety)', the handbook states—paraphrasing the 1963 KUBARK manual—that 'sustained long enough, a strong fear of anything vague or unknown induces regression'. For example, the prisoner 'should be made to believe that he has been forsaken by his comrades'. Referencing the general principle behind the Brazilian fridge torture device, the manual adds that 'constant disrupting patterns will cause him to become disoriented and to experience feelings of fear and helplessness'. Finally, at the end of the section on DDD, the author, again paraphrasing KUBARK, adds a word of caution: 'If the debility–dependency–dread state is unduly prolonged, the subject may sink into a defensive apathy from which it is hard to arouse him. It is advisable to have a psychologist available whenever regression is induced.'

At one stage, the manual appears to suggest that painful techniques should be used throughout an interrogation—not only as a last resort—because 'If pain is not used until late in the "questioning" process and after other tactics have failed, the subject is likely to conclude the "questioner" is becoming desperate'. When pain is to be employed, the manual recommends 'rigid positions such as standing at attention or sitting on a stool for long periods of time' because 'pain which he feels he is inflicting on himself is more likely to sap his resistance'.

Like the original Don Compos *Studies in Intelligence* article and the 1963 KUBARK manual, the 1983 exploitation training manual creates a false distinction between torture and the types of DDD techniques outlined above. The anonymous author aptly cautions that torture produces unreliable information, corrupts those who use it, lowers the moral calibre of organisations and is frowned upon by society. All of these points are true, and perhaps reflect lessons learned from the Phoenix Program. The problem is that the author fails to classify forced standing, humiliation, and sensory deprivation as *real* torture. For the author, these methods are mere 'psychological techniques designed to persuade the subject to want to furnish us with the information we desire'. Studies dating back to the early 1950s revealed that these techniques do indeed constitute torture. A passage from the 1956 Hinkle–Wolff study is telling:

> The effects of isolation, anxiety, fatigue, lack of sleep, uncomfortable temperatures, and chronic hunger produce disturbances of

mood, attitudes, and behavior in nearly all prisoners. The living organism cannot entirely withstand such assaults. The Communists do not look upon these assaults as 'torture'. Undoubtedly, they use the methods which they do in order to conform, in a typical legalistic manner to overt Communist principles which demand that 'no force or torture be used in extracting information from prisoners'. But these methods do, of course, constitute torture and physical coercion. All of them lead to serious disturbances of many bodily processes.

———

6

THE HUMAN COST

The *Human Resource Exploitation Training Manual* wasn't a theoretical field study written by a rogue agent and then filed away. Between 1983 and 1987 it was used extensively by CIA and Army Special Forces advisers to train hundreds of officers from at least seven Latin American countries. In Honduras, its effects on human rights and the rule of law are pronounced.

Honduran officers of the infamous Battalion 316 were the first students to learn the manual's cruel DDD techniques. During the 1980s, Honduras, an impoverished state wedged between Guatemala and El Salvador to its west and Nicaragua to its east, was used by the United States as a base against communist movements in the region. From Honduras, the United States armed death squads in El Salvador and funded counter-revolutionary guerrillas in Nicaragua (the 'Contras') through arms sales to Iran. Battalion 316 was charged with keeping Honduras safe from communist insurgency. Its mission, according to a declassified CIA cable, was 'to combat both domestic and regional subversive movements operating in and through Honduras'.

The battalion was founded in the late 1970s under Gustavo Alvarez Martinez, a fervent anti-Communist who was trained in counterinsurgency at the National Military Academy in Argentina, Fort Bragg in North Carolina, the United States' School of the Americas, and the International Police Academy in Washington, DC. US officials in Central America considered Alvarez to be one of the country's top officers. Upon the insistence of the CIA, he was promoted to head of the Honduran police in 1980, then head of the Honduran military in 1982. In 1989, Alvarez was assassinated by left-wing guerillas. According to John Negroponte, the US Ambassador to Honduras from 1981 to 1985, Alvarez was 'a hard man but effective officer'.

Battalion 316 was created with American funding and guidance. Between 1980 and 1984, US military aid to Honduras increased per year from $3.9 million to $77.4 million. According to General Alvarez's chief of staff, General José Bueso Rosa, 'It was [the Americans'] idea to create an intelligence unit that reported directly to the head of the armed forces. Battalion 316 was created by a need for information. We were not specialists in intelligence, in gathering information, so the United States offered to help us organize a special unit.'

Although formed to gather intelligence, under Alvarez the battalion became a death squad that stalked its prey for weeks in advance. General Alvarez picked the battalion's members, directed its operations and selected targets. Once kidnapped, victims were tortured, killed, and dumped into unmarked graves. Colonel Eric Sanchez, who served under Alvarez, recalled that the General had told him: 'One had to fight Communists with all weapons and in every arena, and not all of them are fair.'

The battalion was trained in interrogation by the US military and the CIA, as well as by Argentinean interrogators active in their own nation's 'dirty war'. One of the first men selected to join the squad was Sergeant Florencio Caballero. According to Caballero: 'I was taken to Texas with twenty-four others for six months between 1979 and 1980. There was an American Army captain there and men from the CIA.' In Texas, the battalion learned methods of DDD later codified in the 1983 manual. There, said Caballero, Americans 'taught me interrogation ... They taught us psychological methods—to study the fears and weaknesses of a prisoner. Make him stand up, don't let him sleep, keep him naked and isolated, put rats and cockroaches in his cell, give him bad food, serve him dead animals, throw cold water on him, change the temperature.' After returning from Texas, Caballero said, he joined an intelligence unit as an interrogator, and they 'seized and investigated subversives'.

Interrogation training was supplemented with a special program three years later. From 8 February to 13 March 1983, members of Battalion 316 attended a 'human resource exploitation' course led by eight CIA instructors along with four Argentineans at a Honduran military base at Lepaterique, a town 25 kilometres west of the capital, Tegucigalpa. Richard Stolz, then Deputy Director for Operations at the CIA, later testified that Caballero was one of the battalion members to attend the course. According to Stolz, 'The course consisted of three weeks of classroom instruction followed by two weeks of practical exercises, which included the questioning of actual prisoners by the students'. Stolz added that the material used in the course—coupled with the 1963 KUBARK manual—became the basis for the *Human Resource Exploitation Training Manual,* which was written by a CIA trainer later that year.

According to Caballero, CIA advisers stressed that fear can induce compliance from some of the most resistant sources. 'If a person did not like cockroaches, then that person might be more cooperative if there were cockroaches running around the room', Caballero said. José Barrera also attended the human exploitation course. The Americans, he said, 'gave us training in surveillance, disguise and photography ... and taught us methods of interrogation'. According to Barrera:

> The first thing we would say [to a prisoner] is that we know your mother, your younger brother, and it's better you cooperate, because if you don't, we're going to bring them in and rape them and torture them and kill them. We would show them photos of their family. We would say, 'We're going to get your mother and rape her in front of you.' Then we would make it seem like we went to get the mother.

While CIA officers taught methods of KUBARK, Argentinean officers taught more violent techniques. Under the Americans' watch, they taught methods of electrical torture and the use of *la capucha,* a rubber hood that was placed on a victim's head to induce suffocation. The effect of physical and psychological torture on Barrera's victims was profound. 'They always asked to be killed. Torture is worse than death', Barrera said.

One victim who survived an encounter with 316 was Inés Murillo, a member of a Marxist guerrilla group operating in Honduras. On 13 March 1983—the same day the CIA course finished in Lepaterique—members of Battalion 316 seized Murillo as she walked along a road with a friend. Murillo was driven to a country house by the masked men of Battalion 316 and shoved into a cold basement. In her damp cell, she was stripped naked, her hands and feet were bound, and she was then punched and kicked repeatedly. Murillo then recalls being immersed in a barrel of water and losing consciousness.

She was given nothing to eat or drink for the first several days. According to Murillo, her captors also fondled her and threatened to rape her if she fell asleep. During this time, interrogators electrocuted her repeatedly. After about ten days, she remembered that one interrogator, Marco Tulio Regalado—a battalion member trained at Lepaterique—came to her cell and gave her beans and tortillas. Regalado spoke to her with a soft voice and told Murillo that the tortures would cease if she revealed her real name. At this point, she said, 'I became hysterical and began to laugh. I wrote my real name and my parents' names'.

Psychologically broken, Murillo was then transferred to a secret jail on the outskirts of Tegucigalpa at a military complex known as INDUMIL, an acronym for *Industrias Militares*. The torture there 'was much more sophisticated', she recalled. 'They tortured my mind and my body.' Sergeant Caballero interrogated her at INDUMIL for hours at a time. 'I remember perfectly well what he did to me', she said. At the secret prison, she was placed in a small cell and forced to strip. Again, she was not allowed to sleep. Every ten minutes men came into her cell and poured ice water on her naked body. In her cell, she also heard the screams of other victims nearly twenty-four hours a day. According to Murillo, 'I heard one of the men say he was going to stick a rod inside the woman. The woman screamed, "No, no!" And then she just screamed. Sometimes it felt as if they were torturing other people to torture me.' Often Murillo was ordered to stand at attention for hours at a time while blindfolded. If she moved, her torturers said, a German shepherd dog would maul her. She recalled that she felt the dog against her legs as it circled around her. 'He growled all the time and barked', Murillo said. 'I thought they were going to let him attack me.' During sessions of forced standing, her captors would refuse to let her go to the toilet, and they taunted her further when she urinated on the floor. According to Murillo: 'They would say to me, "You Communists have no mothers. You have no morals. You have no country."'

During her time at INDUMIL, she recalled seeing an American whom the Hondurans called 'Mr Mike'. The American was well liked by the interrogators. 'I could tell he did not live there, but he was always welcome', she said. One day, she was blindfolded and questioned by a man she believed was Mr Mike. Sergeant Caballero confirmed that an American named 'Mr Mike' had free access to the prison and one time had entered Murillo's cell to ask her questions. 'He saw how she was', Caballero said. Richard Stolz also confirmed Mr Mike's visit to INDUMIL. According to Stolz, a CIA officer went to visit 'the area where Ms Murillo was held'. Said Caballero, 'The Americans knew everything we were doing. They saw what condition the victims were in—their marks and bruises. They did not do anything'.

During the height of 316's reign of terror, the annual State Department Country Reports on Human Rights played down all references to torture in Honduras. According to then Ambassador John Negroponte—appointed Director of National Intelligence by George W. Bush in 2005—America 'worked to promote the restoration and consolidation of democracy in Honduras, including the advancement of human rights'. Negroponte's predecessor, Ambassador Jack R. Binns, disagreed. 'When it comes to subversion, [Alvarez] would opt for tough, vigorous and extra-legal action', Binns said. According to Binns, he reported the actions of 316 to the State Department and was 'begging for them to take some action'. The Reagan administration, he said, failed to act. Instead, they ordered him to stop reporting the abuses and then removed him from his post.

Inés Murillo was eventually released after her father, a former Honduran military officer, threatened to expose the location of INDUMIL. Murillo suffered seventy-nine days with the battalion, but she was lucky to survive. By the time 316 was disbanded in 1984, more than 180 Hondurans had 'disappeared'.

———

In October 1984, a CIA manual instructing Nicaraguan rebels in techniques of guerrilla warfare was leaked to the US House Intelligence Committee. This manual, *Psychological Operations in Guerrilla Warfare*, was compiled in late 1983 by 'John Kirkpatrick', a pseudonym used by a Phoenix veteran and adviser to the Contra rebels working under CIA contract. The handbook states that unpopular government officials can be 'neutralized' with the 'selective use of violence' and recommends the hiring of criminals to carry out 'selective jobs'. When the manual was exposed, Reagan first sought to downplay its importance by claiming that to 'neutralize' a person meant nothing more than 'you just say to the fellow that's sitting there in the office, "You're not in the office any more"'. A follow-up CIA Inspector General Report recommended that Kirkpatrick resign, three agents who assisted him receive letters of reprimand, and two others be suspended without pay. Senator Daniel Patrick Moynihan compared the punishments with cancelling 'weekend privileges for a month'.

Disclosure of the manual led to the CIA's first explicit policy statement regarding interrogations. On 14 January 1985, CIA Headquarters in Langley, Virginia, cabled the following notice to field agents across the globe:

> Interviewing and interrogation of suspects in custody is a method routinely used by police, security and intelligence services around the world. In many countries, the legal and basic rights of the suspect in custody may not be given full consideration, resulting in deprivation of his/her human rights. CIA policy is not to participate in nor to encourage interrogation that results in use of force, mental or physical torture, extremely demeaning indignities or exposure to inhumane treatment of any kind, as an aid to interrogation. CIA policy is to actively discourage the use of these methods during interrogations. CIA should play a positive role in influencing foreign liaison to respect human rights.

This official notice, the first of its kind in CIA history, led one concerned agent to manually edit the *Human Resource Exploitation Training Manual*. Some changes were subtle. For example, the sentence that began 'Whether regression occurs spontaneously under detention or is induced by the "questioner" ...' was changed to read: 'Whether regression occurs spontaneously under detention or is *inadvertently* induced by the "questioner" ...'. (emphasis added). Other items were crossed out completely, like the reference to 'physical violence' on page I-8. A disclaimer added at the front of the manual in March 1985 advised against 'inhumane treatment' but qualified it by adding 'the use of force is not to be confused with psychological ploys ...'. The section on coercion was left largely intact. The sentence 'While we do not stress the use of coercive techniques, we do want to make you aware of them and the proper way to use them' was changed to read: 'While we deplore the use of coercive techniques, we do want to make you aware of them so that you may avoid them'.

A 1988 *New York Times Magazine* article about the abuses of 316 led to closed-door Senate Select Committee Hearings that sought to uncover the extent of US involvement with the battalion. The existence of the 1983 and 1963 CIA manuals surfaced for the first time in a report prepared for the committee. At the hearing, Senator William S. Cohen, who served as Secretary of Defense under President Clinton, was surprised by the manuals' existence—revealing just how little Congress knew about CIA torture training at the time:

> I am not sure why, in 1983, it became necessary to have such a manual. But [also] … upon its discovery, why we only sought to revise it in a fashion which says, 'These are some of the techniques we think are abhorrent. We just want you to be aware of them so you'll avoid them.' There's a lot in this that troubles me in terms of whether you are sending subliminal signals that say, 'This is improper, but, by the way, you ought to be aware of it.'

Deputy Director Stolz countered that while the manual's techniques 'might appear harsh', they didn't qualify as torture. Glossing over the previous forty-plus years of torture research, training and development, Stolz maintained that it was the CIA's policy all along neither to:

> participate directly in nor to encourage interrogation which results in the use of force, mental or physical torture, demeaning indignities or exposure to inhumane treatment of any kind as an aid to interrogation. The policy is to actively discourage the use of these methods during interrogations.

No one at the hearing called Stolz's bluff—this was, after all, the CIA's stated policy beginning only in 1985. Rather, Stolz was thanked for his contribution and praised by the panel for being 'most cooperative'.

The existence of the 1963 and 1983 manuals was revealed publicly for the first time by declassified transcripts of the above exchange.

As part of their research for a story on Battalion 316, on 26 May 1994 the *Baltimore Sun*'s Gary Cohn and Ginger Thompson filed an FOIA request for the KUBARK and human exploitation manuals. At first, the CIA refused to release the manuals and Cohn and Thompson had to run their award-winning series, 'Unearthed: Fatal Secrets', without them. The *Baltimore Sun* articles prompted the CIA to launch their own internal investigation into CIA complicity in Latin American human rights abuse. Two years later a CIA Working Group concluded that it was 'unable to resolve whether [any] CIA employee was present during sessions of hostile interrogation or torture in Honduras'. The panel tracked down Mr Mike and questioned him about his time at INDUMIL. According to the report, '[Redacted] continues to deny the allegation ... [Redacted] states that he never assisted the Hondurans in conducting interrogations, either directly or indirectly, nor has he ever been involved in inflicting torture on a prisoner. [Redacted] cannot offer an explanation for the allegation that he participated in an abusing interrogation.'

After three years of legal struggles with the *Baltimore Sun*, the agency released the KUBARK and human exploitation manuals on 24 January 1997. The paper's bold headline, 'Torture Was Taught By CIA', caught the nation's attention—albeit briefly. After the manuals were declassified, an investigation led by Congressman Joseph P. Kennedy blamed both the CIA and the School of Americas for human rights abuse in Honduras. Kennedy initiated an unsuccessful fight to close down the school, a mission now led by the organisation SOA Watch.

The CIA escaped the exposures unscathed—the addition of a general statement against torture marked the only tangible change to CIA policy. To this day, no one has been held accountable for producing the two manuals. Unlike the CIA, the Department of Defense commenced significant reforms after military-sponsored torture training was disclosed. The seven Spanish-language manuals that discussed torture and assassination were exposed in 1991 when instructors evaluating course materials for military training programs in Colombia stumbled across the material. A Department of Defense inquiry later found that six of the seven manuals written in 1987 contained material 'in violation of legal, regulatory, or policy prohibitions'. Werner E. Michel, assistant to then Secretary of Defense Dick Cheney, concluded that the manuals' discovery 'undermines US credibility and could result in significant embarrassment'. Michel advised that in the future all training materials should be made consistent with US policy and ordered the destruction of 'all other copies of the manuals and associated instructional materials, including computer disks, lesson plans and "Project X" documents'. In 1996, the Pentagon declassified all seven manuals.

In keeping with Michel's decision, all references to Project X were excised from US Army field manuals. On 28 September 1992, a new version of *Intelligence Interrogation* superseded the 1987 edition. The 1992 version deleted all mention of DDD-style techniques, including all references to controlling the lighting and heating and the quantity and quality of food, shelter and clothing given to subjects. Rather than label interrogation an 'art', the 1992 edition stated plainly: 'Interrogation is the process of questioning a source to obtain the maximum amount of usable information. The goal of any interrogation is to obtain reliable information in a lawful manner …'.

The field manual closely conformed to the rules outlined in the *Geneva Convention relative to the Treatment of Prisoners of War* (GPW), which, along with the other three Geneva Conventions, was ratified by the United States on 2 August 1955. GPW states that prisoners of war 'must at all times be humanely treated' (Article 13) and housed 'under conditions as favorable as those for the forces of the Detaining Power' (Article 25). Article 17 states that 'No physical or mental torture, nor any other form of coercion, may be inflicted on prisoners of war to secure from them information of any kind whatever. Prisoners of war who refuse to answer may not be threatened, insulted or exposed to any unpleasant or disadvantageous treatment of any kind'. These articles reflect the broad language of Article 5 of the *Universal Declaration of Human Rights*—signed by the USA in 1948—which specifies that in times of war and peace 'no one shall be subjected to torture or to cruel, inhuman, or degrading treatment'.

Unlike previous editions, the new field manual explicitly banned the use of all physical and mental torture and coercion. 'Experience', it reads, 'indicates that the use of prohibited techniques is not necessary to gain the cooperation of interrogation sources'. It boldly adds:

Use of torture and other illegal methods is a poor technique that yields unreliable results, may damage subsequent collection efforts, and can induce the source to say what he thinks the interrogator wants to hear. Revelation of use of torture by US personnel will bring discredit upon the US and its armed forces while undermining domestic and international support for the war effort.

According to the 1992 edition: 'Torture is defined as the infliction of intense pain to body or mind to extract a confession or information, or for sadistic pleasure'. The manual stresses that torture is subject to prosecution under the Uniform Code of Military Justice (UCMJ), which specifically bans 'Cruelty and Mistreatment' (Article 93), 'Murder' (Article 118) and 'Maiming' (Article 124). Examples of physical torture include: 'electric shock, infliction of pain through chemicals or bondage, forcing an individual to stand, sit, or kneel in abnormal positions for prolonged periods of time, food deprivation, [and] any form of beating'. Furthermore, the manual states that mental torture includes: 'mock executions, abnormal sleep deprivation, [and] chemically induced psychosis'.

In addition to banning the often-used DDD torture methods above, the manual went one step further, stating that all forms of 'coercion' were also off-limits to Army interrogators. Like torture, coercive techniques were punishable under the UCMJ. According to the field manual, coercion is defined as unlawful actions designed to induce or compel another to perform an act against his or her will. Examples of coercion include: 'Threatening or implying physical or mental torture to the subject, his family, or others to whom he owes loyalty [and] intentionally denying medical assistance or care in exchange for the information sought or other cooperation'. Rather than using these techniques, the manual recommends non-violent methods designed to build rapport between subjects and interrogators. These include the direct approach ('questions directly related to information sought'), an incentive approach (rewarding the subject with 'certain luxury items such as candy, fruit, or cigarettes'), an emotional approach ('identify dominant emotions which motivate') or fear-up approach (where 'the interrogator behaves in an overpowering manner with a loud and threatening voice'). The manual concedes that sometimes the application of these techniques may 'approach the line between lawful actions and unlawful actions'. To determine whether the methods are lawful, the manual asks interrogators to consider two tests:

1. Given all the surrounding facts and circumstances, would a reasonable person in the place of the person being interrogated believe that his rights, as guaranteed under both international and US law, are being violated or withheld if he fails to co-operate?
2. If your contemplated actions were perpetrated by the enemy against US PWs [prisoners of war], would you believe such actions violate international or US law?

If the answer to either test is yes, states the manual, 'do not engage in the contemplated action'.

With the 1992 publication of FM 34-52, American interrogation procedure had come full circle. First, the armed forces and the CIA studied communist techniques of coercion. These methods were then tested, refined and exported abroad. Exposed by Congress and the press, the Pentagon removed DDD techniques from official literature. Despite these efforts, the same DDD tortures banned in FM 34-52 were kept alive both in practice and on paper.

———

7

ALIVE AND LEGAL

In 1988, Ronald Reagan declared in Moscow that his reference to the 'Evil Empire' was from 'another time' and 'of course' the Cold War was over. Over the next three years, America's long-time foe fractured at the seams and on 25 December 1991 the Soviet flag was lowered from the Kremlin for the last time. Although the ideological driver behind the development of American torture was dead, the debility–dependency–dread paradigm survived.

The specific DDD tortures and coercive techniques banned in FM 34-52, *Intelligence Interrogation* (1992) lived on in practice at military Survival, Evasion, Resistance and Escape (SERE) schools. As discussed in Chapter 2, SERE trains soldiers to live off the land, outsmart adversaries, and, if captured, resist torture. Resistance is ostensibly achieved via stress inoculation—exposing soldiers to abusive treatment in a controlled setting, on the theory that they can thereby be 'immunised' against the effects of torture. Since the Korean War era, SERE has grown more violent, brutal and deadly. Although the Pentagon remains secretive about the specifics, claiming that revealing its details would only tip off 'the enemy', various reports have surfaced over the years, revealing what goes on in the program.

In the early 1960s, the US Navy opened two SERE schools: a cold-weather facility at Naval Air Station Brunswick in north-western Maine and a warm-weather school at Warner Springs, California, outside San Diego in the Cleveland National Forest. In 1961, a sailor suffocated inside an isolation box during the course at Warner Springs. Six years later, another student suffered a fatal heart attack during an evasion exercise. Despite the deaths, Warner Springs SERE school remained open. In March 1976, one former student filed a US$15 million dollar civil claim against the school for assault and battery. Lieutenant Wendell Richard Young, a Navy pilot with a 'sparkling service record', filed suit after he broke his back during the course. Although he wore a yellow wristband indicating that he had a back condition, an instructor, he alleged, gave him a jarring 'judo flip' that caused the injury. Young's suit was dismissed after the Navy invoked the Feres Doctrine, a legal principle that prevents people injured in the course of military service from successful litigation against the government. Despite his legal loss, Young's allegations shed light on the shadowy world of SERE.

Investigating Young's claims, in 1976 *Newsweek* found that during the 'resistance laboratory phase' at SERE, students were kept in boxes measuring less than half a cubic metre, bombarded with Vietnamese music and subjected to the 'dread water board'. The waterboard is a torture device that dates back to the Italian Inquisition in the sixteenth century. It is used to convince victims they are drowning. According to *Newsweek*, in the variation used at SERE students were 'strapped head down onto an inclined board, with a towel placed over their faces and cold water poured onto it. They choke, gag, retch and gurgle—and it is dangerous enough that a Navy doctor must stand by at all times to prevent the students from accidentally drowning'. In an interview, Lieutenant Young recalled, 'I could hear the gurgling screams of people on the water board, you could hear people being smashed into walls. The pain was quite real—I experienced it'. Torture at Warner Springs didn't end there. Young also alleged that students were forced into 'spitting, urinating and defecating on the American flag, masturbating before guards, and on one occasion, engaging in sex with an instructor'. The SERE camp, said Young, is 'a modern-day Dachau'.

Two weeks after Young filed suit and only four days after *Newsweek* published its own findings, the Pentagon formed a Defense Review Committee to re-examine the 1955 Code of Conduct that spurred wide-scale SERE training. According to the committee, the inquiry was launched amid 'speculation and controversy concerning validity of the Code of Conduct', which holds that POWs are obliged to reveal only their name, rank, service number and date of birth when captured. This protection is drawn word-for-word from Article 17 of the Geneva Convention relative to the Treatment of Prisoners of War.

From May through July 1976, the committee interviewed dozens of ex-POWs about their experiences in Vietnam. Like Korean War POWs, hundreds of Americans captured in Vietnam signed false confessions under torture. The Vietcong held John McCain, now a ranking Republican senator, for more than five years at the infamous Hoa Lo Prison, better know as the Hanoi Hilton. According to McCain, to force a confession guards first beat him 'from pillar to post, kicking and laughing and scratching. After a few hours of that, ropes were put on me and I sat that night bound with ropes'. The brutality continued until he signed a confession. 'For the next four days, I was beaten every two to three hours by different guards', he said. McCain was then presented with a list of charges. 'I signed it', he said. 'It was in their language, and spoke about black crimes, and other generalities … I had learned what we all learned over there. Every man has his breaking point. I had reached mine.'

Another soldier who admitted to 'war crimes' in Vietnam was retired Navy pilot Mike Cronin. Like McCain, Cronin was shot down in 1967 and spent nearly six years in the Hanoi Hilton. To force a confession his captors used rope to bind his neck and ankles together. In the process, his shoulder was dislocated and nerves in his wrist were severed. 'I told lies', he said. 'When you put people in that position, the information you get is not reliable.'

Communications technician Don E. Baily was also tortured after Vietcong forces captured his ship, the USS *Pueblo*. Unlike McCain and Cronin, Baily had SERE training prior to deployment. According to Baily, the 'living conditions in [Vietnamese] prison had been better than in the [SERE] school'. Baily did put his SERE training to use. During his captivity, he said, 'I tried to get the men in my room to understand what I learned in school. I tried to tell them that fear was the biggest thing, that not knowing what was going to happen was sometimes worse than knowing'. VC interrogators beat Baily until he neared death. Despite SERE training, he said he signed an espionage confession 'because there was no alternative'.

The Pentagon SERE inquiry considered accounts such as these in their review of the program. After months of hearings, the panel decided to expand resistance training at SERE. In its final report, the Defense Review Committee found that

> Some PWs [prisoners of war] and detainees had completed
> sophisticated survival, evasion, resistance and escape (SERE)
> training which enabled them to understand their situation and to
> cope with it more effectively; whereas others might only have
> been exposed to a poor quality tape recording of a lecture on the
> Code to 'fill a square'.

To remedy this problem, the group recommended that the
Pentagon standardise SERE training among all branches of the military and expand SERE to include 'lessons learned from previous
USPW [United States Prisoner of War] experiences'. These changes,
they said, will make training more 'realistic and useful'.

In December 1984, the Pentagon issued DOD Directive 1300.7
establishing three levels of SERE training: A, B and C. The resistance
phase of SERE was incorporated in Level C training. According to
the directive, Level C training is for soldiers whose 'assignment has a
high risk of capture and whose position, rank, or seniority make them
vulnerable to greater than average exploitation efforts by a captor'.
Only four military bases are currently authorised to conduct C-level
training, although other bases sometimes conduct their own version of
SERE.

The Air Force's official Level C SERE program is based at
Fairchild Air Force Base in Washington State. In 1966, the Air Force
SERE program shifted to Fairchild from Stead, Nevada. Although
Fairchild's resistance training laboratory (RTL) is shrouded in mystery,
a good indication of what goes on there emerged in the early 1990s.
In 1993, the Air Force Academy in Colorado Springs, Colorado,
launched its own version of SERE for first- and second-year cadets.
The instructors for the academy's SERE course were drawn from the
Air Force's Fairchild SERE school. In Colorado Springs, cadets were
subjected to extensive and varied abuse.

Christian Polintan was a popular straight-A student at the academy.
At SERE he was singled out by administrators to show that if he
could be broken, anyone could be. In 1995, Polintan told the television news program *20/20* that he was forced to parade around as
'the executive officer's sex toy' wearing make-up and a skirt. 'They
made me act like a girl, curtsy and sit on his lap', Polintan said. He was
also tied face down to a table and was groped by another male student.
'They brought in another cadet, a "prisoner" like me, and told him to

take off his clothes and get on top of me and act like he was having sex', Polintan recalled. 'The cadet tried to resist—he said you know that's sick—I don't want to do it ... And they made him get on top of me and act like he's having sex with me.' When Polintan complained to school authorities, he was told the abuse was within SERE guidelines and he was overreacting to 'realistic resistance training'. Polintan dropped out of the academy, disillusioned by his ordeal.

A *20/20* investigation found that at least twenty-four other cadets were subjected to various degrees of sexual assault at the academy's SERE program. One of these cadets was Elizabeth Saum, then nineteen years old. According to Saum, she was singled out for being 'too pretty and too confident'. At SERE she was led to the woods by several guards and ordered to lie on her back and unbutton her shirt. One man then forced her knees apart and demanded to know if she was 'ready for it' while another videotaped the scene. Another time, Saum said, she was handed a stick and ordered to put it down her pants. 'If anyone asked me about it, I was to say it was my masturbating stick', she said. When Saum first went public, the Air Force downplayed the tortures as vital components of a SERE 'sexual exploitation scenario' and an internal investigation found that no 'actionable misconduct occurred'. In 1995, the academy changed course and dropped the resistance portion of SERE training. The following year, Saum sued the Air Force for violating her constitutional rights—a claim that circumvented the Feres Doctrine. The Air Force settled out of court for an estimated US$3 million.

C-Level training for the Navy is equally brutal. It is held in two locations: Naval Air Station Brunswick in Maine and Warner Springs, California. One graduate of the Warner Springs course reported that he was subjected to an array of physical and psychological tortures at the school. According to this student, at Warner Springs:

> We were penned in concrete cell blocks about four foot by four foot by four foot—told to kneel, but allowed to squat or sit. There was no door, just a flap that could be let down if it was too cold outside ... Each trainee was interrogated to some extent, all experienced some physical interrogation such as pushing, shoving, getting slammed against a wall (usually a large metal sheet set up so that it would not seriously injure trainees) with some actually water-boarded (not me).

At the Warner Springs course, instructors also added a cruel torture designed to distress Christian students. According to the graduate,
one of the most traumatic moments at SERE came when an instructor
abused a Bible. He recalled:

> The bible trashing was done by one of the top-ranked leaders of
> the camp, who was always giving us speeches—sort of 'making it
> real' so to speak—because it is a pretty contrived environment.
> [It] happened when this guy had us all in the courtyard sitting for
> one of his speeches. They were tempting us with a big pot of
> soup that was boiling—we were all starving from a few days
> of chow deprivation. He brought out the bible and started going
> off on it verbally—how it was worthless, we were forsaken by
> this God, etc. Then he threw it on the ground and kicked it
> around. It was definitely the climax of his speech. Then he kicked
> over the soup pot, and threw us back in the cells. Big climax. And
> psychologically it was crushing and heartbreaking, and then we
> were left isolated to contemplate this.

The Army's C-Level Training takes place at Camp Mackall and is
considered by some as the military's toughest. At Mackall—a base 56
kilometres outside Fort Bragg that has hosted SERE since 1953—the
SERE course lasts nineteen days total and includes a four-day RTL
phase featuring sleep, food and sensory deprivation. A CNN crew that
visited the school was not permitted to film the resistance portion of
the program but did interview some instructors. 'Is the guy going to
be under stress in captivity? You're dang straight, he is', said Elmer
Adams, an instructor at the Army SERE course. 'So, we're going to
put him under stress here to prepare him for that, just in case …'.
CNN reported that two doctors and one psychologist, sometimes
disguised as interrogators or guards, observe the resistance laboratory
portion of the training. Another instructor told CNN: 'You don't
know what freedom is until you lose it. Here they lose their freedom,
all freedom.'

A graduate of the Mackall Level C course said that his time at
SERE was one of the toughest challenges of his twenty-year Army
career. Interrogators, he recalled in an interview with *Salon*, specifically target students' values and self-esteem. They stomped on a copy
of the Constitution, destroyed an American flag and 'kicked the Bible

around'. Students were also subjected to sexual humiliation. During one interrogation session, he said, '[t]hey had me remove my clothes'. A woman in the room said to him, 'You are fat', and added, 'You have the smallest dick I have ever seen'. The experience, he said, was 'humiliating and degrading'.

Physical tortures at Mackall included DDD-style methods. Students were isolated in cells that were too low to stand up in and too narrow to lie down. They were denied toilet breaks and had to urinate and defecate in their clothes. They were forced to exercise to the point of exhaustion and were sometimes hooded and drenched with cold water. 'If you have ever had a bag on your head and somebody pours water on it, it is real hard to breathe', the former student said. They were also subjected to a variety of stress positions. Students were forced to squat and keep their palms facing up, or to assume a half-crouch and keep their arms extended straight out. In this position, he said, 'Your legs go numb. Your knees go numb. Your feet tingle. It feels like fire. Eventually, you can't hold yourself up'.

The clinical effects of SERE torture are striking. In 2000, psychiatrist Dr C. A. Morgan III and Army psychologist Major Gary Hazlett published a paper in *Special Warfare* titled 'Assessment of Humans Experiencing Uncontrollable Stress: The SERE Course'. The authors analysed saliva samples of more than 200 students participating in the Army C-Level course before, during and after the RTL phase. From the samples, they were able to chart changes in the levels of cortisol and testosterone in students' bodies. Cortisol is a hormone that prepares the body for stress by increasing energy and alertness. It also increases anxiety. The researchers found that cortisol levels of students during periods of stress at SERE 'were some of the greatest ever documented in humans'. Stress levels of the students, based on the amount of cortisol, were found to be higher than those in people undergoing major surgery, soldiers completing Army Ranger training, pilots operating aircraft, and even skydivers making their first jump. The effects of SERE stress on testosterone were equally dramatic. Testosterone maintains sex characteristics in men, and in both sexes repairs tissues, facilitates proper functioning of the immune system and aids the body in dealing with stress. Morgan and Hazlett found that testosterone in men undergoing stress at SERE 'dropped from normal levels to castration levels within eight hours'. According to Hazlett: 'About a third of our guys will measure at a point at which they're no longer producing viable semen, so they're basically shooting blanks at that point.'

The Morgan–Hazlett study revealed that sexual, religious and physical DDD tortures used at Mackall, and by logical extension at the other three Level C SERE centres, deliver incredible levels of stress—enough to make a healthy man sterile. Given these dangers, Morgan and Hazlett cautioned that SERE training should be carefully controlled. 'If the stress level is not high enough, inoculation will not occur; if the stress level is too high, stress sensitization will occur, and the individual will probably perform less effectively when he is stressed again.'

Colonel Rhonda Cornum, an Army flight surgeon who spent eight months as a POW in Iraq during the first Gulf War, is a strong advocate for SERE, but had doubts about the effectiveness of stress inoculation. 'Sometimes you fly really tired, but you don't train that way', she said. There are some things you cannot prepare for, she added. 'Practicing to bleed' is impossible.

Some have suggested that there is a more sinister element to the schools. The Warner Springs graduate who described the Bible thrashing said, 'My gut feeling tells me that the SERE camps were "laboratories" and part of the training program for military counter-intelligence and interrogator personnel'. A former SERE trainer, Paul Bauer, confirmed that SERE—at least in his experience—is used to train interrogators. Bauer worked at a SERE school in the late 1980s and early 1990s. In addition to using non-coercive methods, stress positions, sensory deprivation and humiliation were common, he said. 'I used these techniques on our own and allied troops', he added. 'As a quid pro quo for providing this training, the interrogators involved were also allowed to hone their own skills …'.

———

While SERE kept DDD methods alive, the US Department of Justice kept them legal. In 1988, Reagan signed the UN *Convention Against Torture and Other Cruel, Inhuman or Degrading Treatment or Punishment* (CAT) and submitted it to the Senate, as US ratification procedure requires. According to Reagan: 'Ratification of the Convention by the United States will clearly express United States opposition to torture, an abhorrent practice unfortunately still prevalent in the world today.' In retrospect, the only thing clearly expressed upon ratification was America's intent to keep DDD torture free from judicial oversight.

The CAT was designed to ban all forms of psychological and physical torture. The treaty's definition of torture, as adopted by the UN General Assembly in December 1984, states in Article 1 that it is 'any act by which severe pain or suffering, whether physical or mental, is intentionally inflicted on a person for such purposes as obtaining from him or a third person information or a confession …'. For abuse that falls below the threshold of this definition, Article 16 directs that 'Each State Party shall undertake to prevent in any territory under its jurisdiction other acts of cruel, inhuman or degrading treatment or punishment which do not amount to torture as defined in Article 1'. Finally, Article 3 prohibits any state from sending suspects to another state 'where there are substantial grounds for believing that he would be in danger of being subjected to torture'.

American DDD tortures taught overseas and used at SERE clearly fell within the CAT's definition of torture. In fact, several of these techniques appeared on a list prepared in 1986 by the UN Special Rapporteur on Torture detailing acts that rise to the level of torture. The list included:

> electric shocks; suspension; suffocation; exposure to excessive light or noise; sexual aggression; administration of drugs in detention or psychiatric institutions; prolonged denial of rest or sleep; prolonged denial of food; prolonged denial of sufficient hygiene; prolonged denial of medical assistance; total isolation and sensory deprivation; being kept in constant uncertainty in terms of space and time; threats to torture or kill relatives; total abandonment; and simulated executions.

DDD techniques used by two of America's closest allies—the United Kingdom and Israel—were also found to rise to the level of torture and cruel, inhumane and degrading treatment. In the late 1960s and early 1970s, British interrogators were authorised to use a variety of techniques similar to the methods used at UK stress inoculation schools. As discussed in Chapter 2, British Resistance to Interrogation (R2I) schools established in 1956 were modelled on SERE. At an R2I centre at Chicksands, for example, Special Air Service paratroopers and pilots were hooded, blasted with hours of white noise and stripped naked. British interrogators used these methods in colonies in Kenya, Yemen, Cyprus and Northern Ireland. In 1972, Amnesty International assailed UK security forces in Northern Ireland for using forced standing, hooding, loud noise, sleep deprivation and dietary manipulation. 'The methods used were designed to disorientate and break down the resistance of the prisoners', charged Amnesty International. In 1976, victims of these techniques filed suit in the European Court of Human Rights. In *Ireland v United Kingdom* (1978), the court found that while the five methods did not cause 'suffering of the particular intensity and cruelty implied by the word torture', they constituted 'cruel, inhumane and degrading treatment', in breach of the European Convention on Human Rights. Authorisation for these techniques was rescinded, though R2I training continued.

Beginning in the late 1980s, Israel's Shin Bet was also authorised to use 'moderate physical pressure' against Palestinian detainees. These methods resembled various techniques used at SERE. The Committee Against Torture, the UN body that monitors compliance with the treaty, studied the issue and recommended that Israel immediately cease using a variety of DDD tortures. The techniques referred to were: '(1) restraining in very painful positions, (2) hooding under special conditions, (3) sounding of loud music for prolonged periods, (4) sleep deprivation for prolonged periods, (5) threats, including death threats, (6) violent shaking, and (7) using cold air to chill'. These methods were 'in the Committee's view breaches of Art. 16 and also constitute torture as defined in Art. 1 … This conclusion is particularly evident where such methods of interrogation are used in combination'.

The Israeli Supreme Court banned these techniques. According to Dan Meridor, then head of Israel's Foreign Affairs and Defense Committee, 'What the High Court ruled is that in an interrogation, even during a difficult war against terror where the interrogation is vital, one must preserve basic standards of behavior'.

Since DDD techniques were clearly banned under the CAT, lawyers in the Department of Justice's Office of Legal Counsel (OLC) worked hard to rewrite the CAT's broad definition of torture and its numerous provisions. The OLC provides legal advice to the president and to agencies under the president's direction, namely the CIA. The OLC—perhaps upon insistence of the CIA or even SERE officials—authored nineteen 'reservations', 'understandings' and 'declarations' that excluded American use of DDD torture from treaty effect. The United States wasn't alone in submitting reservations to the CAT. What set America apart was the sheer number—no other state submitted more than four.

Reagan's OLC lawyers took immediate issue with the definition of torture. They believed that torture should constitute only the most egregious physical tortures and suggested the following reservation: 'The United States understands that, in order to constitute torture, an act must be a deliberate and calculated act of an extremely cruel and inhuman nature ...'. This definition, the lawyers opined, excludes sensory deprivation, forced standing and sexual humiliation but includes acts like 'systematic beatings, application of electric currents to sensitive parts of the body and tying up or hanging in positions that cause extreme pain'. Importantly, the Reagan administration found that 'rough treatment as generally falls into the category of "police brutality," while deplorable, does not amount to "torture"'. The OLC also introduced the concept of 'specific intent' into the definition. For an act to constitute torture, they wrote, it must be *specifically intended* to inflict excruciating and agonizing physical or mental pain or suffering' (emphasis added).

The difference between an 'intentional' and 'specifically intended' crime is vast. While an 'intentional' crime is performed deliberately, it lacks a precise objective. A 'specifically intended' crime is wholly different. According to the 1995 case *United States v Blair*, whose importance lies in its clarification of this distinction:

> A specific intent crime is one in which an act was committed voluntarily and purposely with the specific intent to do something the law forbids. In contrast, a general intent crime is one in which an act was done voluntarily and intentionally, and not because of mistake or accident. In short, a specific intent crime is one in which the defendant acts not only with knowledge of what he is doing, but does so with the objective of completing some unlawful act.

The difference between these two mental states can be seen in this illustration of the test used by US courts:

> A person entered a bank and took money from a teller at gunpoint, but deliberately failed to make a quick getaway from the bank in

the hope of being arrested so that he would be returned to prison and treated for alcoholism. Though this defendant knowingly engaged in the acts of using force and taking money (satisfying 'general intent'), he did not intend permanently to deprive the bank of its possession of the money (failing to satisfy 'specific intent').

Torture, as redefined by Reagan's OLC, only occurs if an interrogator committed acts against a suspect with the sole objective of inflicting severe mental or physical pain. If an interrogator inflicts severe pain on a suspect with the aim of extracting information, the interrogator lacks the requisite 'specific intent' to be found guilty of torture. Proving that a torturer had 'specific intent' can be extremely difficult, because it requires not only that the accused intended to do something, but that he or she intended to do it for a particular reason.

In addition to Article 1, OLC lawyers also rewrote Article 16, ostensibly to provide increased 'precision'. According to the United Nations, the phrase 'cruel, inhuman or degrading treatment or punishment' should be interpreted to

extend the widest possible protection against abuses, whether physical or mental, including the holding of a detained or imprisoned person in conditions which deprive him temporarily or permanently of the use of any of his natural senses, such as sight or hearing, or of his awareness of place and the passing of time.

Given the breadth of Article 16, OLC lawyers also targeted it for revision. After all, sensory deprivation and disorientation are core elements of the DDD routine. The OLC proffered:

The United States understands the term 'cruel, inhuman or degrading treatment or punishment', as used in Article 16 of the Convention, to mean the cruel, unusual, and inhumane treatment or punishment prohibited by the Fifth, Eighth, and/or Fourteenth Amendments to the Constitution of the United States.

By binding Article 16 to the US Constitution—as interpreted by US courts—OLC lawyers safeguarded DDD methods yet again. According to Amnesty International this 'reservation has far-reaching implications and can apply to any US laws or practices which may breach international standards for humane treatment but are allowed under the US Constitution, for example, prolonged isolation or the use of electro-shock weapons'.

The Senate did not consider the reservations submitted by Reagan until the first Bush administration took the White House in 1989. When George H. W. Bush took office, his OLC staff expanded the CAT reservations submitted by Reagan. Five 'understandings' dealt directly with torture as defined by Article 1. Bush's reservations to this article kept intact the notion of specific intent and reaffirmed the extremely high threshold of pain required for an act to constitute torture. The concept of torture, according to Bush's Deputy Assistant Attorney General Mark Richard, involves strictly conduct 'the mere mention of which sends chills down one's spine'. Physical torture only includes acts like 'the needle under the fingernail, the application of electric shocks to the genital area, the piercing of eyeballs, etc.', said Richard.

Bush's OLC also added a long list of stipulations regarding mental torture. According to Richard, 'The basic problem with the Torture Convention—one that permeates all our concerns—is its imprecise definition of torture, especially as that term is applied to actions which result solely in mental anguish'. In order to 'overcome this unacceptable element of vagueness', OLC lawyers limited mental torture to only four specific variations, subject to overall severity. According to this understanding:

> the United States understands that, in order to constitute torture, an act must be specifically intended to inflict severe physical or mental pain or suffering and that mental pain or suffering refers to prolonged mental harm caused by or resulting from: (1) the intentional infliction or threatened infliction of severe physical pain or suffering; (2) the administration or application, or threatened administration or application, of mind altering substances or other procedures calculated to disrupt profoundly the senses or the personality; (3) the threat of imminent death; or (4) the threat that another person will imminently be subjected to death, severe physical pain or suffering, or the administration or application of mind altering substances or other procedures calculated to disrupt profoundly the senses or personality.

While the mental anguish resulting from extreme isolation, forced standing, humiliation or extreme disorientation may 'disrupt profoundly the senses of the personality', for these acts to constitute torture they must cause 'prolonged mental harm'. According to Physicians for Human Rights, this rationale 'turns the very idea of the prohibition against torture on its head since the purpose of the laws against torture is to prevent interrogators from using it in the first place, not waiting to see what impact it may have'.

Bush's OLC also kept intact Reagan's understanding of the term 'cruel, inhuman or degrading treatment or punishment'. Like Reagan, Bush opted to bind the definition of these terms to acts prohibited by the Fifth, Eighth, and/or Fourteenth Amendments—not to international standards. The government of the Netherlands strongly objected to this reservation, finding it 'incompatible with the object and purpose of the Convention, to which the obligation laid down in article 16 is essential'.

With these reservations, Bush's OLC omitted the bulk of psychological DDD tortures from the CAT. But what of more traditional torture methods like drowning or beating? In order to safeguard the use of more extreme torture techniques, administration lawyers added a provision that ensured the right to send suspects to states that torture. According to the terms of ratification, 'the United States understands the phrase, "where there are substantial grounds for believing that he would be in danger of being subjected to torture", as used in Article 3 of the Convention, to mean "if it is more likely than not that he would be tortured"'. According to Amnesty, this 'places a higher burden of proof on someone seeking not to be returned to a country where he or she faces the risk of torture than is intended under the treaty'. Given this understanding, a prisoner cannot be extradited to any state where the 'official' chance of torture is higher than 50 per cent. If the United States considers the likelihood to be any less than 50 per cent, a suspect can legally be sent abroad.

Finally, the OLC inserted an understanding noting that the treaty is 'not-self executing', meaning that it is not effective as judicially enforceable US law without federal legislation specifically implementing it. As a result, a private citizen cannot use the CAT as a legal basis for litigation in US courts. According to Kenneth Roth of Human Rights Watch, this assured the Bush administration that 'some new hidden right is not lurking in parts of the treaty for which no reservation, declaration, or understanding was entered'. The clause also acts as an 'insurance policy against the possibility that the Justice Department lawyers might have made a mistake'. This was the second time the Bush administration applied this dubious principle—it also tacked the 'not self-executing' clause on to the UN's *International Covenant on Civil and Political Rights*.

In 1994, the CAT was ratified by the Clinton administration with all nineteen reservations intact. The UN Committee Against Torture considered the record number of US CAT reservations to be unacceptable. In 2000, the committee recommended that the USA 'withdraw its reservations, interpretations and understandings relating to the Convention [and] take such steps as were necessary to ensure that those who violated the Convention were investigated, prosecuted and punished ...'. The committee added that the USA 'enact a federal crime of torture in terms consistent with article 1 of the Convention'. To this day, the United States has not criminalised the distinct act of torture within its borders. This directly violates Article 4, which directs that 'Each State Party shall ensure that all acts of torture are offences under its criminal law'.

The United States did enact CAT implementation legislation for acts occuring *outside* the USA, but these laws are hampered by the treaty's narrow redefinition of torture. The *Torture Victim Protection Act of 1991* (TVPA) allows civil suits in US courts against foreign perpetrators of torture who enter American soil, and the federal torture statute (18 USC §§ 2340–2340A) makes torture a federal crime if perpetrated by any American anywhere outside US jurisdiction. The problem is that the definition of torture in these statutes mimics Bush's OLC definition of torture, including the 'prolonged mental harm' clause.

Not one US court has heard a case involving a violation of the federal torture statute. Several cases have been brought under the TVPA, but prosecutions have been hampered by the statute's narrow terms. For instance, in *Hilao v Estate of Marcos* (1996), the court ruled that a plaintiff who spent eight years in solitary confinement—seven months of which he was shackled to a cot in a hot unlit cell that measured two and a half square metres—was not subjected to 'torture' *per se*. Rather, the court found that the solitary confinement amounted to 'prolonged arbitrary detention'. A similar ruling was reached in *Eastman Kodak v Kavlin* (1997), where a plaintiff was held in a dirty cell in Bolivia for eight days without food. During his captivity, the plaintiff also witnessed several murders. Again, the court found that this treatment did not constitute 'torture' as defined by the Act.

The loose 'more likely than not' standard pioneered by the OLC regarding extradition to states that torture also found its way into US law. Today, suspects are permitted to be transferred to any state provided the USA seeks written 'assurances' that they will not be tortured. Given the lax guidelines, in late 1995 a CIA counterterrorism unit targeting Islamic militants entered an agreement with Egypt to send terrorism suspects for interrogation and trial in Cairo. Egypt is consistently cited by the US State Department in its reports for using torture. In 1996, for instance, the State Department noted that in Egypt:

> Torture is used to extract information, coerce the victims to end their antigovernment activities, and deter others from such activities ... Detainees are frequently stripped to their underwear; hung by their wrists with their feet touching the floor or forced to stand for prolonged periods; doused with hot and cold water; beaten; forced to stand outdoors in cold weather; and subjected to electric shocks. Some victims, including female detainees, report that they have been threatened with rape.

The first suspect sent, or 'rendered', to Egypt was Talaat Fouad Qassem, an Egyptian linked to the assassination of Anwar Sadat. In late 1995, he was kidnapped in Croatia, interrogated by US agents in a ship on the Adriatic Sea, then handed over to Egypt. Human rights experts believe he was tortured, then executed—no record of any trial exists. Another suspect, Shawki Salama Attiya, was seized in Albania in 1998 and flown to Cairo by the CIA in a private jet. Attiya was believed, at the time, to be in contact with Ayman al-Zawahiri, a top al Qaeda deputy. The *New Yorker* reported that Attiya later claimed that he 'suffered electrical shocks to his genitals, was hung from his limbs, and was kept in a cell in filthy water up to his knees'. From 1996 to 1999, Michael Scheuer headed the CIA's counterterrorism unit that established the rendition program. He later recounted that he was 'not sure' whether any assurances were signed before suspects were transferred. According to Fred Hitz, a former CIA Inspector General, 'Based largely on the Central American human rights experience, we don't do torture, and we can't countenance torture [in that] we can't know of it.' But, he added, the CIA 'can use the fruits' of information offered by countries like Egypt.

By so narrowly defining what constitutes torture, the CAT and its implementation legislation essentially legalised it. Painful physical tortures such as forced standing, psychological torture like total isolation, and even the American transfer of suspects to states that torture were all protected—not banned—by US law.

Until October 2006, there was only one law that outlawed the use of DDD tortures inside and outside the United States: the *War Crimes Act of 1996* (WCA). Unlike the TVPA and the federal torture statute, the WCA (18 USC § 2441) was not hampered by language conjured up by the OLC. The law was the result of a chance meeting between ex-Air Force pilot Mike Cronin and Republican Congressman Walter B. Jones in 1996. As noted earlier, Cronin languished six years at the Hanoi Hilton and suffered nerve damage in his hand from the torture he endured. Cronin discussed with Jones his surprise and dismay upon discovering that there was no law enabling a United States prosecutor to try his torturers, and no definitive authority as to whether the Geneva Conventions are self-executing. 'I just thought that was wrong', he said.

Jones was inspired and drafted a new law holding perpetrators to standards set forth in the Geneva Conventions. According to the *Washington Post*, 'Jones and other advocates intended the law for use against future abusers of captured US troops in countries such as Bosnia, El Salvador and Somalia, but the Pentagon supported making its provisions applicable to US personnel because doing so set a high standard for others to follow'. Only two lawmakers attended the congressional hearing on the law and it passed easily in the House and Senate.

The WCA was not a toothless statute. Until it was amended in 2006, the Act's language was closely bound to the internationally recognised language of the Geneva Conventions and applied to all US citizens in the position of either victim or perpetrator. Perpetrators of war crimes were to be punished by up to twenty years in prison or subject to the death penalty if the victim died. A war crime, according to the Act, includes 'a grave breach of the Geneva Conventions'. Grave breaches of Geneva include:

> wilful killing, torture or inhuman treatment, including biological experiments, wilfully causing great suffering or serious injury to

body or health ... wilfully depriving a protected person of the rights of fair and regular trial prescribed in the present Convention, taking of hostages and extensive destruction and appropriation of property, not justified by military necessity and carried out unlawfully and wantonly.

In 1997, the law was amended to include violations of Geneva Common Article 3 as war crimes. Article 3, whose text is repeated in all four Geneva Conventions, constitutes the minimum standard of treatment afforded to persons during conflicts. Specifically, Common Article 3 prohibits:

(a) Violence to life and person, in particular murder of all kinds, mutilation, cruel treatment and torture; (b) Taking of hostages; (c) Outrages upon personal dignity, in particular, humiliating and degrading treatment; and (d) The passing of sentences and the carrying out of executions without previous judgment pronounced by a regularly constituted court affording all the judicial guarantees which are recognized as indispensable by civilized peoples.

Unlike the CAT, TVPA and the federal torture statute, the WCA was designed to hold Americans to the broad provisions of Geneva—and violations were to be punishable by death. But while WCA drew its strength from Geneva, its Geneva-bound language proved to be its undoing in George W. Bush's war on terror.

THE GLOVES COME OFF, PART I

On the evening on 11 September 2001, President George W. Bush gathered with his top staff in the Presidential Emergency Operations Center, a narrow bunker in the White House's East Wing. Bush wanted retribution. 'We are at war and we will stay at war until this is done', he said. 'Nothing else matters. Everything is available for the pursuit of this war. Any barriers in your way, they're gone ... I don't care what the international lawyers say, we are going to kick some ass.' Five days later, Vice President Dick Cheney mirrored these remarks in an appearance on *Meet the Press*. 'We need to make certain that we have not tied the hands, if you will, of our intelligence communities in terms of accomplishing their mission', Cheney said. He continued:

> We also have to work, though, sort of the dark side ... A lot of what needs to be done here will have to be done quietly, without any discussion, using sources and methods that are available to our intelligence agencies, if we're going to be successful. That's the world these folks operate in, and so it's going to be vital for us to use any means at our disposal, basically, to achieve our objective.

Cheney made these comments at Camp David, where earlier he had met with the president, National Security Advisor Condoleezza Rice, Secretary of State Colin Powell, Secretary of Defense Donald Rumsfeld, CIA Director George Tenet, the CIA's Counterterrorism Center (CTC) Director Cofer Black, Attorney General John Ashcroft and other top officials to discuss the United States' response to the attacks. According to Bob Woodward, George Tenet brought to the table a draft presidential finding that, if signed, would give the CIA extensive new powers in America's newly declared 'war on terror'. Tenet said that the 'CIA needed new robust authority to operate without restraint'. First, Tenet sought authorisation for 'targeted killing' missions against top al Qaeda leaders and financiers. He also discussed the importance of expanding CIA powers to 'detain al Qaeda operatives worldwide'. Finally, Tenet stressed that the CIA needed to co-operate closely with brutal security forces in the Middle East. In particular, he singled out intelligence agencies in Egypt, Jordan and Algeria as ideal 'Arab Liaison Services' that could each act as an 'extended mercenary force of intelligence operatives'.

Tenet's requests were well received by the president. On 17 September, Bush signed the presidential finding that Tenet drafted. The finding authorised the CIA to kill, apprehend or detain members of al Qaeda anywhere in the world. Cofer Black, in testimony to Senate and House Intelligence Committees two weeks later, said the agency was granted enormous 'operational flexibility' after the attacks. Said Black: 'This is a very highly classified area. All I want to say is that there was "before" 9/11 and "after" 9/11. After 9/11 the gloves come off.'

Black's Counterterrorism Center, located in the agency's Langley headquarters, was charged with finding bin Laden and thwarting new attacks. According to one CIA officer, in the days following 9/11 the biggest fear at the CTC was that a terrorist would elude capture and wreak havoc in the USA. 'Their logic was: If one of them gets loose and someone dies, we'll be held responsible', he said. Michael Scheuer, former head of the counterterrorism unit that pioneered renditions, was recalled to the CIA in 2001 to act as a CTC adviser. Scheuer recalled the rage of Cofer Black after the attacks. 'He wanted bin Laden's head brought to him on ice', he said. During this time, he added, 'a lot of that kind of warrior rhetoric … came out'.

On 11 November 2001, Ibn al-Shaykh al-Libi—then ranked number seventeen on the State Department's list of most wanted terrorists—was captured in Pakistan. Al-Libi, a Libyan emir, was a leader of an al Qaeda training camp in Khalden, Afghanistan. Shoe-bomber Richard Reid and al Qaeda conspirator Zacarias Moussaoui—both serving life sentences in a Colorado prison for terrorism-related offences—trained at the Khalden camp. At first, al-Libi was handed to the FBI by Pakistani authorities. While the CIA traditionally had interrogated spies and defectors using the KUBARK method of interrogation, the FBI uses a non-violent model of interrogation more akin to the system laid out in the 1992 Army *Intelligence Interrogation* field manual. As a domestic intelligence service, the FBI aims to build cases against criminals using non-coerced evidence that can be submitted in US courts. Over the years, the bureau developed rapport-building techniques to gain the trust of suspects—a tactic that had worked with terrorism suspects exceedingly well before 9/11.

Jack Cloonan, an FBI interrogator from 1977 to 2002, worked on an anti-terror squad investigating the 1993 World Trade Center bombing and the 1998 bombings in Kenya and Tanzania. Using basic police work and rapport-building techniques, Cloonan and his fellow agents gained confessions from suspects that held up in court. In fact, Cloonan's team netted some of the US government's best pre-9/11 intelligence about al Qaeda using those techniques—information that has since proved invaluable in the war on terror. In 1998, Cloonan earned the co-operation of L'Houssaine Kherchtou, known as 'Joe the Moroccan', a member of the al Qaeda cell that bombed the embassies. 'We advised [Kherchtou] of his rights. We told him he could have a lawyer anytime, and that he could pray at any time he wanted', Cloonan told *The American Prospect*. Patrick Fitzgerald, then Assistant US Attorney for New York City, also participated in the interrogation. Cloonan said:

> We spent a lot of time talking about his family, and how disillusioned he was … and from there he really began to open up. The critical moment was when Pat Fitzgerald told Joe, 'Here's the deal: You will come to the US voluntarily; you will plead guilty to conspiracy to kill US nationals abroad; your exposure is anywhere from zero to life, no promises.' I instinctively reached for my briefcase, figuring it was over, but then I added something. I looked at him and I said, 'Before you answer, I think you should go pray. After 10 days with us, I think you have a sense of who we are and what we're about—you know you would not be treated this way by other folks. You may go to prison, but you have the chance to start your life over again, to get rid of this anxiety, to stop running. And I think you should do this for your wife and children.

Kherchtou left the room and came back with his answer. He agreed to testify. Back in New York, he helped convict four al Qaeda plotters. 'FBI agents, as officers of the court, know what the rules are', Cloonan said. 'We have procedures to follow. We firmly believe in this thing called due process, and do not see it as something passé or something that should be seen as an impediment.'

Al-Libi was first interrogated by FBI agents in Afghanistan. Cloonan was in New York, but directed his agents to be respectful. 'I told them, "Do yourself a favor, read the guy his rights. It may be old-fashioned, but this will come out if we don't. It may take ten years, but it will hurt you, and the bureau's reputation, if you don't. Have it stand as a shining example of what we feel is right."' According to Cloonan, his agents were successful using rapport-building techniques. Over the course of several weeks, al-Libi revealed information later used to convict Reid and Moussaoui. But while the FBI worked with their suspect, the CIA grew restless with FBI methods, wanting faster results. A dispute soon erupted over which agency should interrogate al-Libi. According to *Newsweek*:

> FBI officials brought their plea to retain control over al-Libi's interrogation up to FBI Director Robert Mueller. The CIA station chief in Afghanistan, meanwhile, appealed to the agency's hawkish counterterrorism chief, Cofer Black. He in turn called CIA Director George Tenet, who went to the White House. Al-Libi was handed over to the CIA.

Cloonan said that al-Libi was then shuttled away to Cairo via the CIA's rendition program. He recalled:

> My guys told me that a Toyota Tundra with a box in the back pulls up to the building. CIA officers come in, start shackling al-Libi up. Right before they duct tape his mouth, he tells our guys, 'I know this isn't your fault.' And as he's standing there, chained and gagged, this CIA guy gets up in his face and tells al-Libi he's going to fuck his mother. And then off he apparently goes to Cairo, in a box.

Al-Libi's rendition marked a turning point in interrogation operations in the war on terror. From that point forward, interrogations were handled primarily by the CIA, while the FBI—and rapport-building—were sidelined.

Following the al-Libi episode, the CIA began sending other suspects to Cairo, and to other Middle Eastern states known to torture. According to Dan Coleman, an ex-FBI interrogator who had worked with Cloonan, after 9/11 rendition 'really went out of control'. Today more than 100 suspects have been rendered to states known to employ torture. High-value suspects like al-Libi weren't the only suspects sent abroad. Countless others have been transferred as well in a process now known as 'extraordinary rendition'. According to Alberto Gonzales, 'We do not transport anyone to a country if we believe it more likely than not that the individual will be tortured'. An official quoted in the *Washington Post* put it differently: 'We don't kick the [expletive] out of them. We send them to other countries so they can kick the [expletive] out of them.'

Suspects sent abroad for questioning have returned with horrific tales of abuse. The story of Mamdouh Habib has already been told. Transferred to Egypt from Pakistan in late 2001, he has alleged that he was brutally beaten, hung by his arms from hooks, repeatedly shocked, drugged, and nearly drowned by security forces there. Habib's account is not unique. Maher Arar, for instance, is a Canadian citizen of Syrian descent who had a two-hour layover in New York's John F. Kennedy Airport and was pulled aside at passport control. Arar was on his way back home to Montreal after vacationing with his family in Tunis. Five years earlier, he said, he was friends with a man named Nazih Almalki, whose brother was later wanted by the CIA for alleged links to al Qaeda. Maher Arar was first held in an immigration prison in New York for eight days. During this time, he was allowed only one phone call and was questioned about his relationship with Almalki and his views on Israel, Osama bin Laden and al Qaeda. 'They told me that based on classified information that they could not reveal to me, I would be deported to Syria', he said. 'I said that I would be tortured there.' Immigration officials ignored his pleas. He was shackled, chained and given to the CIA. A small plane flew him first to Jordan and he was driven across the border into Syria. The US State Department has cited Syria in human rights reports for systematic use of torture. Methods used by Syrian security forces in 2003, according to the State Department, included:

administering electrical shocks; pulling out fingernails; forcing objects into the rectum; beating, sometimes while the victim is suspended from the ceiling; hyper-extending the spine; bending the detainees into the frame of a wheel and whipping exposed body parts; and using a chair that bends backwards to asphyxiate the victim or fracture the victim's spine.

Arar was held in Syria for more than ten months in a basement cell less than one metre wide by two metres deep. He was spared some of the harsher tortures, though he was beaten by interrogators. 'The cable is a black electrical cable, about two inches thick. They hit me with it everywhere on my body. They mostly aimed for my palms, but sometimes missed and hit my wrists; they were sore and red for three weeks. They also struck me on my hips, and lower back', he said. 'I could hear other prisoners being tortured, and screaming and screaming. Interrogations are carried out in different rooms. One tactic they use is to question prisoners for two hours, and then put them in a waiting room, so they can hear the others screaming, and then bring them back to continue the interrogation.' Under torture he falsely admitted to training in Afghanistan, but he was later released uncharged after his wife led a successful public campaign on his behalf. CIA officials have dubbed cases like Arar's examples of 'erroneous rendition'.

By late 2001, the CIA was inundated with prisoners captured in Afghanistan by the Northern Alliance and Coalition forces during Operation Enduring Freedom. The US-led campaign in Afghanistan, launched on 7 October 2001, netted thousands of detainees. While the US military was charged with detaining rank-and-file fighters ostensibly taken off the battlefield, the CIA assumed responsibility for the 'high value' suspects—those believed to be senior Taliban and al Qaeda leaders. Renditions could not keep up with the flow of fresh detainees and agents wanted greater control over the interrogations than foreign allies offered. At first, the CIA kept these prisoners in metal shipping containers in Bagram Air Base, an abandoned Soviet supply hangar. As space at Bagram grew limited, the CIA looked for a more permanent solution. The agency requested, and was granted, hundreds of millions of dollars to start construction of a private CIA prison network. The first secret prison, known as a 'black site' in CIA and White House documents, was built on the grounds of an old brick factory north of Kabul called the 'Salt Pit'.

When questioning was about to begin in a host country, CIA agents would hand lists of questions to the interrogators, then leave the room—thereby removing direct culpability for any torture that was used. At the Salt Pit, the CIA ran the show. With the exception of a handful of Afghani guards, the prison was fully staffed by the CIA. This arrangement presented new questions regarding the specific methods that could be used during interrogation. According to CIA officials interviewed by the *New York Times*, 'the agency sought legal guidance on how far its employees and contractors could go in interrogating terror suspects'. Michael Scheuer explained: 'At the end of the day, the US intelligence community is palsied by lawyers, and everything still depends on whether the lawyers approve it or not.'

Based on White House and Justice Department memos leaked to the press in the wake of the Abu Ghraib scandal, it appears that the CIA's chief concern was that agents using coercive interrogation techniques could be charged under the War Crimes Act, the 1996 legislation that bound US law to the Geneva Conventions. The WCA expressly outlawed violations of Common Article 3 including 'cruel treatment and torture', 'outrages upon personal dignity, in particular humiliating and degrading treatment', and 'the passing of sentences and the carrying out of executions without previous judgment pronounced by a regularly constituted court'. The WCA also prohibited all Americans from committing 'grave breaches' of Geneva, including 'torture or inhuman treatment, including biological experiments', 'wilfully causing great suffering or serious injury to body or health', or 'wilfully depriving a prisoner of war of the rights of fair and regular trial'. Traditional Cold War interrogation methods outlined in the KUBARK manual patently violate the WCA. Consequently, the CIA requested ways to get around the law.

White House lawyers and attorneys in the Justice Department's Office of Legal Counsel were charged by top officials, chiefly Vice President Dick Cheney, with finding ways to cirvumcent the WCA. The solution they delivered was both elegant and cruelly simple: simply withdraw American support for the *Geneva Convention for the Treatment of Prisoners of War* (GPW). In the words of John Ashcroft, then Attorney General—the highest ranking law enforcement official in the United States at the time—a determination that GPW would not apply would 'provide the highest assurance that no court would subsequently entertain charges that American military officers, intelligence officials, or law enforcement officials violated Geneva Convention rules relating to field conduct, detention conduct, or interrogation of detainees'. According to Alberto Gonzales, then the Chief Legal Counsel to the President and as of 2006 the US Attorney General, invalidation of GPW 'substantially reduces the threat of domestic criminal prosecution under the War Crimes Act'. The WCA was a liability, said Gonzales, in America's war on terror for three main reasons. First, he said, 'some of the language of the GPW is undefined (it prohibits, for example, "outrages upon personal dignity" and "inhuman treatment") and it is difficult to predict with confidence what actions might be deemed to constitute violations of the relevant provisions of GPW.' Second, 'it is difficult to predict the needs and circumstances that could arise in the course of the war on terrorism'. Furthermore, he added, 'it is difficult to predict the motives of prose-cutors and independent counsels who may in the future decide to pursue unwarranted charges based on [War Crimes Act] Section 2441'. Invalidation of Geneva, said Gonzales, would 'provide a solid defense to future prosecution'. For Gonzales, it was crucial that the United States was not bound by the rules of war because 'the nature of the new war places a high premium on other factors, such as the ability to quickly obtain information from captured terrorists and their sponsors in order to avoid further atrocities against American civilians'. He concluded, 'This new paradigm renders obsolete Geneva's strict limitations on questioning enemy prisoners and renders quaint some of its provisions ...'.

This determination marked a tremendous break from both US history and international norms. The four Geneva Conventions are the most internationally recognised treaties in the world, having been ratified by 190 states. Even before they were ratified in the USA, American officials pledged to follow their rules. The Korean War, for instance, broke out on 25 June 1950—one year after Geneva was drafted but five years before it was ratified by the US Congress. At the start of the conflict, General Douglas MacArthur announced, 'My present instructions are to abide by the humanitarian principles of the 1949 Geneva Conventions, particularly common Article Three'. During the Vietnam War, the USA announced that it would apply Geneva—despite its actual behaviour to the contrary. Geneva was also officially recognised in US actions in Panama, Somalia, Haiti, Bosnia and the first Gulf War. On 17 October 2001, General Tommy Franks ordered troops to follow the Geneva Conventions as America invaded Afghanistan. The history was clear. Even the Office of Legal Counsel conceded that 'the United States has never, to our knowledge, suspended any provision of the Geneva Conventions'.

The Geneva Conventions cover all persons, at all times, during all types of conflict. According to the International Committee of the Red Cross, the chief administrator of the convention, 'Every person in enemy hands must have some status under international law ... nobody in enemy hands can fall outside the law'. The Geneva Conventions divide conflicts into two distinct categories: wars of international character and those 'not of an international character'. The former class constitutes traditional state-versus-state conflicts where at least one party is a signatory to the treaty, while the latter includes all other types of conflicts that may occur within the territory of a signatory. By definition, this includes civil war, insurgency, general unrest, and acts of terrorism. Common Article 3, as an absolute minimum, applies to conflicts of non-international character, while the full guarantees stipulated in all four Geneva Conventions apply to persons involved in conflicts of international character.

Leaked OLC memoranda to Pentagon officials provide the best indication of the still-classified advice delivered to the CIA. In a memo to Department of Defense General Counsel William J. Haynes II, the OLC argued that Common Article 3 does not apply to al Qaeda or the Taliban because members of these groups commit acts of international terrorism—technically not acts of 'non-international character'. The OLC also claimed that the full protections of Geneva do not apply to either party. Al Qaeda, they contended, is not protected because the group 'is merely a violent political movement or organization and not a nation-state. As a result, it is ineligible to be a signatory to any treaty'. As for the Taliban, they opined that Afghanistan is simply a 'failed state' that cannot carry out treaty obligations. The OLC stated that Taliban and al Qaeda fighters are not POWs as defined by the GPW but are 'enemy aliens' who fall outside all known domestic and international law.

The authors of these memos, namely then Deputy Assistant Attorney General John Yoo and Special Counsel Robert J. Delahunty, ignored a range of facts in their determination. First and foremost, they overlooked Common Article 1, which holds all signatories to respect the conventions 'in all circumstances'. They also twisted the definition of 'non-international character' to suit their needs. As the Supreme Court later affirmed in the landmark *Hamdan v Rumsfeld* (2006) case, this term applies to all individuals involved in a conflict in the territory of a signatory. Afghanistan ratified Geneva in 1956—as such, Common Article 3 applies to both al Qaeda and Taliban fighters operating in that country. Furthermore, the question of whether Afghanistan is a failed state is irrelevant—the Taliban's rise to power in 1996 did not alter in any way the physical territory of Afghanistan. Since then, the country has maintained its borders with all neighbouring states; thus, both al Qaeda and the Taliban operate in the territory of a signatory.

In addition to the minimal safeguards of Common Article 3, both the Taliban and al Qaeda are also entitled to full protections of Geneva. The Taliban and al Qaeda are intertwined militarily and constitute the de facto armed forces of Afghanistan. According to the International Committee of the Red Cross, a captured combatant is 'either a prisoner of war and, as such, covered by the Third Convention [GPW], [or] a civilian covered by the Fourth Convention [GPC] ... There is no intermediate status'. To qualify for POW status, the conventions state that combatants must satisfy four specific criteria:

(a) being commanded by a person responsible for his subordinates;
(b) having a fixed distinctive sign that is recognisable at a distance;
(c) carrying arms openly; and
(d) conducting their operations in accordance with the laws and customs of war.

If captured fighters do not fit the above criteria—which in many cases Taliban and al Qaeda fighters may not—they are not to be considered POWs, but are 'protected persons' subject to the broad provisions of the GPC. If there is any confusion as to the status of a person, Article 5 of the GPW provides that 'persons shall enjoy the protection of the present Convention until such time as their status has been determined by a competent tribunal'. Finally, even if a 'protected person' is later discovered to be 'a spy or saboteur, or as a person under definite suspicion of activity hostile to the security of the Occupying Power', he or she still, according to the GPC, must 'nevertheless be treated with humanity and ... not be deprived of the rights of fair and regular trial'.

Perhaps sensing the shortcomings of their argument, administration laywers developed a range of back-up rationales that would still exclude al Qaeda and Taliban from the Geneva Conventions. The OLC opined that the president's authority is at its apex during times of war and that any law that restricts the president's powers in that area, including those concerning the treatment of prisoners, would be unconstitutional. Following a precedent set when Bush opted out of elements of the Anti-Ballistic Missile Treaty of 1972, administration lawyers also argued that the president can nullify portions of Geneva, or even the entire document, if he saw it as in the nation's best interest. According to John Ashcroft, 'When a President determines that a treaty does not apply, his determination is fully discretionary and will not be reviewed by the federal courts'. Jay S. Bybee, then Assistant Attorney General, seconded Ashcroft's opinion. In a memo to Alberto Gonzales, Bybee argued that 'the President possesses the power to interpret treaties on behalf of the Nation ... This includes, of course, the power to apply treaties to the facts of a given situation'. A presidential determination that Geneva does not apply, he said, would 'eliminate any legal "doubt" as to the prisoners' status, as a matter of domestic law, and would therefore obviate the need for Article 5 tribunals'.

The bulk of these arguments for presidential power were engineered by David Addington, then Chief Counsel to the Vice President and later Cheney's chief of staff. 'Addington's fingerprints were all over these policies', said Lawrence Wilkerson, former Secretary of State Colin Powell's top aide. According to another administration lawyer, 'Torture isn't important to Addington as a scientific matter, good or bad, or whether it works or not. It's more about his philosophy of presidential power. He thinks that if the President wants torture he should get torture. He always argued for maximum flexibility'.

The OLC's radical interpretation of both Geneva and the US Constitution, placing al Qaeda and Taliban fighters outside the bounds of international and domestic law, was met by fierce criticism in the State Department. According to Colin Powell, Geneva 'was intended to cover all types of armed conflict and did not by its terms limit its application'. In a memo to Gonzales, Powell stressed that the decision to nullify Geneva places US troops abroad at greater risk of ill-treatment upon capture. Abiding by Geneva, he added, 'preserves US credibility and moral authority by taking the high ground'. The State Department's legal adviser, William H. Taft IV, agreed with Powell. Taft wrote to Gonzales that the United States should base 'its conduct not just on its policy preferences but on its international legal obligations'. Taft specifically called on the Bush administration to adhere to UN Resolution 1193. This 1998 resolution was adopted eight days after US forces struck al Qaeda training facilities in Taliban-held Afghanistan in retaliation for the embassy bombings in Nairobi and Dar es Salaam. The resolution decreed that 'all parties to the conflict [in Afghanistan] are bound to comply with their obligations under international humanitarian law and in particular the Geneva Conventions ...'. The USA, al Qaeda and the Taliban were all parties to the conflict and therefore bound to comply with Geneva in keeping with Resolution 1193.

The warnings of Taft and Powell fell on deaf ears. On 19 January 2001, Donald Rumsfeld rescinded Tommy Franks' order for US troops to follow the Geneva Conventions in Afghanistan. Bush officially voided Geneva's applicability to al Qaeda and the Taliban three weeks later on 7 February 2002. Paraphrasing Gonzales, Bush said:

> The war against terrorism ushers in a new paradigm, one in which groups with broad, international reach commit horrific acts against innocent civilians, sometimes with the direct support of states. Our Nation recognizes that this new paradigm— ushered in not by us, but by terrorists—requires new thinking in the law of war ...

Bush used the faulty opinions of the OLC to justify his decision. According to Bush, Common Article 3 does not apply because the acts of al Qaeda and the Taliban are not 'non-international' in nature. Furthermore, he said, 'al Qaeda detainees do not qualify as prisoners of war' because al Qaeda is not a 'High Contracting Party' or signatory. As for the Taliban, Bush stated that 'Taliban detainees are unlawful combatants and, therefore, do not qualify as prisoners of war' under the GPW. According to Bush, 'unlawful combatants'—an ambiguous term last used during World War II—were not to be treated according to the guidelines of Geneva, but 'to the extent appropriate and consistent with military necessity, in a manner consistent with the principles of Geneva'.

———

With both the Geneva Conventions and the War Crimes Act out of the way, the CIA had a free hand to conduct aggressive interrogations in Afghanistan. The next question the agency faced was where to turn for firsthand expertise on coercive techniques. Top officials made a logical choice. SERE staff have intimate knowledge about the upper limits of DDD torture—isolation, forced standing and humiliation— and its effects on the human body and mind. Before 9/11, the primary function of psychologists and medics affiliated with SERE was to monitor the mental and physical health of students to ensure their safety. After 9/11, they were asked to aid in the interrogations of terrorism suspects. According to Jonathan Moreno, a bioethicist at the University of Virginia interviewed by the *New Yorker*, the rationale was simple: 'If you know how to help people who are stressed, then you also know how to stress people, in order to get them to talk.'

The Army's top SERE expert on coercive interrogation is Colonel Louie Banks, PhD. He has been responsible for the training and over-sight of all Army SERE psychologists, and in the early 1980s Banks helped to design the Resistance Training Laboratory at Camp Mackall's SERE program. As discussed in Chapter 7, a 2000 study found that students at Mackall experience greater stress than skydivers and people undergoing surgery. In late 2001, Banks was reassigned from North Carolina to Afghanistan. According to the American Psychological Association (APA), Banks 'spent four months over the winter of 2001/2002 at Bagram Airfield, supporting combat operations against Al Qaeda and Taliban fighters'. In an interview with the *New Yorker*, Banks was elusive about the specifics of his role, but conceded: 'I just consulted generally on what approaches to take. It was about what human behavior in captivity is like.'

Banks wasn't the only SERE doctor sent to Afghanistan. Bryce E. Lefever, PhD, supervised Navy SERE training between 1990 and 1993. According to the APA, during this time Lefever 'insured the safe training of high-risk-of-capture personnel undergoing intensive expo-sure to enemy interrogation, torture, and exploitation techniques'.

In 1998 he joined the Navy SEALs and in 2002 he too was deployed to Afghanistan, where he 'lectured to interrogators and was consulted on various interrogation techniques'.

In March 2002, James Mitchell, a former SERE psychologist, was observed participating in a CIA interrogation overseas. According to one official, Mitchell suggested that rougher methods be used in order to elicit a psychological condition known as 'learned helplessness'. The same month Mitchell, Banks and Lefever were consulting with interrogators, six 'enhanced' interrogation techniques were authorised for agency use. All six techniques are used at SERE. According to several disaffected CIA officials, who believe 'the public needs to know the direction their agency has chosen', the methods included:

1. The Attention Grab: The interrogator forcefully grabs the shirt front of the prisoner and shakes him.
2. The Attention Slap: An open-handed slap aimed at causing pain and triggering fear.
3. The Belly Slap: A hard open-handed slap to the stomach. The aim is to cause pain, but not internal injury.
4. Long Time Standing: Prisoners are forced to stand, handcuffed and with their feet shackled to an eye bolt in the floor for more than forty hours.
5. The Cold Cell: The prisoner is left to stand naked in a cell kept near fifty degrees [Fahrenheit]. Throughout the time in the cell the prisoner is doused with cold water.
6. Water Boarding: The prisoner is bound to an inclined board, feet raised and head slightly below the feet. Cellophane is wrapped over the prisoner's face and water is poured over him.

According to ABC News (US), these coercive techniques were personally authorised by George Bush via a 2002 presidential finding co-signed by Condoleezza Rice and John Ashcroft. It is also likely that in early 2002 the OLC wrote several specific memos authorising each individual technique, finding that each method didn't rise to the level of torture as defined by narrow terms specified in US law.

One of the first victims of the SERE techniques was Ibn al-Shaykh al-Libi—the high-value detainee initially rendered to Egypt. By the time the Salt Pit was set up and authorisation for coercive techniques was secured, al-Libi was back in US custody in Afghanistan. According to CIA officers involved in his case, al-Libi was progressively subjected to the six SERE techniques over the course of two weeks. The day al-Libi broke down, they said, he was stripped, waterboarded, forced to stand in a cold cell, and doused with ice water.

On 28 March 2002, Pakistani forces apprehended Abu Zubaydah, al Qaeda's alleged logistics chief who ran a series of guesthouses in Pakistan and Afghanistan. Zubaydah was handed over to American authorities—replacing al-Libi as the highest-ranking al Qaeda member in US custody—and was rendered to Thailand to a newly constructed CIA black site. At first, the FBI took the lead in his interrogation, but as in the case of al-Libi, CIA agents appealed for greater access and in a matter of weeks had assumed full control of the interrogation. 'When you are concerned that a hard-core terrorist has information about an imminent threat that could put innocent lives at risk, rapport-building and stroking aren't the top things on your agenda', said one official familiar with the case. Zubaydah was then subjected to a range of harsh SERE techniques, including the cold cell and food, sleep and light deprivation. Although he co-operated with the FBI—for example, confirming the identity of al Qaeda plotter Khalid Sheikh Mohammed from a photograph—he refused to talk under CIA torture. According to officials interviewed by the *New York Times*, 'Zubaydah's resistance began after the agency interrogators began using more stringent tactics'. By the summer of 2002, CIA interrogators seemingly had grown unhappy with the six approved techniques. According to *Newsweek*, 'frustrated CIA officials went to OLC lawyer Yoo for an opinion on bolder methods'.

While the Geneva Conventions and the WCA were no longer impediments, the CIA was concerned that harsher interrogation methods might create a basis for prosecution in the International Criminal Court (ICC) or violate the UN Convention Against Torture. Although the Bush administration withdrew the United States' signature from the Rome Statute in May 2002, the ICC, under limited circumstances, can still prosecute states not party to the treaty. Still, in a memo dated 1 August 2002, Yoo argued that American interrogators need not worry about ICC laws outlawing torture. According to the Rome Statute, torture is defined as the 'intentional infliction of severe pain or suffering, whether physical or mental, upon a person in the custody or under the control of the accused'. Further, torture may be considered a crime against humanity if it is 'part of a widespread and systematic attack directed against any civilian population' (Article 7) or if it is committed against persons 'protected under the provisions of the relevant Geneva Conventions' (Article 8). Using the invalidation of the War Crimes Act as a legal basis, Yoo argued that because 'unlawful combatants' were not subject to the protections of Geneva, the terms of Article 8 could not apply either. Yoo also found that Article 7 did not apply. 'If anything', he wrote, 'the interrogations are taking place to elicit information that could prevent attacks on civilian populations'. According to Yoo, Americans were thus immune to the reach of the ICC 'even if certain interrogation methods being contemplated amounted to torture …'. As for the Convention Against Torture, for Yoo it was a non-issue. According to Yoo, the United States' obligations under the CAT 'are identical to the standard set' by the federal torture statute, USC § 2340. As discussed earlier, § 2340 was crafted using the language from America's reservation to the CAT. Added Yoo, 'so long as the interrogation methods do not violate § 2340, they also do not violate our international obligations under the Torture Convention'.

Specific conduct permissible under the federal torture statute was explored in another August memo signed by Jay S. Bybee, but written with extensive input from David Addington. The federal torture statute bans the use of torture by any American outside the USA. It defines torture as an 'act committed by a person under the color of law specifically intended to inflict severe physical or mental pain or suffering (other than pain or suffering incidental to lawful sanctions) upon another person within his custody or physical control'. According to the Bybee–Addington memo—easily the most outrageous of all the infamous torture memos—a variety of defences 'would negate any claim that certain interrogation methods violate the statute'.

Bybee and Addington argued that the phrase 'specifically intended' in § 2340's definition of torture enables interrogators to evade prosecution under the statute. They wrote: '[S]howing that an individual acted with a good faith belief that his conduct would not produce the result that the law prohibits negates specific intent.' In other words, if an interrogator can show that he didn't know he was causing severe pain to a detainee, the interrogator is not guilty of torture. 'A good faith belief need not be a reasonable one', they added.

This is crucial when it comes to psychological torture. The torture statute defines 'severe mental pain or suffering' as:

the prolonged mental harm caused by or resulting from—
(a) the intentional infliction or threatened infliction of severe physical pain or suffering;
(b) the administration or application, or threatened administration or application, of mind-altering substances or other procedures calculated to disrupt profoundly the senses of the personality;
(c) the threat of imminent death; or
(d) the threat that another person will imminently be subjected to death, severe physical pain or suffering, or the administration or application of mind-altering substances or other procedures calculated to disrupt profoundly the senses or personality.

According to Bybee and Addington, severe mental pain arising from the four listed acts constitutes torture only if they cause 'lasting psychological harm, such as seen in mental disorders like post-traumatic stress disorder'. They continued, 'Thus, if a defendant has a good faith belief that his actions will not result in prolonged mental harm, he lacks the mental state necessary for his actions to constitute torture'.

While this defence works well in instances of psychological torture such as isolation, disorientation or humiliation, it would be harder for an interrogator to claim he didn't 'know' he was causing severe pain to a detainee if he was beating him or forcing him to stand for forty hours at a time. For this reason, Bybee and Addington argued that for a physical act to constitute torture under § 2340, 'it must be of an intensity akin to that which accompanies serious physical injury such as death or organ failure'. If the physical pain does not reach this level of severity, they said the act is not torture.

Another avenue to impunity, Bybee and Addington suggested, was to argue that the war on terror constitutes a state of war where any behaviour, as directed by the president, could be allowed. The influence of Addington, who believes in strong presidential wartime powers, is particularly evident in this portion of the memo. According to the memo, the president's 'authority is at its height in the middle of a war ... [and] Congress may no more regulate the President's ability to detain and interrogate enemy combatants than it may regulate his ability to direct troop movements on the battlefield'. Bybee and Addington based this expansive understanding of executive power from Civil War-era litigation. In the *Prize Cases* (1862), for example, the Supreme Court explained that whether the president 'in fulfilling his duties as Commander in Chief' had appropriately responded to the secession of the southern states was a question 'to be decided by him'. Nowhere in the lengthy memo did Bybee and Addington mention *Youngstown Sheet and Tube Co. v Sawyer* (1952), a landmark Supreme Court decision on executive authority. In this case the court rejected an argument that President Harry S. Truman had constitutional authority to direct the Secretary of Commerce to seize the nation's steel mills during a strike. Justice Hugo Black wrote the majority opinion stating that the executive, even in a time of war, could not act beyond the limits of constitutional power. According to Black, the President's power 'must stem either from an act of Congress or from the Constitution itself'. Conveniently overlooking this significant judgment, the OLC memo concludes that any effort to apply the torture statute 'in a manner that interferes with the President's direction of such core war matters as the detention and interrogation of enemy combatants thus would be unconstitutional'. Remarkably, Bush's unfettered power even extends to individuals acting on his behalf. According to Bybee and Addington:

> If a government defendant were to harm an enemy combatant during an interrogation in a manner that might arguably violate Section 2340A, he would be doing so in order to prevent further attacks on the United States by the al Qaeda terrorist network. In that case, we believe that he could argue that his actions were justified by the Executive branch's constitutional authority to protect the nation from attack.

Taken as a whole, White House and the OLC lawyers argued that any American could torture anyone deemed to be a terrorist using any method, at any time, for any reason. Upon its exposure, Harold Hongju Koh, dean of the Yale Law School, called the memo 'embarrassing' and 'abominable'. According to Koh, 'If the president has commander-in-chief power to commit torture, he has the power to commit genocide, to sanction slavery, to promote apartheid, to license summary execution'. On the eve of Alberto Gonzales' Senate confirmation hearings for Attorney General, the OLC rescinded this memo. While a new OLC directive scaled back references to 'organ failure' and 'death', it stated in a footnote that policy decisions regarding interrogation techniques based on the earlier memo are still valid.

Immediately after Yoo and Bybee issued their August memos—or possibly even before—Abu Zubaydah's interrogation grew brutal. The CTC sent out a special interrogation team to interrogate Zubaydah using several new, even harsher, SERE techniques. According to the *New York Times*, the 'group included an agency consultant schooled in the harsher interrogation procedures to which American special forces are subjected in their training'. Under the supervision of this unnamed SERE official, interrogators employed 'deafening blasts of music' and the selective use of drugs. While in US custody, Zubaydah was being treated for gunshot wounds to his abdomen and groin, injuries he received during his capture in Pakistan. CIA interrogators decided to give him painkillers only if he co-operated. According to one unnamed official familiar with the case, pain control for a wounded detainee 'is a very subjective thing'.

Interrogations also grew worse for detainees at other CIA black sites. In November 2002, for example, an Afghan detainee suffered through various SERE tortures at the Salt Pit in Afghanistan. A junior CIA agent directing his interrogation ordered Afghan guards to strip the man naked, chain him to a concrete floor outside his cell and leave him there overnight. Sometime during the night the man died of hypothermia and the next day he was buried in an unmarked grave near the prison. 'He just disappeared from the face of the earth', an official familiar with the case told the *Washington Post*. As the techniques were authorised, no one has been charged with the inmate's death. The agent directing the interrogation has since been promoted.

On 1 March 2003, the CIA scored their biggest catch in the war on terror: Khalid Sheikh Mohammed, the man whom Zubaydah identified under FBI interrogation. Mohammed, known commonly by the initials KSM, is alleged to be the al Qaeda operations chief behind the 1993 World Trade Center bombings, the 1998 bombings of US embassies in East Africa, the 2000 USS *Cole* bombing in Yemen that left seventeen US sailors dead, and the attacks of 9/11. Along with KSM, his wife and children were arrested as well. After three days in

Pakistani custody, he was transferred to the CIA, who whisked him away to Bagram and then to an undisclosed black site known only as 'Hotel California', located possibly in Iraq. Journalist Mark Bowden discussed KSM's conditions of confinement in the *Atlantic Monthly*. KSM was fed infrequently, waterboarded, kept in a cell where he was unable fully to recline or to stand up, and doused with cold water. It is likely that threats were made against his family, Bowden said. The CIA also administered mind-altering drugs, recalling the earliest days of CIA mind control research. Said Bowden:

> On occasion he might be given a drug to elevate his mood prior to interrogation; marijuana, heroin, and sodium pentothal have been shown to overcome a reluctance to speak, and methamphetamine can unleash a torrent of talk in the stubbornest subjects, the very urgency of the chatter making a complex lie impossible to sustain. These drugs could be administered surreptitiously with food or drink, and given the bleakness of his existence, they might even offer a brief period of relief and pleasure, thereby creating a whole new category of longing—and new leverage for his interrogators.

According to one 1950s–era CIA study, 'used in combination with the system of psychological and physiological pressures ... [drugs] will, in many cases, accelerate and exacerbate the profound fatigue, confusion, loss of critical judgment, and breakdown of resistance which is a consequence of the full course of control techniques'. Fifty years later, it appears that in a secret CIA prison halfway across the globe, American interrogators had stumbled back into the agency's long-forgotten past.

9

GUANTÁNAMO

Shafiq Rasul's hood was removed and he was photographed naked. Soldiers then gave him a bright orange jumpsuit. After he was dressed, his hands and feet were shackled, black thermal mittens were placed on his hands and blacked-out goggles, earmuffs and a surgical mask were affixed to his head. On the plane, prisoners were attached to one another by chains and then padlocked onto the floor. 'My legs were in a painful position but if I tried to move to get comfortable they would kick you', said Rasul. 'When we eventually landed, it was obviously somewhere very hot. We could tell as we came off the airplane that it was in the middle of the day, it was very light and very hot. I had no idea where we were.' Dragged off the runway and forced onto a bus, Rasul was ordered not to move. The bus then boarded a ferry that sailed into a fenced enclosure. Although his journey has all the hallmarks of a rendition, Rasul was not in the custody of the CIA. 'On our arrival at the camp somebody lifted the earmuffs I was wearing and shouted into my ear, "You are now the property of the US Marine Corps."' He had arrived at Guantánamo Bay, Cuba.

Like the CIA, the Pentagon was given unprecedented new power in the war on terror. On 13 November 2001—one day after Coalition forces took Kabul—George Bush signed a military order that placed all 'international terrorists' not held by the CIA under the authority of the Department of Defense. The 13 November order applies to any individual the president has 'reason to believe' is a member of al Qaeda or anyone causing or seeking to cause harm to the United States, its citizens, or its economy. The order ambiguously states that while suspects are to be treated 'humanely', they are to be detained 'in accordance with such other conditions as the Secretary of Defense may prescribe'. The November order also states that 'if', not when, the individual is to be tried, he or she must be tried by military commission. Rules for the commissions later issued by the Pentagon authorised the death penalty, allowed statements made under torture, and stipulated that suspects could be barred from attending their own trials and seeing the evidence against them. Responding to questions surrounding the order, Dick Cheney said, 'We think it guarantees that we'll have the kind of treatment of these individuals that we believe they deserve'.

Lawyers in the Department of Justice's Office of Legal Counsel were asked by top Bush officials to find an ideal location to house 'international terrorists'. The November order states that detainees subject to the directive shall 'not be privileged to seek any remedy or maintain any proceedings in any court of the United States, or any State thereof, any court of any foreign nation, or any international tribunal'. Put simply, detainees were to be kept in a place outside the law. The chief obstacle was habeas corpus—the right to be brought before a federal court to determine whether one's imprisonment is lawful. According to the OLC, a 'habeas petition would allow a detainee to challenge the legality of his status and treatment'. Further, it could 'interfere with the operation of the system that has been developed to address the detainment and trial of enemy aliens'.

There was one solution to the 'problem' of habeas. If no US court could claim jurisdiction, it was argued, no claims under habeas could be made. OLC laywers first singled out the US-controlled islands of Midway, Wake and Tinian as ideal locations to hold terrorism suspects, but further research found that federal courts excercised unquestioned jurisdiction over these islands. In December 2001, Patrick F. Philbin and John Yoo, then Deputy Assistants to the Attorney General, were asked to consider the naval station at Guantánamo Bay. This base is unique in many ways. It is the only American military installation located inside the territory of a state that does not have formal diplomatic relations with the USA. A former Guantánamo base commander, Rear Admiral Jack Fetterman, once described Guantánamo as like 'any other base ... except that it happens to be a 45-mile square chunk of real estate at the southeastern tip of a Communist country and is ringed by 17 miles of a 10-foot high cyclone fence topped by barbed wire'. The United States acquired the base in the last days of the Spanish-American War. The 1903 lease granted the US land on the south-eastern tip 'for use as coaling or naval stations only, and for no other purpose'. The lease stipulated that the United States would exercise 'complete jurisdiction and control over and within said areas' but would recognise 'the continuance of the ultimate sovereignty of the Republic of Cuba over and above' the leased areas. In 1934, a treaty reaffirmed the original agreement, adding that termination of the lease can only occur if the USA abandons the property or the two governments 'agree to a modification of its present limits'. After the failed CIA-sponsored Bay of Pigs invasion, Fidel Castro turned off the supply of all power and water to the base and demanded that the USA vacate the area. Instead, the USA held firm to the territory and began supplying its own utilities. According to Castro: 'The naval base is a dagger plunged into the Cuban soil ... a base we are not going to take away by force, but a piece of land we will never give up.' As stipulated in the treaty, every year the United States sends a cheque to Castro for US$4085. Castro has not cashed a cheque since 1961.

After studying the history, Philbin and Yoo suggested that because the base is in the 'sovereign territory of Cuba', as stipulated by the terms of the lease, foreign detainees had no venue to file habeas petitions in the United States. This determination ignored a line of litigation that placed Guantánamo Bay in the firm jurisdiction of US courts. The most relevant precedent regarding jurisdictional issues at Guantánamo is the 1966 Pellicier murder case. On 13 February 1965, Pellicier, a Cuban working on the base, killed an unarmed Jamaican man with a machete. In normal circumstances, a suspect like Pellicier would be tried in the host country, but by this time Cuba had sealed off all links to the base. After some deliberation, the Navy Judge Advocate General and Attorney General reasoned that the base is within the 'special maritime territorial jurisdiction of the United States'. Pellicier was then flown to the USA and indicted for murder in a Miami court. Although the Cuban was found to be insane before the trial started, the Pellicier precedent has stood. In *United States v Lee* (1977), for example, a Jamaican man was brought to the USA from Guantánamo to stand trial, while in *Burtt v Schick* (1986) a military court of appeals issued a writ of habeas corpus to a Marine confined at Guantánamo. In a case involving Haitian refugees temporarily housed at the base, in *Haitian Centers Council Inc v McNary* (1992) the presiding judge found that 'Guantánamo Bay is a military installation that is subject to the exclusive control and jurisdiction of the United States'. Inexplicably, Philbin and Yoo concluded that 'a federal district court could not properly exercise habeas jurisdiction over an alien detained' at Guantánamo.

The importance of placing Guantánamo outside the jurisdiction of courts is clear when you consider the facility's stated purpose. The official mission of the Pentagon's military intelligence unit, Joint Task Force Guantánamo (JTF GTMO), is to provide 'safe, humane care and custody of detained enemy combatants and gather intelligence in support of the global war on terror'. Central to this mission is the creation of a place free of judicial interference where interrogators can control every aspect of a detainee's life. According to Army Colonel Donald D. Woolfolk, the deputy commander JTF GTMO in 2002:

> The need to maintain the tightly controlled environment, which has been established to create dependency and trust by the detainee with his interrogator, is of paramount importance. Disruption of the interrogation environment, such as through access to a detainee by counsel, undermines this interrogation dynamic. Should this occur, a critical resource may be lost, resulting in a direct threat to national security.

The influence of the CIA's KUBARK model is unmistakable. With Guantánamo, the Pentagon sought to design a centre where inmates—later termed 'unlawful combatants' outside the protections of the Geneva Conventions—could be held in perfect DDD conditions. Lowell E. Jacoby, Director of the Defense Intelligence Agency (DIA), the Pentagon's intelligence gathering arm, has also stressed the importance of dependency in long-term interrogation–detention operations. According to Jacoby:

> Anything that threatens the perceived dependency and trust between the subject and interrogator directly threatens the value of interrogation as an intelligence-gathering tool. Even seemingly minor interruptions can have profound psychological impacts on the delicate subject–interrogator relationship. Any insertion of counsel into the subject–interrogator relationship, for example—even if only for a limited duration or for a specific

purpose—can undo months of work and may permanently shut down the interrogation process.

For nearly three years, Guantánamo interrogators enjoyed an environment free from judicial review. This changed after the Supreme Court ruled in mid 2004 that detainees held at Guantánamo were indeed entitled to habeas protection. The worst accounts of torture surfaced during these thirty intervening months—a time of impunity where human rights violations were not aberrations, but the norm.

On 6 January 2002, construction began on Guantánamo of a series of metal cages, dubbed Camp X-Ray, which held the initial batch of al Qaeda and Taliban suspects. Rasul and two friends, Asif Iqbal and Rhuhel Ahmed, arrived at the prison on 12 January. Together they have been dubbed the 'Tipton Three' after the town in the UK where the three lived, worked and went to school. David Hicks arrived with or immediately after the Tipton Three. They all were residents of Camp X-Ray, which closed only weeks before Mamdouh Habib arrived at the prison.

Like Habib and later more than 300 others, the Tipton Three were released from Guantánamo uncharged. Since their return to the UK, they have detailed an array of abuses spanning their time at the prison. FBI reports corroborating the bulk of their allegations were declassified in late 2004—nearly six months after their statements were first taken. The Tipton Three said their diets and physical activities were restricted at X-Ray. According to Iqbal, prisoners were not allowed to exercise in the two- by two-metre cage and during the daytime they were forced to sit in total silence. 'We couldn't lean on the wire fence or stand up and walk around the cage', he said. Their captors intentionally starved them, he added. According to Iqbal:

> We were fed three times a day, but given very little time to eat the food. The quantity of food we were given was also very little. It is not an exaggeration to say that sometimes we were only allowed about one minute in which to eat our food … Occasionally it would be in packets and we would not be able to open the packet before the food was taken back.

According to the men, at night they were required to sleep with their hands outside their blankets—a style reminiscent of KGB protocol. Toilet facilities were equally controlled. If the detainees needed to defecate, they first had to ask permission from a guard. According to Rasul:

> Very often the guards would refuse to take us to the portaloo outside and therefore people started to use the buckets [used for washing] in the cells. Many of the people who were detained in Camp X-Ray were ill, often suffering from dysentery or other diseases and simply couldn't wait until the guards decided they would take them to the toilet. I think the guards also knew how important cleanliness is to Muslims and took a sick pleasure from seeing us degraded like this.

If the guards agreed to take him, the prisoner was first shackled, then escorted to a portable toilet outside the detention block. He would then have to use the toilet while shackled, with the door open, and with the guard staring directly at him—a procedure outlined in the 1983 human exploitation manual.

The three British detainees recalled seeing David Hicks at X-Ray. 'David Hicks and us three (when we were together) would always talk about our interrogations', said Rasul. Iqbal added: 'He was a very surprising sight. A tiny white guy not more than 5'3" with a lot of tattoos on him. He told us he had endured an extremely bad experience having been held on a ship where he had been interrogated by Americans and hooded and beaten.' The men also saw Mamdouh Habib in mid 2002. By this time, a new permanent facility known as Camp Delta had been built. Unlike X-Ray, Delta featured cells with toilets and sinks. Rasul saw Habib when he arrived at Delta. He recalled:

> Habib himself was in catastrophic shape, mental and physical. As a result of his having been tortured in Egypt where he was taken from Bagram and then brought back, he used to bleed from his nose, mouth and ears when he was asleep ... He got no medical attention for this. We used to hear him ask but his interrogator said that he shouldn't have any. The medics would come and see him and then after he'd asked for medical help they would come

back and say if you co-operate with your interrogators then we can do something.

Conditions worsened for all inmates in late 2002 after a high-value detainee named Mohammad al-Qahtani was discovered among the nearly 600 prisoners at the base. One month before the 9/11 attacks, al-Qahtani was detained in the Orlando International Airport in Florida upon arrival from London. Immigration officials noticed he was nervous, evasive and hostile. He only had US$2800 in cash and no return ticket. After questioning him for ninety minutes, immigration officials fingerprinted al-Qahtani and deported him back to the UK.

In the summer of 2002, FBI agents at Guantánamo Bay discovered that the fingerprints of Detainee 063 matched those of the suspicious man deported from Orlando. Since arriving in February 2002, Detainee 063 had said little to interrogators. Upon the discovery of his true identity, Detainee 063 was reclassified as a 'very high-value target detainee'. Pentagon officials dubbed al-Qahtani the 20th Hijacker, a title he shared for some time with convicted al Qaeda plotter Zacarias Moussaoui.

Al-Qahtani was the Pentagon's first high-value detainee. Since the al-Libi episode in November 2001, the CIA siphoned off top al Qaeda suspects captured abroad and whisked them away to brutal intelligence services in the Middle East or to CIA black sites. The Pentagon, on the other hand, was charged with holding the flotsam and jetsam of those ostensibly taken off the battlefield. While Dick Cheney claimed in 2002 that the inmates at Guantánamo constitute the 'worst of a very bad lot', a variety of credible sources directly refute this. A CIA analysis in 2002 found that more than half of the detainees didn't belong there, while a more recent 2006 survey by a European inspection team found only thirty to forty 'real' terrorists at the prison. According to Brigadier General Martin Lucenti, Deputy Commander of Joint Task Force Guantánamo in 2004, 'of the 550 [detainees] that we have, I would say most of them, the majority of them, will either be released or transferred to their own countries … Most of these guys weren't fighting. They were running'. An investigation using data provided by the Pentagon found that 40 per cent of the detainees are not affiliated with al Qaeda and only 8 per cent have fought for a terrorist group. The majority of the detainees, roughly

60 per cent, are merely accused of being 'associated with' terrorists—
an amorphous category that includes unknowingly supporting a
charity that is deemed by the USA to be sympathetic to terrorist
causes. Finally, 86 per cent of detainees at Guantánamo weren't even
captured by US forces, but were delivered to Coalition officials by
Pakistani authorities or Northern Alliance generals eager to collect on
bounties. Hicks, for example, was turned in by Northern Alliance
forces for US$1000. The Tipton Three, captured by the Northern
Alliance while assisting displaced Afghani refugees on the Afghan–
Pakistan border, were also turned over for bounty. One leaflet dropped
across Afghanistan by the United States in early 2002 depicted piles
of US twenty-dollar bills overlaid with the words: 'Reward for Information Leading to the whereabouts or capture of Taliban and al Qaeda
leadership'. Another flyer was more explicit. Under a picture of a
traditional Afghan city and a smiling elder, the text on the front said:
'Get wealth and power beyond your dreams—help the anti-Taliban
force to rid Afghanistan of murderers and terrorists.' On the back, it
continued: 'You can receive millions of dollars for helping the anti-
Taliban force catch al Qaeda and Taliban murderers. This is enough
money to take care of your family, your village, your tribe for the rest
of your life—pay for livestock and doctors and school books and
housing for all your people.'

With al-Qahtani, for the first time in more than six months
interrogators believed they finally had someone of value. The Pentagon
held on to al-Qahtani and blocked CIA moves to render him elsewhere.
According to Pentagon spokesman Larry DiRita, al-Qahtani was
'believed capable of unlocking an enormous amount of specific and
general insights into 9/11, al Qaeda operations and ongoing planning
for future attacks'. But al-Qahtani insisted that he came to the USA
merely to open a used car dealership and pursue a hobby in falconry.
'We were getting nothing out of him … This guy had been trained in
resistance techniques and was using them', said Army General James T.
Hill of the US Southern Command.

Military intelligence was at first restrained from increasing
the pressure on al-Qahtani by the camp commander, Brigadier General
Rick Baccus. The General favoured the FBI's non-violent rapport-
building techniques. According to the *Financial Times*, Baccus 'faced
constant pressure from military intelligence officials to bend army doctrine for the treatment of prisoners'. Baccus said military intelligence

interrogators wanted him to make detainees' lives 'less comfortable'. He refused—and was promptly replaced.

In October 2002, Major General Geoffrey Miller—an Army administrator with no prior detention or interrogation experience—took over Baccus's assignment. Miller lost several friends in the 9/11 attacks on the Pentagon and according to James J. Yee, then a chaplain at Guantánamo, Miller channelled his anger onto prisoners at the base. Yee, who often clashed with the General, said that Miller would repeatedly tell prison staff 'the war is on' and stress the need to get tough. According to Yee, 'Soldiers know that when you are in combat there's considerable leniency in the rules and the leaders, including General Miller, wanted to put them in that frame of mind'.

As commander of JTF GTMO, Miller instituted two changes at the prison that had dramatic effects not just on the interrogation of al-Qahtani, but on all other detainees as well. First, Miller placed military police (MP) under the command of military intelligence (MI). According to military historian Major James F. Gebhardt, 'An inherent conflict exists between guarding and protecting the rights of detainees (the MP mission) and extracting the maximum intelligence from a source under the law (the MI mission)'. The result, according to one military lawyer, was 'to allow for intelligence to dominate how military police treated detainees'.

Second, Miller brought SERE and Guantánamo officials together. One result of this meeting was the creation of Behavioral Science Consultation Teams (BSCTs). In many ways, BSCTs (pronounced 'biscuits') resemble the small teams of doctors, psychologists and psychiatrists at SERE who oversee the Resistance Training Laboratory phase to ensure that students do not suffer serious injuries. BSCT teams at Guantánamo have a similar, but more sinister purpose. A former interrogator told the *New York Times*, 'Their purpose was to help us break them'. According to Dr Darryl Matthews, a psychiatrist interviewed by the *New Yorker*, 'As psychiatrists, we know how to hurt people better than others. We can figure out what buttons to push. Like a surgeon with a scalpel, we have techniques and we know what the pressure points are'.

Colonel Louie Banks, the SERE administrator initially deployed to Afghanistan, was sent to Guantánamo in late 2002 and advised the Pentagon that members of BSCTs should have a SERE background. In turn, BSCT doctrine was formulated with the aid of SERE officials. According to the *New England Journal of Medicine,* the BSCT program is based largely on the premise that:

> acute, uncontrollable stress erodes established behavior (e.g., resistance to questioning), creating opportunities to reshape behavior. Complex reward systems (e.g., the creation of multiple camp 'levels' with different privileges) promote co-operation. Stressors tailored to the psychological and cultural vulnerabilities of individual detainees (e.g., phobias, personality features, and religious beliefs) are key to this approach and can be devised on the basis of detainee profiles.

According to the official BSCT Standard Operating Procedures (SOP), a team comprises a clinical psychologist, a psychiatrist, and a mental health specialist whose foremost mission is to 'consult on interrogation approach techniques'. It is also the BSCT's job to inform interrogators about 'cultural issues pertaining to the detainee population' and to provide 'input into the development of strategies for increasing positive behavior, such as implementation of incentive programs, reinforcement programs for positive behavior, and increasing access to recreational and social activities'. Oddly, teams are also supposed to craft 'strategies for increasing pro-American sentiment' among detainees. Finally, it adds, 'BSCT personnel have full and direct access to JTF Commander to consult on all aspects of JTF mission'.

The second outcome of the meeting between SERE and Guantánamo officials was a new list of interrogation techniques prepared for MI. According to General James T. Hill:

> The staff at Guantánamo working with behavioral scientists, having gone up to our SERE school and developed a list of techniques which our lawyers decided and looked at, said [they] were OK. I sent that list of techniques up to the Secretary [Rumsfeld] and said, in order for us to get at some of these very high-profile, high-value targets who are resistant to techniques, I may need greater flexibility. But I want a legal review of it and [I want] you to tell me that, policywise, it's the right way to do business. He did that.

The paper trail is revealing. In a memo dated 11 October 2002, Jerald Phifer, Director of Joint Task Force 170, the intelligence task force at Guantánamo at the time, requested approval of the following 'Category I' and 'Category II' 'counter-resistance' techniques adapted from SERE. These included: yelling at the detainee, stress positions ('like standing … maximum four hours'), isolation for up to thirty days, deprivation of auditory stimuli, twenty-hour interrogations, removal of all comfort items ('including religious items'), removal of clothing, forced grooming ('shaving off facial hair'), and using detainees' individual phobias ('such as fear of dogs') to induce stress. These techniques, according to a companion report, 'are not intended to cause gratuitous, severe, physical pain or suffering or prolonged mental harm, but are instead intended to induce cooperation over a period of time by weakening the detainee's mental and physical ability to resist'.

In addition to the techniques listed above, Phifer also sought official approval for four 'Category III' techniques. Some of these closely parallel the techniques authorised for the CIA in March 2002. They included:

(1) the use of scenarios designed to convince the detainee that death or severely painful consequences are imminent for him and/or his family;
(2) exposure to cold weather or water ('with appropriate medical monitoring');
(3) use of a wet towel and dripping water to induce the misperception of suffocation; and
(4) use of mild, non-injurious physical contact such as grabbing, poking in the chest with the finger, and light pushing.

Diane E. Beaver, an Army Staff Judge Advocate who reviewed the request, concluded that 'the proposed strategies do not violate applicable federal law'. Beaver relied heavily on the weakness of US torture law and the legal arguments of the CIA torture memos. According to Beaver: 'The federal torture statute will not be violated so long as any of the proposed strategies are not specifically intended to cause severe physical pain or suffering or prolonged mental harm.' Beaver also found that the methods could be employed 'so long as the force used could plausibly have been thought necessary in a particular situation to achieve a legitimate government objective …'. Noting that interrogation techniques listed in the 1992 Army FM 34-52, *Intelligence Interrogation,* 'are constrained by' the Geneva Conventions, Beaver recommended 'that the proposed methods of interrogation be approved'.

The request for advanced techniques was then forwarded up the chain of command. Michael B. Dunlavey, Major General of Joint Task Force 170, wrote that the harsh methods 'will enhance our efforts to extract additional information'. Concurring with Beaver, he found that 'these techniques do not violate US or international law'. Next up the chain was James T. Hill. Although Hill was 'troubled' by the permissibility of threatening the life of a detainee, he wrote that he had the 'desire to have as many options as possible at my disposal'. He requested that the techniques be quickly reviewed by the Pentagon in order 'to maximize the value of our intelligence collection mission'.

Ultimately, the request was forwarded to Donald Rumsfeld. General Counsel William J. Haynes II advised while 'all Category III techniques may be legally available, we believe that, as a matter of policy, a blanket approval of Category III techniques is not warranted at this time'. On 2 December 2002, Rumsfeld signed off on all of the Category II techniques and authorised the fourth Category III technique. Blanket authorisation was rescinded less than a month later, and replaced with authorisation pending approval prior to application of the harshest techniques. Despite the minor change in policy, the bulk of category II and III techniques were used at Guantánamo indiscriminately under General Miller. A handwritten note penned by Rumsfeld on the bottom of the December memo is telling. Rumsfeld was clearly dissatisfied with the time limit on forced standing. Next to his signature, Rumsfeld scribbled: 'I stand for 8–10 hours a day. Why is standing limited to four hours? D.R.'

———

Mohammad al-Qahtani's interrogations grew tougher even before Rumsfeld's official authorisation of SERE techniques. Miller was ordered personally to see to it that al-Qahtani was broken, and he kept Rumsfeld informed in weekly briefs about his progress. Added the *New Yorker,* '[W]hen General Miller assumed his administrative role at Guantánamo he became impatient with the FBI interrogations, and insisted that harsher methods be used'. As with the interrogation of Ibn al-Shaykh al-Libi in Afghanistan and Abu Zubaydah in Thailand, the FBI was side-lined from al-Qahtani's interrogation and JTF interrogators took over.

By early November 2002, al-Qahtani was 'totally isolated (with the exception of occasional interrogations) in a cell that was always flooded with light', as recorded by FBI agents in a declassified document—one of more than 10 000 released to the American Civil Liberties Union following a 2003 FOIA request. FBI agents, the document adds, also 'observed that a canine was used in an aggressive manner to intimidate detainee #63'.

An interrogation logbook obtained by *Newsweek* documenting al-Qahtani's interrogation from 22 November 2002 through 11 January 2003 picks up where the FBI accounts leave off. This chilling logbook tracks events minute by minute. Its authenticity was confirmed by Pentagon spokesman Larry DiRita, who said various JTF GTMO interrogators and observers compiled it as the interrogation proceeded. An entry on 25 November 2002 is typical in its cold retelling of events:

0940: Detainee was given three and one-half bags of IV. He started moaning and told the MPs he's willing to talk so he can urinate. SGT A entered the booth and asked the following questions: Who do you work for? (Detainee answered: Al Qaida), Who was your leader? (Detainee answered: Usama bin Laden), Why did you go to Orlando? (Detainee answered: I wasn't told the mission), Who was meeting you? (Detainee answered: I don't know), Who was with you on the plane? (Detainee answered: I was by myself). SGT R told detainee he was wasting SGT R's time. Detainee told SGT A he was willing to drink.

1000: Detainee again said he has to go to bathroom. SGT R said he can go in the bottle. Detainee said he wanted to go to the bathroom because it's more comfortable. SGT R said 'You've ruined all trust, you can either go in the bottle or in your pants.' Detainee goes in his pants. SGT A continued approach.

1030: Assessment—Detainee has a greater deal of animosity toward SGT R. He is beginning to understand the futility of his situation. He has to understand that his antics will not stop the interrogation at all. We feel he is slowly realizing that he will not outlast the battle of wills. He is much closer to compliance and cooperation now than at the beginning of the operation.

The logbook is littered with references to a person known as 'Maj. L'. This is Major John Leso, a BSCT psychologist who sat in on many of al-Qahtani's interrogation sessions. On 27 November, for instance, the log states:

> 1000: Control puts detainee in swivel chair at MAJ L's suggestion to keep him awake and stop him from fixing his eyes on one spot in booth. Detainee struggled with MP when MP moved chair. Control used 'onion' analogy to explain how detainee's control over his life is being stripped away. Control gives detainee three facts: we are hunting down Al Qaida every day, we will not stop until they are captured or killed, we control every aspect of your life. Detainee did not speak but became very angry with control.

Under BSCT supervision, al-Qahtani's treatment, in the words of the 1963 KUBARK manual, 'plunged into the strange'. On 19 December, interrogators tried a different tactic:

> 1115: Detainee offered water—refused ... Began teaching the detainee lessons such as stay, come, and bark to elevate his social status up to that of a dog. Detainee became very agitated.

> 1230: Detainee taken to bathroom and walked 30 minutes.

> 1300: Detainee offered food and water—refused. Dog tricks continued and detainee stated he should be treated like a man. Detainee was told he would have to learn who to defend and who to attack. Interrogator showed photos of 9-11 victims and told detainee he should bark happy for these people. Interrogator also showed photos of Al Qaida terrorists and told detainee he should growl at these people. A towel was placed on the detainee's head like a burka with his face exposed and the interrogator proceeded to give the detainee dance lessons. The detainee

became agitated and tried to kick an MP. No retaliation was used for the kick and the dance lesson continued.

At one stage, interrogators performed a puppet show 'satirizing the detainee's involvement with Al Qaida', according to the log. Other times, he was forced to stand for the US national anthem, led around the room on a leash, interrogated in a room lit only with red lights, or drenched with water in a control method called 'drink water or wear it'. JTF interrogators also used sex and religion. Sometimes he was sat upon by female interrogators while other times pictures of naked women were hung around his neck. Al-Qahtani was also kept naked in his cell, and women's underwear was sometimes placed on his head. On 19 December, interrogators constructed a shrine to Osama bin Laden and forced al-Qahtani to pray to it. According to the log: 'Detainee was apprehensive and started to walk out of booth. Detainee was not allowed to leave and interrogator played the call to prayer. Detainee began to pray and openly cried'.

BSCT-directed SERE techniques involving sex and religion weren't reserved only for al-Qahtani. In late 2002, SERE methods were introduced at Guantánamo for use on all detainees at the prison. Various documents declassified by the Pentagon directly cite or indirectly refer to the new SERE techniques. According to a sworn statement by the former Interrogation Control Element (ICE) chief at Guantánamo, SERE instructors were sent to Guantánamo in December 2002. 'When I arrived at GTMO', he said, '[Redacted] my predecessor, arranged for SERE instructors to teach their techniques to the interrogators at GTMO. The instructors did give some briefings to the Joint Interrogation Group (JIG) interrogators'.

On 10 December 2002, formal SERE Standard Operating Procedures were issued to the Special Agent in Charge of the Criminal Investigation Task Force (CITF) at Guantánamo. The CITF's mission is to investigate enemy combatants and either refer their cases to the Pentagon for prosecution in tribunals or recommend that their cases be dropped and the detainees released. According to the CITF agent, 'the SERE methods were designed for use in a battlefield environment as a means of collecting tactical intelligence (e.g. to uncover enemy plans, determine enemy strength, movement, weapons capabilities and logistical support, etc.)'. The Special Agent suggested that the methods were too violent to be used by domestic law enforcement agencies (LEA) because they do not elicit accurate information that would hold up in court. The SERE SOP 'clearly does not apply to LEA (CITF and FBI) interrogators' because 'LEA has the additional responsibility of seeking reliable information/evidence from detainees to be used in subsequent legal proceedings'. The new SERE procedures, the agent adds, are 'applicable only to military and civilian interrogators assigned to JTF-GTMO'.

An e-mail message sent on 17 December 2002 between Guantánamo officials also referred to the new techniques. 'Greetings from GTMO', it began. 'Its [sic] just how you left it [—] plenty of sun and iguanas, not enough of the fairer sex. Attached is a response drafted by [Redacted] and I regarding an attempt by LTC [Redacted]'s replacement to establish the SERE model of interrogation as policy here. Please let us know your thoughts.' All other details are redacted.

According to British detainee Shafiq Rasul, conditions grew harsher 'around the end of 2002. That is when short-shackling started, loud music playing in interrogation, shaving beards and hair, putting people in cells naked, taking away people's "comfort" items … moving some people every two hours depriving them of sleep, the use of A/C air …'. According to Rasul, one day:

> I was taken into a room and short shackled. This was the first time this had happened to me. It was extremely uncomfortable. Short shackling means that the hands and feet are shackled together forcing you to stay in an uncomfortable position for long hours. Then they turned the air conditioning on to extremely high so I started getting very cold. I was left in this position on my own in the room for about 6 or 7 hours, nobody came to see me. I wanted to use the toilet and called for the guards but nobody came for me. Being held in the short shackled position was extremely painful but if you tried to move the shackles would cut into your ankles or wrists. By the time that I was eventually released to be taken back to my cell I could hardly walk as my legs had gone completely numb. I also had severe back pains.

Rasul's account is mirrored in an e-mail sent from one concerned FBI agent to superiors:

On a couple of occassions [sic], I entered interview rooms to find a detainee chained hand and foot in a fetal position to the floor, with no chair, food, or water. Most times they had urinated or defacated [sic] on themselves and had been left there for 18, 24 hours or more. On one occassion [sic], the air conditioning had been turned down so far and the temperature was so cold in the room, that the barefooted detainee was shaking with cold. When I asked the [military police guards] what was going on, I was told that interrogators from the day prior had ordered this treatment, and the detainee was not to be moved. On another occassion [sic], the A/C had been turned off, making the temperature in the unventilated room probably well over 100 degrees. The detainee was almost unconscious on the floor with a pile of hair next to him. He had apparently been literally pulling his own hair out throughout the night.

In addition to SERE techniques, BSCTs were expanded to all detainees by late 2002. Interrogators found their support invaluable. According to one FBI official: 'I've met with the BISC (Biscuit) people several times and found them to be a great resource. They know everything that's going on with each detainee, who their [sic] talking to, who the leaders are, etc. I've encouraged the interview teams to meet with them prior to doing their interviews.'

Under the guidance of BSCTs, military intelligence implemented a prison-wide system of incentives and rewards. Rasul recalled:

Towards the end of December 2002 a new system was introduced, although we weren't aware of it as a system as such, whereby detainees would be placed on different levels or tiers depending on their level of co-operation and their behavior in the camp. At the beginning I was placed on Level 2, the second highest level. This meant that I had all the so called comfort items, including toothpaste, soap, cups etc. The only better position to be would have been Level 1 where you were also given a bottle of water.

According to the *Washington Post*, BSCTs helped interrogators zero in on the inmates' specific fears. After reviewing a prisoner's medical file, one BSCT doctor suggested ways to manipulate the prisoner's severe phobia of the dark. Another time, a BSCT doctor suggested ways to exploit a detainee's longing for his mother. BSCTs also recommended crossing sexual and religious boundaries to illicit stress using techniques similar to those used with SERE students. According to Rasul, sex tactics increased after General Miller initiated the BSCT program:

> We didn't hear anybody talking about being sexually humiliated or subjected to sexual provocation before General Miller came. After that we did … It was clear to us that this was happening to the people who'd been brought up most strictly as Muslims. It seemed to happen most to people … of most interest to the interrogators.

Erik Saar, a former Army translator at Guantánamo, also observed an increase in the use of sex tactics in late 2002. 'Sex, I believe, came from the BSCTs,' he said. 'I have a hard time thinking it was a couple of rogue interrogators, if that's what the Army says, because it was very systematic. It wasn't hidden.' Saar recounted an incident when a female interrogator smeared fake menstrual blood on the face of a Saudi detainee, an account that closely parallels the allegations of Mamdouh Habib. According to Saar, the detainee 'began to cry like a baby'. The female interrogator then jeered: 'Have a fun night in your cell without any water to clean yourself.'

Female interrogators used more than fake menstrual blood to unnerve Muslim detainees. According to T. J. Harrington, Deputy Assistant Director of the FBI's Counterterrorism Division, an agent saw the following scene in late 2002:

> The detainee was shackled and his hands were cuffed to his waist. [Redacted] observed [Redacted] apparently whispering in the detainee's ear and caressing and applying lotion to his arms (this was during Ramadan when physical contact with a woman would have been particularly offensive to a Moslem male). On more than one occasion the detainee appeared to be grimacing in pain and [Redacted] hands appeared to be making some contact with the detainee. Although [Redacted] could not see her hands at all times. He saw them moving toward the detainee's lap. He also observed the detainee pulling away and against

the restraints. Subsequently, the marine who … had been in the interrogation room with [Redacted] during the interrogation re-entered the observation room. [Redacted] asked what had happened to cause the detainee to grimace in pain. The marine said [Redacted] had grabbed the detainee's thumbs and bent them backwards and indicated that she also grabbed his genitals. The marine also implied that her treatment of the detainee was less harsh than her treatment of others by indicating that he had seen her treatment of other detainees result in detainees curling into a fetal position on the floor and crying in pain.

Guantánamo interrogators also employed more bizarre forms of religious abuse. The FBI witnessed a variation of the SERE flag desecration technique. An agent reported in an e-mail that he saw a 'detainee sitting on the floor of the interview room with an Israeli flag draped around him, loud music being played and a strobe light flashing'.

Koran desecration was also widely reported. Many of these accounts corroborate Mamdouh Habib's claims. According to Asif Iqbal, 'The behavior of the guards towards our religious practices as well as the Koran was also, in my view, designed to cause us as much distress as possible. They would kick the Koran, throw it into the toilet and generally disrespect it'. Other inmates complained of an incident where the Koran was wrapped inside an Israeli flag and then stomped on—an act that led to a mass suicide attempt at the prison. A Pentagon investigation later confirmed that guards defiled at least five Muslim holy books. In particular, a two-word obscenity was written on one Koran, a soldier deliberately kicked another Koran, and in one incident a guard's urine splashed on a Koran 'inadvertently'.

The implementation of SERE techniques drove a wedge between FBI and JTF interrogators at Guantánamo. In one e-mail, an agent angrily stated that harsh techniques 'have produced no intelligence of a threat neutralization nature to date and CITF believes that techniques have destroyed any chance of prosecuting this detainee'. The author of the e-mail was infuriated by the fact that Department of Defense (DOD) interrogators were impersonating FBI agents while interrogating a detainee. According to the agent, 'If this detainee is ever released or his story is made public in any way, DOD interrogators will not be held accountable because these torture techniques

were done [by] the "FBI" interrogators. The FBI will be left holding
the bag before the public'. In another e-mail, one FBI interrogator—
the same agent who met with BSCT staff and found their help
invaluable—noted that several interrogators with the DIA's Defense
Human Intelligence Service (DHS) were:

> showing a detainee homosexual porn movies and using a
> strobe light in the room. We moved our interview to a different
> room! We've heard that DHS interrogators routinely identify
> themselves as FBI Agents and then interrogate a detainee for
> 16–18 hours using tactics as described above and others (wrap-
> ping in Israeli flag, constant loud music, cranking the A/C down,
> etc.). The next time a real Agent tries to talk to that guy, you can
> imagine the result.

According to another agent, JTF interrogators were encouraged
to 'use aggressive interrogation tactics' that FBI agents believed were
'of questionable effectiveness and subject to uncertain interpretation
based on law and regulation'. General Miller, the same agent stated,
preferred to use methods that 'could easily result in the elicitation of
unreliable and legally inadmissible information'. Still another internal
FBI memo penned in 2004 cites 'the FBI's continued objection to the
use of SERE (Search, Escape, Resistance and Evasion) techniques to
interrogate prisoners'. According to the memo, in late 2002 FBI personnel 'raised concerns over interrogation tactics being employed by
the US military'. The memo adds: 'We are not aware of the FBI
participating directly in any SERE interrogations. It should be noted
that FBI concerns and objections were documented and presented
to Major General Geoffery [sic] Miller, who oversaw GTMO
operations.'

Several meetings between FBI representatives and the Pentagon
over the use of SERE techniques are discussed at length in a 2004
e-mail sent by an FBI interrogator chief at Guantánamo to
T. J. Harrington. According to the e-mail:

> [W]e met with Generals Dunlevey [sic] & Miller explaining our
> position (Law Enforcement techniques) vs DoD. Both agreed the
> Bureau has their way of doing business and the DoD has their
> marching orders from the Sec Def. Although the two techniques

differed drastically, both Generals believed they had a job to accomplish ...

The same topic also cropped up in talks with the Department of Justice (DOJ). 'In my weekly meetings with the DOJ', the FBI agent states, 'we often discussed [Redacted] techniques and how they were not effective or producing intel that was reliable ... We all agreed [Redacted] were going to be an issue in the military commission cases'. The agent also discussed a meeting he had with General Miller and the Pentagon Detainee Policy Committee over the use of SERE techniques. 'I voiced concerns that the intel produced was nothing more than what the FBI got using simple investigative techniques ... The conversations were somewhat heated ... [Redacted] finally admitted the information was the same info the Bureau obtained. It still did not prevent them from continuing the "[Redacted] methods."'

The cumulative effects of BSCT-directed SERE torture were profound. By late 2002, alleged '20th Hijacker' Mohammad al-Qahtani was showing signs of complete mental collapse. According to one FBI agent, he was 'evidencing behavior consistent with extreme psychological trauma (talking to non-existent people, reporting hearing voices, crouching in a corner of the cell covered with a sheet for hours on end)'. Under enhanced methods, General Hill said al-Qahtani began giving interrogators 'some pretty good stuff'. In particular, al-Qahtani fingered thirty fellow prisoners, claiming they were all Osama bin Laden's personal bodyguards. The Pentagon, in turn, used his statements to justify the continued detention of dozens of detainees at the prison. But in late 2005, al-Qahtani retracted all of the statements he had made to JTF interrogators. According to his lawyer, Gitanjali S. Gutierrez, in their meetings al-Qahtani 'painfully described how he could not endure the months of isolation, torture and abuse, during which he was nearly killed, before making false statements to please his interrogators'. A senior Pentagon official later conceded to *Time* magazine that his 'most valuable confessions came not during the period covered in the [interrogation] log or as a result of any particular technique but when al-Qahtani was presented with evidence coughed up by others in detention'.

Confessions made by the Tipton Three were similarly suspect. Asif Iqbal teetered on the verge of insanity after months of SERE tortures. According to Iqbal:

I started to suffer what I believe was a break down. I couldn't take it any more. I asked to speak to a psychologist but all they said was that I should be given Prozac which I didn't want to have. The other prisoners who had this were just like zombies and put on loads of weight. I was having flash backs and nightmares … and couldn't sleep at night.

At one point the men were shown a grainy video featuring Osama bin Laden speaking to a group of seated followers. Interrogators pushed all three men to admit they were gathered in the audience. Rasul recalled:

I said it wasn't me but [a female interrogator] kept pressing that I should admit it. She was very adamant. She said to me 'I've put detainees here in isolation for 12 months and eventually they've broken. You might as well admit it now so that you don't have to stay in isolation.' Every time I tried to answer a question she insisted I was lying. She kept going on and on at me, pressuring me, telling me that I was lying, telling me that I should admit it. Eventually I just gave in and said 'okay, it's me'. The reason I did this was because of the previous five or six weeks of being held in isolation and being taken to interrogation for hours on end, short shackled and being treated in that way. I was going out of my mind and didn't know what was going on. I was desperate for it to end and therefore eventually I just gave in and admitted to being in the video.

Iqbal and Ahmed also confessed to being in the Osama bin Laden video. According to Rasul, 'When you are detained in those conditions, you are entirely powerless and have no way of having your voice heard. This has led me and many others to "co-operate" and say or do anything to get away'. The British government later found that all three men had been in Britain at the time of the alleged al Qaeda training session. After their whereabouts were established, all three were transferred from Guantánamo to the UK where they were released uncharged.

The Tipton Three recalled that both Habib and Hicks appeared to be near mental collapse. In 2003, both Australians were held in Camp Echo, a squat concrete complex outside Camp Delta that housed inmates scheduled for tribunals. They were kept in total isolation. According to Rasul:

> The impression we have is that the point of keeping people in complete isolation in Camp Echo was so that they would in every way be under the control of the people who held them there. They would have no other information than what they were given by the guards or the interrogators and would be obliged to put all their trust in what they said and would know nothing whatsoever about what was happening in the outside world or even in Guantánamo Bay.

Rasul added that Habib complained bitterly about Echo. Habib had told him there was

> no natural light at all there. Even when you went to the shower, which was 'outside', it was still sealed off so you couldn't see any natural light at all. You couldn't tell what time of day or night it was. You were in a room and a guard was sitting outside watching you 24 hours a day. That was his job, just to sit outside the cell and watch you.

Habib verified Rasul's account. Camp Echo, he said, was the worst. 'They're not going to let anyone out of there with their minds.'

Hicks spent more than eighteen months in Camp Echo. 'David Hicks? He's finished', said Habib. The Tipton Three also recalled its brutal effects upon the Australian. The last time they saw him, Rasul said:

> We thought that he had gone downhill. By downhill we mean that he seemed to be losing all hope and more willing to co-operate as a result. We were interrogated a lot but he used to get interrogated every two to three days, sometimes every day. He was told that if he didn't co-operate he would never go home. It started when he was moved to Delta, that he began to be moved all the time. They wouldn't let him settle with anyone ... [We] had the impression that he was being forced to make admissions, the 'force' consisting of offers of benefits if he co-operated and removal of anything that could make life slightly easier if he did

not. We were aware for instance that he needed essential medical treatment for a hernia and that he was told he would only get it if he co-operated.

After fifteen months in detention, ABC's *Four Corners* program revealed that Hicks signed the following statement: 'I believe that al-Qaeda camps provided a great opportunity for Muslims like myself from all over the world to train for military operations and jihad. I knew after six months that I was receiving training from al-Qaeda, who had declared war on numerous countries and peoples.' While elements of the confession are supported by Hicks' own admissions in interviews with Australian Federal Police at Guantánamo and in letters home, the fact that it was made under duress is unavoidable.

The best gauge of Hicks' mental state comes from Hicks himself. Unlike Habib, who wrongly believed his family was killed during his detention, Hicks often sent letters home to Adelaide. In 2003, Hicks wrote to his father Terry:

Dear Dad, I feel as though I'm teetering on the edge of losing my sanity after such a long ordeal—the last year of it being in isolation. There are a number of things the authorities could do to help to improve my living conditions, but low morale and depression seems to be the order of the day. They're also making sure that I'm disadvantaged as possible when it comes to defending myself.

A recent letter revealed an even greater decline. Hicks wrote:

I've reached the point where I'm highly confused and lost— overwhelmed, if you like. I suffer extreme mood swings every half hour, going from one extreme to the other. I can no longer picture what happens outside. My entire world has become this little room, and everything beyond is nothing but an echo. Love, David.

10

THE GLOVES COME OFF, PART II

On 1 May 2003, President Bush strode triumphantly across the tarmac of the USS *Lincoln* and declared under a banner that read 'Mission Accomplished' that major combat operations in Iraq were officially over. 'The battle of Iraq is one victory in a war on terror that began on September the 11th 2001—and still goes on', said Bush. Three months later, US forces were engaged in an increasingly deadly ground war. Since Bush's triumphant speech, the insurgency in Iraq had grown stronger and better organised. In turn, the Pentagon demanded better intelligence from the field.

On 14 August 2002, Captain William Ponce, an Army military intelligence (MI) officer, wrote an e-mail to interrogators stationed throughout Iraq soliciting a 'wish list' of techniques they'd like to use on detainees. In the e-mail, Ponce introduced the concept of unlawful combatants, a term originally used only to describe al Qaeda and Taliban fighters captured in Afghanistan. Iraq, in contrast, is a theatre of war where the Geneva Conventions explicitly apply. While lawful combatants, said Ponce, 'receive protections of the Geneva Conventions and gain combat immunity for their warlike acts, as well as become prisoners of war if captured', unlawful combatants 'may be treated as criminals under the domestic law of the captor … [and] may include spies, saboteurs, or civilians who are participating in the hostilities'. Ponce wrote: 'The gloves are coming off gentlemen regarding these detainees, Col. [Steven] Boltz has made it clear that we want these individuals broken. Casualties are mounting and we need to start gathering info to help protect our fellow soldiers from further attacks … MI ALWAYS OUT FRONT!'

Four days later, an interrogator from the 4th Infantry Division, stationed in Tikrit, requested authorisation for techniques above and beyond the limits of the 1992 Army interrogation field manual. According to the interrogator, 'There are a number of "coercive" techniques that may be employed that cause no permanent harm to the subject'. These include striking the subject with a telephone book, low-voltage electrocution, closed-fist blows, and inducing muscle fatigue—techniques that 'often call for medical personnel to be on call for unforeseen complications'. A veteran interrogator with the 3rd Armored Cavalry Regiment, based in Qaim in western Iraq, also responded to Ponce's request. 'Our intelligence doctrine is based on former Cold War and WWII enemies', he complained, adding that 'today's enemy' understands 'force, not psychological mind games or incentives'. The interrogator suggested a range of techniques used by 'SERE instructors' including 'close confinement quarters, sleep deprivation, white noise, and … harsher fear-up approaches'. In particular, 'fear of dogs and snakes appear to work nicely'. He added: 'I firmly agree that the gloves need to come off.'

These discussions were used in part to develop a new list of interrogation techniques that would be permissible in Iraq. On 10 September and 14 September 2003, Lieutenant General Ricardo A. Sanchez, then top Army commander in Iraq, authorised a coercive interrogation program for military interrogators that he said was 'modelled' on the one implemented at Guantánamo Bay. The fact that Iraqi detainees were subject to the protections of the Geneva Conventions did not appear to limit the range of techniques approved. Among others, Sanchez authorised stress positions ('sitting, standing, kneeling, prone, etc.'), sleep management ('not to exceed 72 continuous hours'), isolation (subject to 'medical and psychological review'), yelling, loud music and/or light control ('used to create fear, disorient detainee, and prolong capture shock'), a harsh 'fear-up' approach ('significantly increasing the fear level in a detainee'), 'futility' ('invoking the feeling of futility in a detainee') and finally, the presence of military working dogs ('exploits Arab fear of dogs'). Sanchez noted that these techniques should be used if 'the detainee is medically and operationally evaluated as suitable (considering all techniques to be used in combination)' and that they are performed in 'the presence or availability of qualified medical personnel'.

The September memos are rife with contradictions. Sanchez himself notes that these techniques were to be used in 'a theatre of war in which the Geneva Conventions apply', but one technique listed, called 'Incentive/Removal of Incentive', consists of 'providing a reward or removing a privilege, above and beyond those that are required by the Geneva Convention, from detainees'. In brackets, Sanchez adds:

> Caution: Other nations that believe detainees are entitled to EPW [Enemy Prisoner of War] protections may consider that provision and retention of religious items (e.g. Koran) are protected under international law ... Although the provisions of the Geneva Convention are not applicable to the interrogation of unlawful combatants, consideration should be given to these views prior to application of the technique.

Another example of this conflict appears after the description of 'environmental manipulation'. Here, Sanchez adds: 'Caution: Based on court cases in other countries, some nations may view application of this technique in certain circumstances to be inhumane. Consideration of these views should be given prior to use of this technique.'

The muddled directives 'have caused a great deal of confusion as to the status of detainees', said a staff sergeant with the 104th Military Battalion. One interrogator who requested guidance from superiors was required to attend a presentation by two military lawyers. According to the interrogator, first the lawyers showed slides. He recalled:

> Some of the slides were about the laws of war, the Geneva Convention, but it was kind of a starting-off point for them to kind of spout off, you know: why we don't have to follow these Geneva Convention articles and so forth. Like, you know, inhumane and degrading treatment, well, this specifically relates to POWs, so we don't have to do this. So basically, we can do inhumane and degrading treatment. And then they went on to the actual treatment itself, what we were doing, what we'd signed off on and those types of things: cold water and nudity, strobe lights, loud music—that's not inhumane because they're able to rebound from it. And they claim no lasting mental effects or physical marks or anything, or permanent damage of any kind, so it's not inhumane ... I was very annoyed with them because

they were saying things like we didn't have to abide by the Geneva Conventions, because these people weren't POWs … It just went against everything we learned …

According to Tony Lagouranis, another Army interrogator stationed in Iraq: 'Early on, it seemed like as long as you didn't seriously injure or kill a prisoner, you were within the guidelines … Death crosses the line, but you know, torture doesn't.' A sergeant with the 82nd Airborne Division agreed. He said: 'Leadership failed to provide clear guidance so we just developed it. They wanted intel. As long as no PUCs [Persons Under Control] came up dead it happened. We heard rumors of PUCs dying so we were careful. We kept it to broken arms and legs and shit.'

On 12 October, Sanchez issued a new directive rolling back some of the SERE techniques authorised in the September memos. The October memo did not ban the use of coercive techniques, but directed that approval should first be sought before the techniques are employed. The October directive includes the following advice:

> In employing each of the authorized approaches, the interrogator must maintain control of the interrogation. The interrogator should appear to be the one who controls all aspects of the interrogation, to include the lighting, heating, and configuration of the interrogation room, as well as the food, clothing and shelter given to the security detainee.

This familiar passage was lifted nearly word-for-word from the superseded 1987 version of the *Intelligence Interrogation* field manual. Its content reflects Project X material from the 1960s—material that was ordered destroyed in 1992 after the exposure of Mobile Training Team (MTT) and School of the Americas torture training.

To phase in the SERE techniques, the Pentagon reactivated MTTs. Their mission wasn't to teach torture to Latin Americans: it was to teach it to Americans. From 7 to 21 October 2003, a five-person Mobile Training Team was dispatched from Fort Huachuca, the original depository of Project X material, to provide training at the infamous Abu Ghraib prison. Even before Americans arrived, the sprawling 105-hectare British-built complex had a dark reputation. At its peak under Saddam Hussein, up to 50 000 men and women were housed at the prison, with as many as 150 prisoners crammed into cells designed for twenty-four. Torture chambers and rooms with gallows, complete with hidden trapdoors, were spread throughout the facility. Immediately following the fall of Baghdad in April 2003, Iraqis looted and destroyed the prison, leaving only a smoldering shell. Rather than dismantle the remains of a building that was once the ultimate symbol of Baathist oppression, US forces renovated it. On 4 August 2003, Abu Ghraib reopened, complete with new showers, ceiling fans, toilets, windows and tiled floors. The prison took on detainees from a nearby facility at the Baghdad International Airport known as Camp Cropper and from Camp Bucca, a prison in southern Iraq near Basra. According to Brigadier General Janis L. Karpinski, the commander initially in charge of the military police (MP) at Abu Ghraib, a stay at Abu Ghraib was like a lavish vacation. The 'living conditions now are better in prison than at home', Karpinski said in December 2003. 'At one point we were concerned they wouldn't want to leave.'

The MTT sent to Abu Ghraib had previously worked with interrogators at Guantánamo and observed detention operations at Bagram Air Base in Afghanistan. At Abu Ghraib, the MTT taught interrogators and private contractors a range of SERE techniques. One of the MTT teachers, a soldier identified as Sergeant First Class Walters, later approached military investigators because he was concerned, he said, that 'he may have contributed to the abuse at Abu Ghraib'. According to Walters, he was asked by a civilian interrogator at the prison for 'ideas as to how to get these prisoners to talk'. Walter recalled:

> I told him that I'd heard that dogs had been used successfully and that they could be intimidating. I told him the story about the dog that was trained to bark on cue and suggested that he talk to the MPs about the possibilities. I told him that the basic approach strategies would be most successful within the first few hours of capture, because that's when a prisoner's stress level was highest and once they become accustomed to the environment, their stress level decreases and their resistance increases. I told him that these prisoners are captured by soldiers, taken from their familiar surroundings, blindfolded and put into a truck and brought to this place; and then they are pushed down a hall with guards barking orders and thrown into a cell, naked; and that not knowing what was going to happen or what the guards might do

caused them extreme fear. I told him that he should explain to the guards how this fear works to his advantage and tell them not to get friendly with the prisoners, or try to converse with them or give them cigarettes and stuff. I told him that the guards should appear as though they could be harsh, abrasive and … I used some extremely harsh words to describe the level of fear that the prisoner should feel. I told him that this fear, the guards, this place all come together to create a harsh environment and that this sets the stage for the interrogator. I told him that he should be the first friendly face the prisoner sees, and that the prisoner will want to talk to relieve his fear. I suggested he have someone take some pictures of what seemed to be guards being rough with prisoners, so he can use them to scare the prisoners.

Walters told investigators: 'I did not intend for any prisoner to get hurt. My only intent was for the prisoner to imagine what could happen.'

The Red Cross was the first agency to cite systematic torture at the prison. The worst abuses took place at the 'hard site', a block of 203 concrete cells that held 'high priority' detainees. The International Committee of the Red Cross (ICRC) inspected Abu Ghraib on 21–23 October 2003 and visited this section of the prison. According to the ICRC report issued to American forces following the visit, Red Cross officials found inmates 'completely naked in totally empty concrete cells and in total darkness, allegedly for several consecutive days'. According to a military intelligence officer interviewed by the ICRC, this technique was 'part of the process'. The ICRC also observed violent SERE techniques in use, including inmates:

[b]eing forced to remain for prolonged periods in stress positions such as squatting or standing with or without the arms lifted. Hooding, used to prevent people from seeing and to disorient them … used in conjunction with beatings thus increasing anxiety as to when blows would come … Being held in solitary confinement combined with threats (to intern the individual indefinitely, to arrest other family members, to transfer the individual to Guantánamo), insufficient sleep, food or water deprivation … Exposure while hooded to loud noise or music, prolonged exposure while hooded to the sun over several hours,

including during the hottest time of the day when temperatures could reach 50 degrees Celsius (122 degrees Fahrenheit) or higher … Acts of humiliation such as being made to stand naked against the wall of the cell with arms raised or with women's underwear over the head for prolonged periods while being laughed at by guards, including female guards, and sometimes photographed in this position …

The effects of these tortures were significant and shocking. ICRC medical delegates found that one prisoner held in solitary confinement 'was unresponsive to verbal and painful stimuli. His heart rate was 120 beats per minute and his respiratory rate 18 per minute. He was diagnosed as suffering from somatoform (mental) disorder, specifically a conversion disorder, most likely due to the ill-treatment he was subjected to during interrogation.' Other inmates at the hard site were 'presenting signs of concentration difficulties, memory problems, verbal expression difficulties, incoherent speech, acute anxiety reactions, abnormal behavior and suicidal tendencies'. ICRC doctors concluded that '[t]hese symptoms appeared to have been caused by the methods and duration of interrogation'. Despite these damning observations—made before the bulk of the Abu Ghraib photos were taken—American officials did nothing to remedy the situation. In fact, when the Red Cross came back to inspect the prison in January and March 2004, Colonel Thomas M. Pappas, then head of military intelligence, and Colonel Mark Warren, a Pentagon legal adviser, barred inspectors' access to eight 'high value' detainees, including one detained in a cell measuring less than one by two metres and devoid of any windows, bedding or toilet. Inspectors noted that a picture of the character Gollum from the *Lord of the Rings* films was taped to the door, a reference to the nickname given to the inmate by prison staff.

Military police at Abu Ghraib carried out the bulk of the torture. They were placed under the command of MI following a visit by General Geoffrey Miller, then commander at Guantánamo. From 31 August to 9 September 2006, Miller—along with nine other officials from Guantánamo—toured half a dozen prisons in Iraq, including Abu Ghraib. The team was sent to suggest ways to produce greater yields of 'actionable intelligence'. In his report to Pentagon superiors, Miller wrote that 'the detention operation does not yet set conditions for successful operations'. Miller recommended that MP

and MI unify, an arrangement in place at Guantánamo. 'It is essential',
Miller said, 'that the guard force be actively engaged in setting the
conditions for successful exploitation of the internees'.

According to Sergeant Samuel Provance, an MI officer at the
prison, 'Setting the conditions for interrogations was strictly dictated
by military intelligence. They weren't the ones carrying it out, but
they were the ones telling the MPs to wake the detainees up every
hour on the hour', or to limit their food, leave detainees naked, or
force them to wear women's underwear, he told the *Washington Post*.
According to the lawyer representing Staff Sergeant Ivan 'Chip'
Douglas, one of the seven low-level reservists charged in the wake of
the scandal, the interrogation plans directing harsh tortures were never
written down. 'Everybody is far too subtle and smart for that ...
Realistically, there is a description of an activity, a suggestion that it
may be helpful and encouragement that this is exactly what we needed',
he said. Douglas was sentenced to eight years in prison. Charles Graner,
later sentenced to ten, testified: 'I nearly beat a military intelligence
detainee to death with military intelligence there. We treated each
military detainee specifically on how the handler wanted.' The direc-
tions, said convicted reservist Megan Ambuhl, were specific. 'Laugh
and point at his penis while naked, run him into things ... strip him
[of] all clothing, bedding, diet manipulation, cut his clothes off with a
knife, etc.', she recounted. Lynndie England, the cherub-faced reservist
featured in some of the most sexually explicit images and sentenced to
three years, also alleged that she was following orders from superiors.
'I was told to stand here, point thumbs up, look at the camera and take
the picture', she said. 'They were for psy-op [psychological operations]
reasons, and the reasons worked. I mean ... to us, we were doing
our job, which meant we were doing what we were told. And the
outcome was what they wanted. They just told us, hey, you're doing
great. Keep it up.'

The worst abuses at the prison took place between October and
December 2003. During this time, 'sadistic, blatant, and wanton' acts of
cruelty were inflicted on detainees, according to a report by Major
General Antonio M. Taguba. This investigation was launched in January
2004 after military police reservist Specialist Joseph Darby slipped a
compact disc containing the now infamous torture photos to superiors. 'It violated everything I personally believed in and all I'd been
taught about the rules of war', said Darby, who was later awarded the

prestigious John F. Kennedy Profile in Courage Award. Antonio Tuguba led the first of nearly a dozen Pentagon investigations into the abuse at Abu Ghraib. The mandate given to Tuguba—like all other investigators hand-picked by top Pentagon officials—was to catalogue the actions of low-level soldiers, not to analyse how policy crafted in Washington affected conditions at the prison. The reason for the narrow mandate is self-evident: the torture was condoned at the top.

Tuguba interviewed scores of detainees at the prison. Ameen Sa'eed al-Sheikh, a Syrian taken to Abu Ghraib in October 2003, said that when he arrived at the hard site:

> They received me there with screaming, shoving, pushing and pulling. They forced me to walk from the main gate to my cell. Otherwise they would have broken my leg. I was in a very bad shape. When I went to the cell, they took my crutches and I didn't see it since. Inside the cell they asked me to strip naked; they didn't give me blanket or clothes or anything. Every hour or two, soldiers came, threatening me they were going to kill me and torture me and I'm going to be in prison forever and they might transfer me to Guantánamo Bay … Sometime they said, 'We will make you wish to die and it will not happen.' The night guard came over, his name is Graner, open the cell door, came in with a number of soldiers. They forced me to eat pork and put liquor in my mouth. They put this substance on my nose and forehead and it was very hot … One of them told me he would rape me. He drew a picture of a woman to my back and makes me stand in shameful position holding my buttocks. Someone else asked me, 'Do you believe in anything?' I said to him, 'I believe in Allah.' So he said, 'But I believe in torture and I will torture you.' Then they handcuffed me and hung me to the bed. They ordered me to curse Islam and because they started to hit my broken leg, I cursed my religion. They ordered me to thank Jesus I'm alive. And I did what they ordered me. This is against my belief. They left me hang from the bed and after a while I lost consciousness.

Tuguba concluded that torture at Abu Ghraib was physical, psychological and sexual in scope. Detainees were punched, slapped, kicked, forcibly arranged in sexually explicit positions, forced to remain nude for days at a time, forced to wear women's underwear, positioned into piles and jumped upon, subjected to mock executions, forced to masturbate and simulate fellatio, positioned into painful positions for hours and held in solitary confinement for weeks at a time. Inmates were also threatened with live firearms, doused in cold water, beaten with chairs and broom handles, threatened with rape, sodomised with chemical glow sticks, and bitten by unmuzzled attack dogs.

Explicit sexual tortures were likely the products of behavioural science teams sent into Abu Ghraib after Miller's visit. In his September assessment, Miller observed that BSCTs 'are essential in developing integrated interrogation strategies and assessing interrogation intelligence production'. As at Guantánamo, BSCTs at Abu Ghraib helped design and calibrate the interrogation regimes of inmates. According to Colonel Pappas, 'A physician and a psychiatrist are on hand to monitor what we are doing [during interrogations] ... The doctor and psychiatrist also look at the files to see what the interrogation plan recommends; they have the final say as to what is implemented'.

Behavioural scientists at Abu Ghraib instructed interrogators that Arabs 'really hate being sexually humiliated', said interrogator Tony Lagouranis, who was stationed at Abu Ghraib in January 2004. According to another Pentagon inquiry into prisoner abuse, authored by Major General George Fay, military intelligence interrogators started 'directing nakedness' soon after the arrival of BSCTs in order 'to humiliate and break down detainees'. In turn, the Fay report noted, forced nudity likely 'contributed to an escalating "de-humanization" of the detainees and set the stage for additional and more severe abuses to occur'.

Lagouranis also noted that BSCTs at Abu Ghraib encouraged the notion that violent tactics were the best way to break down Arab detainees. According to Lagouranis:

> Soon as I got to Abu Ghraib, we were given a brief by a psychiatrist, an Army psychiatrist. He didn't know anything about Arabs or Arabic or Islam, but he'd read a few books and told us things like, 'Don't expect to ever get a timeline out of an Arab. They can't think like that, they can't think linearly; they have to think associatively.' ... Or that 'Arabs, it's part of their culture to lie,' you know. 'They just lie all the time and don't even know that they're doing it.'

Lagouranis said that racist beliefs about Arabs 'added to the frustration and probably contributed to this culture of abuse'. In particular, the belief that Arabs are especially terrified of dogs—reflected in Sanchez's 10 September authorisation of the use of dogs—led to wide-scale abuses. Colonel Pappas later testified to investigators that he personally approved the use of dogs to frighten detainees. 'In my view, it was to establish control', he said. In one particularly disturbing case, one Army specialist said he witnessed an MP and a dog handler taunt juvenile detainees with an unmuzzled canine. In an interview with investigators with the Fay inquiry, the specialist recalled:

> The MP guard and MP Dog Handler opened a cell in which two juveniles ... were housed. The Dog Handler allowed the dog to enter the cell and go nuts on the kids, barking and scaring them. The kids were screaming, the smaller one hiding behind [Redacted]. The Handler allowed the dog to get within about one foot of the kids. Afterward, I heard the Dog Handler say that he had a competition with another Handler to see if they could scare detainees to the point that they would defecate. He mentioned that they had already made some urinate, so they appeared to be raising the competition.

In addition to pointing out cultural vulnerabilities, it appears that BSCT staff corrupted the traditional roles of doctors and nurses at Abu Ghraib. After the arrival of the BSCT teams, medical staff charged with serving the detainee population's health began tacitly to condone the abuse. Although it was 'outside the scope of this investigation', Fay noted that 'medical personnel may have been aware of detainee abuse at Abu Ghraib and failed to report it'. For example, Medic Reuben Layton observed the MPs' treatment of the Syrian detainee Ameen Sa'eed al-Sheikh, but didn't alert the Criminal Investigation Division (CID). Instead, Layton advised guards to stop beating his wounded leg and not to suspend him by his wounded shoulder. In another case, Nurse Helga Margot Aldape-Moreno later told investigators she saw a 'pyramid of naked guys who had sandbags over their heads ... almost like cheerleaders'. Sergeant Ivan 'Chip' Frederick punched one of the detainees in the chest and the prisoner collapsed to the ground. Aldape-Moreno simply examined the man, recorded that he had an 'anxiety attack', then left him with the guards. Once, medics even let

Graner stitch up wounds he inflicted on detainees. In a statement
deemed credible by Tuguba, detainee Shalan Ṣaid al-Sharoni said he
saw MPs brutally beat six naked Iraqi generals. According to
al-Sharoni:

> they beat them up until they dropped on the floor and one of
> them his nose was cut and the blood was running from his nose
> and he was screaming but no one was responding ... The doctor
> came to stitch the nose and the [Specialist Charles] Grainer [sic]
> asked the doctor to learn how to stitch and it's true, the guard
> learned how to stitch. He took the string and the needle and he
> sat down to finish the stitching until the operation succeeded ...
> And after that they beat up the rest of the group until they fall to
> the ground.

A host of long established medical ethical guidelines explicitly
ban medical complicity in torture. The provisions of the Hippocratic
Oath and the Nuremburg Code are reaffirmed in instruments such as
the World Medical Association's *Declaration of Tokyo of 1975* and the
UN *Principles of Medical Ethics Relevant to the Protection of Prisoners
Against Torture*. According to Principle 4 of this resolution:

> It is a contravention of medical ethics for health personnel,
> particularly physicians:
>
> (a)   To apply their knowledge and skills in order to assist in
>   the interrogation of prisoners and detainees in a manner
>   that may adversely affect the physical or mental health
>   or condition of such prisoners or detainees ...
>
> (b)   To certify, or to participate in the certification of, the
>   fitness of prisoners or detainees for any form of treatment
>   or punishment that may adversely affect their physical
>   or mental health and which is not in accordance with
>   the relevant international instruments, or to participate
>   in any way in the infliction of any such treatment or
>   punishment ...

According to Dr Robert Jay Lifton—a noted psychiatrist who
studied communist methods of coercion for the US Air Force in the
1950s—the mere presence of BSCT and non-BSCT doctors at Abu

Ghraib, and by logical extension at Guantánamo, helped to 'confer an aura of legitimacy' to the violence. 'Even without directly participating in the abuse', said Lifton, doctors 'by virtue of their medical authority helped sustain it'.

In addition to the advice of BSCTs, medical staff complicity, authorisation of SERE techniques, MTT training, and the placement of military police under MI control, there was one more significant factor that fostered abuse at Abu Ghraib. Soon after Geoffrey Miller's visit, significant numbers of interrogators in civilian clothing—believed to be both CIA and special forces interrogators—began to arrive at the prison. Their presence most likely stemmed from Miller's suggestion that greater 'internee access' be granted to CIA and special forces officials operating in Iraq. According to Walter Diaz, an MP at the prison, interrogators in civilian clothes routinely beat Iraqi prisoners behind closed doors. Said Diaz, 'We'd lock the door for them and leave. We didn't know what they were doing ... [but] we heard a lot of screaming'. One detainee who did not survive a violent CIA interrogation was Manadel al-Jamadi. He died in a position dubbed a 'Palestinian hanging': he was first handcuffed, then strung up against a shower room window by his wrists. When he was removed, one MP noted, blood gushed from his mouth 'as if a faucet had been turned on'. Mark Swanner, the CIA agent directing his interrogation, has not been charged. MP commander Janet Karpinski, the highest ranking officer disciplined in connection with torture at Abu Ghraib, claimed that she didn't know who was operating in her prison. The CIA and special forces interrogators used only first names. 'I thought most of the civilians there were interpreters, but there were some civilians that I didn't know. I called them the disappearing ghosts ... [They were] always bringing in somebody for interrogation or waiting to collect somebody going out', she said. General Fay found that these ghosts—plus the 'ghost detainees' they kept off the official prison register—contributed to the culture of violence in the prison. In particular, he said their activities 'led to a loss of accountability, abuse, reduced interagency cooperation, and an unhealthy mystique that further poisoned the atmosphere at Abu Ghraib'.

Investigative reporter Seymour Hersh revealed that some of the ghosts at the prison were members of a secret hit squad created under a Pentagon Special Access Program (SAP). Pentagon SAPs are black operations shielded from normal budgetary oversight. During the

Cold War, SAPs were used to build aircraft such as the Stealth bomber and to fund secret sabotage missions against the USSR. According to Hersh, Rumsfeld created a new SAP after 9/11 to hunt down Osama bin Laden and members of al Qaeda. These forces, composed of Army Special Forces, Rangers, Delta Force units, and Navy SEALs, operated with little or no oversight. Their tactics were so violent, Hersh noted, that the CIA refused to work with the group at Abu Ghraib. According to one official briefed on their existence, their mission was to 'Grab whom you must. Do what you want'.

While little is known about the precise interrogation methods used by SAP personnel behind closed doors at Abu Ghraib, a good indication of SAP techniques comes from statements made by ex-officers and ex-detainees of Task Force 6-26. An internal Pentagon investigation revealed that some SAP personnel were assigned to this task force, a shadowy unit based until 2005 at Camp Nama, a former Baathist torture chamber on the outskirts of Baghdad International Airport. Task Force 6-26 was formed in mid 2003 from two Special Operations units: one that hunted bin Laden in Afghanistan and another that sought Saddam Hussein. From 2003 to 2006, the new task force, initially known as Task Force 121 and today as Task Force 145, hunted Abu Musab al-Zarqawi—the Jordanian insurgency leader later killed by US air strikes. Suspected insurgents apprehended in their search for Zarqawi were received at Nama before being taken to Abu Ghraib for detention. Few rules, if any, governed the conduct of 6-26. Posted throughout Nama was a sign that reminded interrogators 'NO BLOOD, NO FOUL'.

The torture techniques at Nama were heavily influenced by SERE. According to one former 6-26 interrogator, the unit's most violent interrogations took place in the 'black room', a bare space with no windows, 3.6 by 3.6 metres in size. 'The door was black, everything was black', he said. In the 'black room' interrogators used a variety of SERE techniques. He recalled that:

> usually in the black room nobody was sitting down. It was standing, stress positions, and so forth. The table would be for the boom box and the computer. We patched it into the speakers and made the noise and stuff. Most of the harsh interrogations were in that room ... Sleep deprivation, environmental controls, hot and cold, water ... I never saw anybody who was hot, you know,

but it was cold a lot of times or we used cold water, we poured cold water onto them. [Certain times interrogators would] take clothes from the prisoners and so forth … loud music, strobe lights—they were used as well.

SERE torture was not limited to the black room. Outside there was a courtyard where various harsh interrogations took place. One involved a detainee believed to be linked to Zarqawi. According to the interrogator:

He was stripped naked, put in the mud and sprayed with the hose, with very cold hoses, in February. At night it was very cold. They sprayed the cold hose and he was completely naked in the mud, you know, and everything. [Then] he was taken out of the mud and put next to an air conditioner. It was extremely cold, freezing, and he was put back in the mud and sprayed. This happened all night. Everybody knew about it. People walked in, the sergeant major and so forth, everybody knew what was going on, and I was just one of them, kind of walking back and forth seeing [that] this is how they do things.

According to the interrogator, they had to get approval prior to using the techniques. 'There was an authorization template on a computer, a sheet that you would print out, or actually just type it in. And it was a checklist. And it was all already typed out for you, environmental controls, hot and cold, you know, strobe lights, music, so forth … I never saw a sheet that wasn't signed', he said. Abuse by the unit grew so extreme that the FBI banned its interrogators from participating with 6-26—a measure the CIA took as well. One detainee who suffered through a host of SERE tortures at Nama later recounted:

The interpreter told me to take off my clothes … So I took off all my clothes. Then he put the bag back over my head. I was taken to another room that had black walls and an air conditioner. Water was poured on the bag, my neck and shoulders, the air conditioner was turned very cold and I was made to stand in front of it. The only light in the room was a flashlight. There was a stereo in the room. They made me listen to a bad movie in

English language, then some American music, then sounds of children crying. A box was put over my head and something wet on my neck. I was told to walk from wall to wall. I could not see and walked into the walls, which would press the box into my chest. This caused me pain which lasted a couple of weeks. The interrogator asked if I would now tell the truth. I told him I had said everything I know. He asked me if I was tough enough to continue. I told him no. He put me in front of the air conditioner and poured more cold water on me, keeping me wet. Then he put an MRE [Meals Ready to Eat, the military's pre-packaged food] in each of my hands and made me push them towards the ceiling. I held them up for a while then my arms began to drop. Someone punch me in my spine, below my shoulder blades with a fist. I passed out ...

An Army CID inquiry into this detainee's allegations was stymied on several fronts. One CID unit stated that they were 'unable to thoroughly investigate ... due to the suspects' and witnesses' involvement in Special Access Program's (SAP) and/or the security classification of the unit they were assigned to during the offense under investigation'. Another investigator noted that '6-26 had a major computer malfunction which resulted in them losing 70 percent of their files; therefore they can't find the cases we need to review'. Still another agent found that it was impossible to investigate people known only by pseudonyms. Due to lack of evidence, the investigation was closed and the detainee's allegation was judged to have been 'unfounded'. According to one frustrated CID official: 'This investigation meets the necessary requirements and does not need to be reopened. Hell, even if we reopened it we wouldn't get anymore information than we already have.'

In contrast to Abu Ghraib, no BSCTs or MTTs directed the torture at Nama. Instead, it appears that members of the Task Force used their personal knowledge of SERE to torture prisoners. Task Force 6-26 was composed mainly of special forces, and since 1984, Level C SERE training has been mandatory for all special forces soldiers. According to senior SERE psychologist Colonel Louie Banks, in 2004—while Task Force 6-26 operations at Nama were at their peak—he discovered that many former students were using the techniques they learned at SERE against prisoners. According to the

New Yorker, this problem grew so widespread that Banks 'introduced a new requirement at SERE: graduates must sign a statement promising not to apply the program's counter-resistance methods to US-held detainees'. Banks later recalled, 'We did this when we learned people were flipping it'.

Soldiers at Camp Nama weren't the only ones to flip SERE techniques. SERE instructors deployed to Iraq also flipped the program's DDD-style methods. On 10 November 2003, Abed Hamed Mowhoush, an Iraqi Major General, walked into Forward Operating Base 'Tiger' in Qaim to inquire about the arrest of his four sons. Members of the 3rd Armored Cavalry—the same division where an interrogator responded to Ponce's 'wish list' by noting that he 'firmly agreed the gloves must come off'—arrested Mowhoush on the spot. During Saddam's reign, the General was a high-ranking official in the Republican Guard and was suspected by Americans to be supporting the insurgency. During the first few days of his detention, interrogators noted his co-operation and Mowhoush admitted to commanding a group of Saddam loyalists responsible for several attacks. A week into his detention, interrogators grew unhappy with his answers. An interrogation report (which cites Abed as 'Abid') dated 18 November states: 'Previous interrogations were non-threatening; Abid was being treated very well. Not anymore ... The interrogation session lasted several hours and I took the gloves off because Abid refused to play ball.'

Mowhoush's lead interrogator was Warrant Officer Lewis Welshofer, who had worked for several years as an instructor at a SERE program at Hickam Air Force Base in Hawaii. On 24 November 2003, Welshofer stood by as the General was savagely beaten by CIA and special forces interrogators, along with members of an Iraqi paramilitary squad called the Scorpions. The next day, Welshofer increased the pressure. First he took him up to the roof of the detention centre, held him down and poured water on his head. Later that evening, he arranged a meeting between Mowhoush and his youngest son, Muhammad. During their brief time together, the sixteen-year-old was subjected to a mock execution. Muhammad and his brothers were released uncharged. Today, he is convinced that his father thought he died.

On 26 November, Welshofer forced Mowhoush into a sleeping bag, slapped him, covered his mouth, wrapped the sleeping bag with wire, and then sat on the General's chest. Mowhoush died while in the bag. According to an autopsy, the cause of death was 'asphyxiation due to smothering and chest compression'. Although at least two others took part in the fatal interrogation, Welshofer was the only person charged in the murder.

During his court martial, Welshofer repeatedly justified his actions by claiming he used these same techniques on American soldiers in the SERE program without incident. Welshofer said: 'I do not believe that I ever operated outside acceptable methods of intelligence collection. While an outside spectator may view the interrogation techniques as being tough, I would point out that these techniques were meant to elicit information from resistant sources.' He claimed that the sleeping bag technique was a commonly used SERE method. According to Welshofer:

> This position is designed to see if a person is claustrophobic. In SERE … we frequently used close confinement positions, both as a group and as an individual stress position … This position capitalizes on the subject's fear of tight places. Anyone who is claustrophobic gives an almost immediate response. While using the sleeping bag technique someone who squirms or screams and is obviously having an adverse reaction is allowed out as soon as they start to provide information (incentive) … When the sleeping bag was used on the general, he was able to control his breathing … I believe the technique used was acceptable.

Transcripts from the court martial proceedings document Welshofer's unfolding SERE defence:

> Defense [attorney]: You also poured water on the General, what technique was that?
> Welshofer: Fear up harsh.
> Defense: Was that a technique they taught [during regular training]?
> Welshofer: No sir.
> Defense: Why did you think you could use it?
> Welshofer: It's a technique we used in Hawaii.
> Defense: Describe it.

Welshofer: We laid the General on his back and I poured bits of
     water on him intermittently.
Defense: Where?
Welshofer: On his face.
Defense: Was he able to move?
Welshofer: Yes sir, he was able to move his face from side to side.

When Welshofer's superior officer, Company Commander Major
Jessica Voss, observed Welshofer slapping Mowhoush, she asked him if
it was a necessary technique. 'He explained it was something he learned
in SERE school. He said it was open-handed. It was intended to shock
the detainee, not hurt him', Voss testified. Welshofer also noted that
covering Mowhoush's mouth was yet another SERE technique:

Defense: Why did you place your right hand over his mouth
     [while the General was in the sleeping bag]?
Welshofer: I have a rule with detainees. I forbid them to use the
     word 'Wallah'. You know, 'I shot the RPG [rocket propelled
     grenade], Wallah.' In this case I had to enforce the rule ... I
     covered the mouth three, maybe, five, maybe 10 seconds ... It
     was like enough with the Wallah ...
Defense: At any time did you do anything to impair the General's
     breathing?
Welshofer: No sir.
Defense: Is there anything you may have done that may have
     impaired the General's breathing whether you intended to or
     not?
Welshofer: No sir.

The prosecutor asked Welshofer specifically about use of the word
'Wallah':

Prosecutor: What is wrong with saying Wallah?
Welshofer: In Hawaii, you try to identify something to throw
     them out of their comfort zone. You identify something and
     take it away.
Prosecutor: You took away his god?
Welshofer: Basically, yes, I took away his Wallah.
Prosecutor: And what does that mean?

Welshofer: It's like we say 'I swear to God.'

Prosecutor: You took away his god?

Welshofer: I took away one of his comfort items.

After one week of testimony, the six-person jury sided with Welshofer. He wasn't convicted of murder, for which he would have faced up to a life sentence, but of a lesser charge: negligent homicide. He was fined US$6000 and sentenced to sixty days' confinement in his home. No jail sentence was imposed.

———

THE DUAL STATE

O n the morning of 6 September 2006, top officials gathered at the Pentagon to announce the release of a new Army field manual on interrogation. Across the Potomac River, President Bush readied himself for a national televised address from the White House's East Wing. The Pentagon press conference started first.

'The Army has taken pretty dramatic steps over the last two and a half years to improve our human intelligence capabilities and capacity, to include interrogation ... And by interrogation, I really mean getting truthful answers to time-sensitive questions on the battlefield', began Lieutenant General John Kimmons, Army Deputy Chief of Staff for Intelligence. He then unveiled the *Human Intelligence Collector Operations* field manual, which replaced the 1992 version of *Intelligence Interrogation*. Cully Stimson, the Deputy Assistant Secretary of Defense for Detainee Affairs, added that it 'incorporates the lessons we have learned over the past few years in waging the global war on terror'. This was quite an understatement.

The *Human Intelligence Collector Operations* manual expressly bans all coercive techniques previously used in Guantánamo, Iraq and Afghanistan. The new standards are explicit: 'All prisoners and detainees, regardless of status, will be treated humanely. Cruel, inhuman and degrading treatment is prohibited.' The prohibited acts all seem to have been lifted from the Tuguba report. They include 'forcing an individual to perform or simulate sexual acts or to pose in a sexual manner; exposing an individual to outrageously lewd and sexually provocative behavior; intentionally damaging or destroying an individual's religious articles'. In a separate section, the manual also bans the following tech-niques during interrogation: 'Placing hoods or sacks over the head of a detainee; using duct tape over the eyes; Applying beatings, electric shock, burns, or other forms of physical pain; "Waterboarding"; Using military working dogs; Inducing hypothermia or heat injury; Conducting mock executions; Depriving the detainee of necessary food, water, or medical care.' In short, it bans most of the SERE tech-niques previously authorised by Donald Rumsfeld and Ricardo A. Sanchez. The manual also includes a clear condemnation of methods stressed by Major General Geoffrey Miller, who had since taken an early retirement amid fallout from Abu Ghraib. The new manual offers clear directives that separate the roles of military intelligence and military police. It reads: 'The standard MP security and internment functions are the only involvement the MPs have in the interrogation process. MPs will not take any actions to set conditions for inter-rogations (for example, "softening up" a detainee). For purposes of interrogation, military working dogs will not be used.'

The manual didn't stop there. It also explicitly incorporated the findings of *Hamdan v Rumsfeld*, a Supreme Court decision from two months earlier. In *Hamdan*, the court found that Common Article 3 applies to all enemy combatants detained by the United States. This ruling was a direct rebuke to the Bush administration for its assertion that al Qaeda and Taliban suspects fell outside the basic protections of Geneva.

Abiding by the decision of the court, the Pentagon reaffirmed in the new field manual that Common Article 3 applies to all detainees, including 'unlawful enemy combatants'. According to the manual, unlawful enemy combatants 'engage in acts against the United States or its coalition partners in violation of the laws and customs of war during an armed conflict' and the category is 'not limited to ... Taliban or al Qaeda forces'. Lawful combatants are entitled to all protections afforded POWs as stipulated in the *Geneva Convention relative to the Treatment of Prisoners of War*, while unlawful enemy combatants are subject only to the minimum standards of Common Article 3. Furthermore, it adds, there is one additional interrogation technique that is permissible for unlawful enemy combatants, subject to prior approval. It is called 'separation'. This is by far the harshest technique authorised by the manual. It involves keeping the detainee in isolation for up to thirty days. According to the manual:

Separation does not constitute sensory deprivation, which is prohibited. For the purposes of this manual, sensory deprivation is
defined as an arranged situation causing significant psychological
distress due to a prolonged absence, or significant reduction, of
the usual external stimuli and perceptual opportunities. Sensory
deprivation may result in extreme anxiety, hallucinations, bizarre
thoughts, depression, and anti-social behavior. Detainees will not
be subjected to sensory deprivation.

The manual lists several safeguards during the use of separation—
again obliquely referencing the torture at Abu Ghraib and elsewhere.
Detainees should be protected from excessive noise and dampness,
excessive or inadequate heat, light or ventilation, and inadequate bedding and blankets. It adds that 'use of separation must not preclude the
detainee getting four hours of continuous sleep every 24 hours. Use of
hoods (sacks) over the head, or of duct tape or adhesive tape over the
eyes, as a separation method is prohibited'.

The manual also incorporates elements of FBI interrogation
technique and includes an entire section on rapport-building methods.
'Building rapport', it begins, 'is an integral part of the approach
phase. The establishment of rapport begins when the HUMINT
[human intelligence] collector first encounters the source ...'. The
manual permits the use of 'futility' and 'fear-up', but stresses that they
may be employed only humanely. For example, when using 'fear–up',
an interrogator 'must be extremely careful that he does not threaten
or coerce a source ... [because] conveying a threat may be a violation
of the UCMJ'. Furthermore, only two techniques are added that
were not present in the 1992 manual: the good cop/bad cop technique employing two interrogators at the same time and a false flag
technique in which interrogators use false identities as a ruse 'to build
rapport'.

In addition to banning all torture and coercion, the manual discusses how these techniques are damaging for all parties involved. A
disclaimer notes:

Use of torture is not only illegal but also it is a poor technique
that yields unreliable results, may damage subsequent collection
efforts, and can induce the source to say what he thinks the
HUMINT collector wants to hear. Use of torture can also have

many possible negative consequences at national and international
levels.

Although separation could easily spill over into sensory deprivation if not carefully monitored, overall the new field manual represents
a fundamental shift in interrogation policy back to the humane standards
outlined in the 1992 field manual. General Kimmons ended the press
conference with an almost moving account of why the Pentagon
had so radically changed course. The *Hamdan* ruling, it appears, only
reinforced the lessons of Abu Ghraib. According to Kimmons:

> No good intelligence is going to come from abusive practices. I
> think history tells us that. I think the empirical evidence of the
> last five years, hard years, tell us that. Moreover, any piece of
> intelligence which is obtained under duress, through the use
> of abusive techniques, would be of questionable credibility, and
> additionally it would do more harm than good when it inevi-
> tably became known that abusive practices were used. And we
> can't afford to go there. Some of our most significant successes
> on the battlefield have been—in fact, I would say all of them,
> almost categorically all of them, have accrued from expert inter-
> rogators using mixtures of authorized humane interrogation
> practices in clever ways, that you would hope Americans would
> use them, to push the envelope within the bookends of legal,
> moral and ethical, now as further refined by this field manual. We
> don't need abusive practices in there. Nothing good will come
> from them.

————

It would give me great pleasure to end this book on such a high note.
I would love to conclude: 'After fifty-plus years of torture, Abu Ghraib
exposed the errors of American interrogation policy, and now all
torture is banned.' But I cannot. The Army field manual applies only
to agents of the Pentagon—all Army, Navy, Marine and Air Force
interrogators. The CIA, of course, does not abide by the new manual.

At 1.33 p.m. on 6 September 2006, George Bush began his speech.
He started by evoking the horror of 9/11 and segued into American
detention policy. He then revealed one of the CIA's worst-kept secrets:

the existence of black site prisons outside the United States. 'In addition to the terrorists held at Guantánamo, a small number of suspected terrorist leaders and operatives captured during the war have been held and questioned outside the United States, in a separate program operated by the Central Intelligence Agency', said Bush. Until this time, administration officials denied or simply 'refused to confirm' the existence of the program. James Pavitt, who headed covert operations at the CIA when the black site program was created, was relieved. 'Finally', he said, 'the burden of this program will not rest only on the shoulders of the CIA'.

The *Hamdan* ruling derailed two programs of the Bush administration: the Pentagon's military tribunal system and CIA black site interrogation operations. The tribunal system was unconstitutional because the Supreme Court found that the tribunals didn't constitute 'regularly constituted courts' as defined by Common Article 3. At Guantánamo, all impending cases, including David Hicks', were put on hold while new plans were drawn up. But at the CIA, the mood after *Hamdan* was more tense. The Office of Legal Counsel could no longer assure agents that techniques like waterboarding, induced hypothermia and forced standing for forty hours were still legal. Since Geneva applied, so too did the War Crimes Act. Many agents grew afraid they would be liable under the Act and bought special insurance policies to cover any civil judgments made against them. 'Aggressive' CIA interrogation techniques, said Director of National Intelligence John Negroponte, suddenly became 'problematic'.

Rather than follow the lead of the Pentagon and swear off coercion, President Bush decided on a different path. During his televised speech, Bush announced that Common Article 3 is 'vague and undefined' and could be 'interpreted in different ways by American or foreign judges'. He added that 'some believe our military and intelligence personnel involved in capturing and questioning terrorists could now be at risk of prosecution under the War Crimes Act—simply for doing their jobs in a thorough and professional way'. Bush then announced new legislation that would redefine breaches of Common Article 3 so CIA interrogators can continue to use SERE techniques. 'You can't ask a young professional on the front line of protecting this country to violate law', Bush later said.

The 6 September speech didn't end there. Bush also announced that fourteen prisoners held by the CIA had been transferred to

Guantánamo. These included Khalid Sheikh Mohammed and Abu Zubaydah—two men known to have suffered through the CIA's most violent methods. According to Bush, the 'CIA used an alternative set of procedures … I cannot describe the specific methods used … But I can say the procedures were tough, and they were safe, and lawful, and necessary.' In order for the men to 'face justice', said Bush, Congress must authorise a new military tribunal system and provide 'clarity' to the War Crimes Act. Politically it was a smart manoeuvre—with mid-term elections only months away Bush's advisers doubted that anyone in Congress would oppose the plan. Democrats who spoke out against it could be branded 'soft on terror'. By all accounts, the plan worked.

After the speech, the White House introduced new legislation ostensibly to 'clarify' portions of the War Crimes Act. One source told the *Washington Post* that the techniques sought by the administration 'include prolonged sleep deprivation and forced standing or other stress positions'. After some initial superficial modifications of the bill based on criticism by fellow Republicans, the White House released a final version of the *Military Commissions Act of 2006* (MCA) on 21 September—eight days before Congress was to adjourn for recess. The bill 'preserves the most single—most potent tool we have in protecting America and foiling terrorist attacks, and that is the CIA program to question the world's most dangerous terrorists and to get their secrets', said Bush. 'I hope the Congress will send me legislation before it wraps up their business next week.'

The MCA is sweeping in its authority and shocking in its contents. Among other things, it strips the writ of habeas corpus—the right to challenge grounds for detention—from all foreign nationals held by the United States anywhere across the globe. Non-citizens are also not permitted to file any claim relating to aspects of their 'detention, transfer, treatment, trial, or conditions of confinement'. The Act allows both secret evidence and coerced evidence to be admitted during trials of unlawful enemy combatants if it is considered relevant to the case. It defines an unlawful enemy combatant as *any* person who 'purposefully and materially supported hostilities against the United States'—an incredibly broad category that is not specific to the battle-field in Afghanistan or elsewhere. Further, it is a designation that the 'President or the Secretary of Defense' has the authority to make—with no check or balance. The Act then tears into the Geneva

Conventions. According to the MCA, no person—not even a US citizen—can invoke the rights guaranteed by Geneva in a court of law. Only the president, it states, can determine what is and what is not a breach of the conventions with respect to war crimes.

The MCA also narrows the scope of the War Crimes Act, and drags the clear standards of Common Article 3 into the grey zone. Under the original War Crimes Act, as amended in 1997, any violation of Common Article 3 is a war crime punishable under US law. A 'violation' of Common Article 3 is a broad category that outlaws 'outrages upon personal dignity' and 'humiliating and degrading treatment'. The MCA, retroactively applying new provisions, replaces 'violation' with 'grave breach' as the punishable criminal act. 'Grave breach' is a narrower category that outlaws only 'torture' and 'cruel or inhuman' treatment.

The MCA's ban on 'torture' is problematic but familiar—it is the same as the one laid out in the narrow federal torture statute: that is, acts that must be *specifically intended* to cause severe mental and physical pain. The MCA's key faults lie in its ban on 'cruel or inhuman' treatment. It stipulates that for an act to be 'cruel or inhuman' it must produce 'serious' physical or mental pain. A 'serious' act of physical pain is one that inflicts 'bodily injury' and involves either '(a) substantial risk of death; (b) extreme physical pain; (c) a burn or disfigurement of a serious nature (other than cuts, abrasions, or bruises); or (d) significant loss or impairment of the function of a bodily member, organ, or mental faculty'. Physical pain that does not fall into these categories is not, by definition, 'cruel or inhuman'. Mental pain is similarly limited. This type of pain is 'cruel or inhuman' only if it stems from any of the four predicate acts listed in the federal torture statute. These four acts include:

(a) the intentional infliction or threatened infliction of serious physical pain or suffering;
(b) the administration or application, or threatened administration or application, of mind-altering substances or other procedures calculated to disrupt profoundly the senses or the personality;
(c) the threat of imminent death; or
(d) the threat that another person will imminently be subjected to death, serious physical pain or suffering, or the administration or application of mind-altering substances or other procedures calculated to disrupt profoundly the senses or personality.

Finally, serious mental pain only constitutes 'cruel or inhuman' treatment if the mental suffering stems from one or more of the four acts above *and* produces 'non-transitory mental harm (which need not be prolonged)'. This means that only mental pain that is not brief yet not necessarily prolonged can be considered 'cruel or inhuman' and thus violate the War Crimes Act.

Confused? You're supposed to be. By making these standards murky, the Bush administration gives the OLC the necessary wiggle-room to define a range of coercive techniques as once again legal. While new OLC memoranda on torture are classified, the argument most likely goes like this: CIA interrogation techniques are not 'torture' because they do not inflict severe mental or physical pain. CIA techniques are also not 'cruel or inhuman'. Waterboarding produces brief mental pain (through the threat of imminent death) because the gag reflex kicks in for only a fraction of a second. Due to its transitory nature, it does not produce serious mental pain, thus it is not 'cruel or inhuman'. Hypothermia, sleep deprivation and hand-slaps do not produce serious physical pain because they do not inflict a bodily injury. While they may cause serious mental pain, they do not stem from any of the four predicate acts. This same analysis can apply to forced standing if limited in duration. (If it is not limited in duration, forced standing can inflict a bodily injury, via extreme physical pain and impairment of the function of a bodily member or organ.) In this way, waterboarding, hypothermia, sleep deprivation, slaps, and limited stints of forced standing all fall outside the range of acts outlawed under the amended War Crimes Act. The MCA makes all these changes retroactive back to 1997—immunising interrogators, and their superiors, from any litigation stemming from the use of these techniques.

The Act's opacity was its greatest strength. By deliberately obfuscating the definition of 'cruel or inhuman' treatment, the Bush administration concealed the true implications of the legislation from Congress. Stephen J. Hadley, the president's National Security Advisor, refused to brief Congress on precisely which techniques the CIA employed and what would be banned under the Act. 'If there's public discussion of techniques, then the terrorists are able to train against them', said Hadley, ignoring the fact that the US military explicitly outlined in the new field manual what its interrogators can and cannot do. As the *Boston Globe* reported: '[F]ewer than 10 percent of the members of Congress have been told which interrogation techniques have been used in the past, and none of them know which ones would be permissible under proposed changes to the War Crimes Act.' Some members of Congress seemed content with this arrangement. 'I don't know what the CIA has been doing, nor should I know', said Senator Jeff Sessions, an Alabama Republican who supported the Act.

In this atmosphere of secrecy, confusion and wilful blindness, the MCA was put to a vote. The few Democrats who criticised the ban were branded cowards—ineffectual leaders who preferred to 'coddle' terrorists rather than interrogate them. The bill passed on party lines in the House of Representatives 253 to 168 and in the Senate 65 to 34. On 17 October 2006, President Bush signed it into law.

———

In *The Dual State* (1941), Ernst Fraenkel argued that two modes of law characterised Nazi Germany: the normative and the prerogative. The former was administered by the courts; it protected and enforced ordinary statutes and regulations. The latter was controlled by the ruling party and was characterised by 'unlimited arbitrariness and violence unchecked by any legal guarantees'. These two spheres of law—one mundane and traditional, the other lawless and malicious— coexisted in the Nazi state.

America today is no Third Reich, but the legal parallels are striking. The United States now has a small body of prerogative law written by the ruling party for agents of the executive (the CIA), while normal federal, state and international law (reflected in the new Army field manual) exist for everyone else. There is a gross disparity between the authorised interrogation methods of the CIA and military rules for interrogation. One agency is permitted to violate the ban on torture contained in Common Article 3 while the other clearly cannot. Asked to explain the schism, Stephen A. Cambone, the Pentagon's Undersecretary of Defense for Intelligence, responded curtly: 'Each of us has our task to do.'

The current arrangement will perpetuate the confusion that plagued military interrogators after 9/11. Knowing that it is essentially legal for the CIA to torture will no doubt tempt interrogators— perhaps even detectives in American police departments—to use these same techniques. On a deeper level, the fact that the president has not repudiated these techniques will foster a variety of myths. As of late 2005, 61 per cent of Americans polled believed torture could be justified while 63 per cent said they supported secret detention and interrogation of terrorism suspects. Perhaps torture will lose its dark allure if its facts are laid bare.

Torture is self-defeating. The use of torture has been shown only to harden the wills of the enemies upon whom it has been used. The Tupamaros in Uruguay, for instance, only turned to direct violence after its members were tortured under the direction of Dan Mitrione. Tom Parker, a former agent for MI5, the British intelligence service, shared this view. 'The US is doing what the British did in the nineteen-seventies, detaining people and violating their civil liberties', he said. 'It did nothing but exacerbate the situation. Most of those interned went back to terrorism. You'll end up radicalizing the entire population.' An American Army sergeant of the 82nd Airborne who oversaw the use of numerous SERE tortures on detainees in Iraq perhaps said it best: 'If he [was] a good guy ... now he's a bad guy because of the way we treated him.'

Today, the images of Abu Ghraib are used as a powerful recruiting tool for al Qaeda across the globe. Christopher Hitchens has aptly described the fallout from the photos as a 'moral Chernobyl'. Before the Abu Ghraib scandal broke, a Coalition Provisional Authority poll showed that 63 per cent of Iraqis supported the occupation. One month after Abu Ghraib, the number dropped to 9 per cent. George Bush, in a rare moment of reflection on the deepening crisis in Iraq, said: 'I think the biggest mistake that's happened so far, at least from our country's involvement in Iraq is Abu Ghraib. We've been paying for that for a long period of time.' His comments are accurate, but puzzling: today the CIA is authorised to commit the same offences.

Burton L. Gerber, a former Moscow CIA station chief who spent thirty-nine years with the agency, has spoken out about torture's self-defeating character. 'Foreign nationals agree to spy for us for many different reasons; some do it out of an overwhelming admiration for America and what it stands for, and to those people, I think, America being associated with torture does affect their willingness to work with us', he said. 'But one of my arguments with the agency about ethics, particularly in this case, is that it's not about case studies, but philosophy. Aristotle says the ends and means must be in concert; if the ends and means are not in concert, good ends will be corrupted by bad means.'

Merle L. Pribbenow, another CIA veteran, was stationed throughout South-East Asia during his twenty-seven years with the agency. While working in Saigon, Pribbenow briefly took part in the interrogation of Nguyen Van Tai, the high-ranking Vietcong officer in the CIA's 'snow white cell'. Pribbenow also said that torture corrupts the moral standing of the United States. 'We, as Americans, must not let our methods betray our goals', he said. Another agent, in an interview with the *National Journal*, agreed that torture degrades the United States in the eyes of the world. He asked: 'Do you fight the enemy in the gutter, the same way, or maintain some kind of moral high ground?' He added, 'It's not just about what it does or doesn't do, but about who, and where, we as a country want to be'.

Like the United Kingdom, Israel later banned methods like induced hypothermia, stress positions and sensory deprivation. The Supreme Court found that despite 'the harsh reality of terrorism' against Israel, the methods of the Shin Bet were not grounded in the rule of law. 'This is the destiny of a democracy, as not all means are acceptable to it, and not all practices employed by its enemies are open before it', Court President Aharon Barak wrote in his lengthy decision. 'Although a democracy must often fight with one hand tied behind its back, it nonetheless has the upper hand.'

Torture is unnecessary. Some pundits and politicians have argued that torture is a necessary evil needed today to fight terrorism. 'The world changed on 9/11. Some people get that and some people don't', said Representative Tom Davis, a Virginia Republican who voted for the MCA. The necessity argument most often falls back on the so-called ticking time bomb case: a scenario where a bomb is planted in a hidden location and only torture can wring out answers from a reluctant suspect before the bomb goes off. Lawyer Alan Dershowitz has argued that in situations like this a judge should issue a 'torture warrant'—legal authorisation for severe torture such as the insertion of sterilised needles under a suspect's fingernails. Although the ticking time bomb scenario appears often on television, in reality it is incredibly improbable. In *A Question of Torture*, historian Alfred W. McCoy debunks this overworked rationale. He writes:

The fundamental flaw in this fanciful scenario is its pretzel-like, ex post facto logic. It assumes an improbable, even impossible, cluster of variables that runs something like this. First, the FBI or CIA captures a terrorist. Second, the capture takes place at the precise moment between a plot's launch and a bomb's burst. Third, the interrogators somehow have sufficiently detailed knowledge of the plot to know they must interrogate this very person and do it now, right now. Fourth, these same officers who have sufficient intelligence to know all about this specific terrorist and his ticking bomb are, for some unexplained reason, missing just a few critical details that only torture can divulge. Put simply, this constellation of circumstances is so far-fetched that the logic of Dershowitz's argument is sophistic if not spurious.

Even if we could justify torture in these (extremely unlikely) hypothetical circumstances, we could never be confident that we are actually *in* such a situation.

Seasoned academics are not the only critics who hold this opinion. During the 6 September Pentagon press conference, Cully Stimson, Deputy Assistant Secretary of Defense for Detainee Affairs, made the point that reality is far removed from television. 'So it's not like Sipowicz from the TV show [*NYPD Blue*] where they take them in the back room', he said. 'You're not going to get trustworthy information, as I understand it, from detainees. It's through a methodical, comprehensive, vetted, legal—and now transparent in terms of techniques—set of laydown that allows the interrogator to get the type of information that they need.'

Torture does not yield reliable information. From Vietnam, to Latin America, to Guantánamo Bay, physical and psychological torture has led to fanciful confessions designed to please interrogators and stop the sensation of pain. Given that the core elements of American torture—forced standing, humiliation and deprivation—were drawn from communist adversaries, this fact is not surprising. The KGB excelled in obtaining signatures from prisoners, but not the truth. George Bush has claimed that 'tough' techniques were effective on high-value detainees like Khalid Sheikh Mohammed and Abu Zubaydah. For example, during his 6 September address Bush claimed that under CIA questioning Zubaydah disclosed that KSM planned the 9/11 attacks and went by the nickname 'Muktar'. According to Bush, 'This was a vital piece of the puzzle that helped our intelligence community pursue KSM'. This claim was false on two fronts. According to the *New York Times*, Zubaydah identified KSM under FBI report-building techniques—not violent CIA methods. Second, various intelligence experts did not agree that this information was as crucial as Bush made out. In *The One Percent Doctrine* (2006), for example, Ron Suskind reported that a tipster collected US$25 million after leading the CIA directly to KSM. Intelligence officials told the *Washington Post* that Suskind's account is correct. Furthermore, the September 11 Commission reported that the CIA already knew KSM's alias as early as August 2001—more than six months before Zubaydah was captured.

Bush also claimed that under the CIA's 'alternative set of procedures', KSM revealed details of 'plots to kill innocent Americans'. Bush's claim is only vaguely based on fact. According to officials interviewed by *Newsweek*:

> KSM did reveal some names and plots. But they haven't panned out as all that threatening: one such plot was a plan by an al Qaeda operative to cut down the Brooklyn Bridge—with a blow torch. Intelligence officials could never be sure if KSM was holding back on more serious threats, or just didn't know of any.

Overall, *Newsweek* labeled President Bush's claims a 'confusing morass of stonewalling, half-truths and moral posturing wrapped up in politics and legalisms. The whole truth remains concealed behind a veil of government secrecy'.

One name that was absent from George Bush's 6 September speech was that of Ibn al-Shaykh al-Libi—the CIA's first victim of coercive SERE techniques. Sometime in 2003, al-Libi was rendered to a temporary CIA black site at Guantánamo. According to CIA officials, he initially revealed under torture a treasure trove of information about links between Saddam Hussein and al Qaeda. In particular, al-Libi claimed that Iraq had provided training in 'poisons and deadly gases' for al Qaeda—a claim that was restated repeatedly by the Bush administration in the lead-up to the war in Iraq. In October 2002, for instance, the president said in a speech in Cincinnati: '[W]e've learned that Iraq has trained Al Qaeda members in bomb making and poisons and gases'. The claim was also repeated by then Secretary of State

Colin Powell to bolster support for the Iraq war in his February 2003 speech to the United Nations. According to Powell, a 'senior al Qaeda terrorist' told interrogators that an al Qaeda militant was sent to Iraq three times between 1997 and 2000 to acquire 'poisons and gases'. The meetings between Iraq and al Qaeda were 'successful', said Powell.

While this claim helped to win over critics, it was false. As early as 2002, doubts were raised about al-Libi's tortured confessions. According to one Defense Intelligence Agency estimate, 'it is more likely this individual is intentionally misleading the debriefers'. After the invasion of Iraq, interrogators confronted al-Libi with new evidence that contradicted his claims. An official familiar with the case said that al-Libi 'subsequently recounted a different story'.

Torture is corruptive. Once officially condoned, torture cannot be contained. As we've seen, the SERE techniques approved only for the CIA in February 2002 quickly spread to Guantánamo, then Iraq. There is also evidence that the same methods were used in Afghanistan as well. As discussed in Chapter 8, at least three SERE psychologists were sent to Afghanistan in early 2002 to give advice about interrogation. In August 2002—the same month the OLC found that for an act to constitute torture it must produce pain akin to 'organ failure or death'—nine coercive interrogation tactics were approved for use at Bagram for Army interrogators. These methods closely resembled the CIA's SERE techniques. Among others, the expanded list included 'the use of dogs, stress positions, sleep management, [and] sensory deprivation'. By late 2002, the Fay report confirmed that Army interrogators at Bagram 'were removing clothing, isolating people for long periods of time, using stress positions, exploiting fear of dogs and implementing sleep and light deprivation'. A military intelligence officer at Bagram interviewed in early 2004 noted that Persons Under Control, or PUCs, were subjected to SERE techniques prior to interrogation. 'We keep the PUCs awake for the first twenty-four hours that they are here. We make them stand for twenty-four hours. We also keep them blindfolded for the first twenty-four hours', said the officer. The CIA, he said, 'guard their own PUCs' because 'they can't use drugs or prolonged sensory deprivation in our facility'.

Torture spreads because it is a seductive option for interrogators looking for easy answers. Rapport-building approaches to interrogation, such as those favoured by the FBI and now the Pentagon, require patience on the part of the interrogator. Torture is an easy alternative for interrogators too lazy to devote the time and effort to getting a suspect to talk. It's only a matter of time until '*Khong, danh cho co*'—'If they are innocent, beat them until they become guilty'—becomes the mantra of an agency where physical and mental coercion is officially condoned.

SERE techniques constitute torture. Approved CIA methods of interrogation have been termed by the White House and right-wing media as merely 'torture lite', an 'alternative set of methods', 'tough' techniques, or 'counter-resistance' methods. According to the conservative editors of the *Wall Street Journal*, acts permitted by the MCA like hypothermia, waterboarding and sleep deprivation are not '"torture" or even "abuse," as some Administration critics dishonestly charge'. Instead, they merely 'make life uncomfortable for al Qaeda prisoners'.

Euphemisms do not erase the fact that these methods constitute torture under internationally recognised definitions of the term. The original UN definition of torture from the CAT—the one uncorrupted by the United States' various understandings—states that torture is 'any act by which severe pain or suffering, whether physical or mental is intentionally inflicted on a person for such purposes as obtaining from him or a third person information or a confession …'. The range of techniques still used today in SERE schools and by the CIA clearly fall under this definition. According to the UN Committee Against Torture, stress positions, hooding and hypothermia 'constitute torture as defined in Article 1'. This is a view shared by the US State Department. Each year, the State Department's Country Reports on Human Rights have taken other countries to task for using these techniques. According to the 2005 report, rendition partners like Jordan, Syria and Egypt, in addition to extreme physical tortures like burning, pulling out fingernails, and beating, also use 'methods of torture' that include 'sleep deprivation', 'extended solitary confinement', and 'dousing victims with cold water'.

These techniques have been rightly called torture for decades. For example, in their 1956 report for the CIA, Hinkle and Wolff aptly noted that:

[t]he effects of isolation, anxiety, fatigue, lack of sleep, uncomfortable temperatures, and chronic hunger produce disturbances of

mood, attitudes, and behavior in nearly all prisoners. The living organism cannot entirely withstand such assaults. The Communists do not look upon these assaults as 'torture'. Undoubtedly, they use the methods which they do in order to conform, in a typical legalistic manner, to overt Communist principles which demand that 'no force or torture be used in extracting information from prisoners'. But these methods do, of course, constitute torture and physical coercion. All of them lead to serious disturbances of many bodily processes.

Nearly sixty years ago, the *Wall Street Journal* took a similar view, though of course back then they weren't talking about the United States using these techniques. Describing methods used by Communists in Bulgaria, the *Journal* noted that 'a favorite militia torture is to stand a person on his tiptoes, arms outstretched, his fingertips touching the wall'. Bulgarian police also used:

> psychological tortures including simulating terrifying sounds outside an already exhausted man's cell in the middle of the night, and the endless interrogations themselves—calling the victim in from his cell at any hour of the day or night, repeatedly, day after day, never allowing him to get enough sleep to think clearly or finally, to care. It is this sort of thing which reduces human beings to dithering idiots, which produce those amazing confessions ...

According to the newspaper, these were 'confessions by torture'.

SERE techniques profoundly disrupt the body and mind. The 'harsh' methods used by the CIA and no longer authorised for the US military constitute torture because they inflict severe mental and physical pain. At Abu Ghraib, the Red Cross found that detainees had 'concentration difficulties, memory problems, verbal expression difficulties, incoherent speech, acute anxiety reactions, abnormal behavior and suicidal tendencies' due to 'methods and duration of interrogation'. At Guantánamo, the FBI noted that Mohammad al-Qahtani was 'talking to non-existent people, reporting hearing voices, crouching in a corner of the cell covered with a sheet for hours on end' after suffering through months of SERE torture.

Sleep deprivation and forced standing—used both in Stalin's prisons and CIA black sites today—inflict enormous damage. As Hinkle and Wolff reported, hours of forced standing produce ankles and feet that 'swell to twice their normal circumference' and eventually produce a 'delirious state, characterized by disorientation, fear, delusions and visual hallucinations'. Although it sounds innocuous, sleep deprivation is described as one of the cruelest forms of torture. József Cardinal Mindszenty—the stimulus for America's early fascination with mind control—was released from prison in December 1956 and was allowed to take up residence in the US embassy in Budapest to serve out his sentence. Mindszenty later told reporters that he was kept awake for twenty-nine nights to force his confession. He called it 'unspeakable brutality'. Associated Press reporter William Oatis and American businessman Robert Vogeler also admitted to imagined crimes after days without sleep. One of the best descriptions of the effects of this torture comes not from these men, but from former Israeli Prime Minister Menachem Begin. In the 1930s, Begin was also imprisoned by the Soviets and kept awake for days. According to Begin:

> In the head of the interrogated prisoner a haze begins to form. His spirit is wearied to death, his legs are unsteady, and he has one sole desire: to sleep, to sleep just a little, not to get up, to lie, to rest, to forget ... Anyone who has experienced this desire knows that not even hunger or thirst are comparable with it ... I came across prisoners who signed what they were ordered to sign, only to get what the interrogator promised them. He did not promise them their liberty. He promised them—if they signed—uninterrupted sleep!

The fact that these tortures do not leave permanent marks can be deceptive. According to Physicians for Human Rights, 'The lack of physical signs can make psychological torture seem less significant than physical torture, but the consensus among those who study torture and rehabilitate its victims is that psychological torture can be more painful and cause more severe and long-lasting damage even than the pain inflicted during physical torture'. According to Peter Kooijmans, the United Nations Special Rapporteur on Torture from 1985 to 1993:

Often a distinction is made between physical and mental torture. This distinction, however, seems to have more relevance for the means by which torture is practised than for its character. Almost invariably the effect of torture, by whatever means it may have been practised, is physical *and* psychological. Even when the most brutal physical means are used, the longterm effects may be mainly psychological; even when the most refined psychological means are resorted to, there is nearly always the accompanying effect of severe physical pain.

Waterboarding, as a form of mock execution, cruelly fuses both the mental and physical. In October 2006, Vice President Dick Cheney confirmed that waterboarding is one of the CIA's 'alternative' techniques. Using it on suspected terrorists, he said, is a 'no-brainer'. According to a former SERE intructor:

> Waterboarding is a torture. Period ... I ran a waterboard team at SERE and administered dozens of students through the process as a tool to show what the worst looks like, short of death. This is why there is a doctor and a psychologist standing right next to the student ... to do it safe and to help the student recover ... It is not a simulation, when applied you are, in fact, drowning at a controlled rate ... we just determine how much and how long— you'll break. Everyone breaks.

Although the pain of choking and sheer terror is brief, this torture leaves lasting effects. Dr Allen Keller, the Director of the Program for Survivors of Torture in New York, told the *New Yorker* that some victims he treated after they were waterboarded remained 'traumatized for years'. One patient, he said, 'couldn't take showers, and panicked when it rained'.

One Uruguayan torture victim who now lives in Australia still cannot escape from the pain he endured. Interviewed by ABC Radio's Ian Walker, Ramon refused to talk specifically about his encounters with the Uruguayan police:

> Ramon: One of the reasons why I haven't spoken about my personal experience in this interview, and I wouldn't, I think I can't. That's how it has impacted on me, I can't speak to you about this.

Ian Walker: It's too painful? What is it?

Ramon: Yes, I certainly admit that. But I can speak about the general experience of the Uruguayan people, but that's as far as I've gone, and this is twenty years down the track. So I guess if you want an answer to that, a more blunt answer is that it's taken me twenty years, and I've not been able to deal with it yet. There isn't a single day when you don't think, or you don't remember, or you don't go through in your mind the experience that you went through twenty years ago.

American torture could leave similar scars. As of November 2006, Australia's David Hicks is still detained at Guantánamo. In July 2006, his civilian lawyer, David McLeod, said Hicks was 'very, very depressed'. McLeod added: 'He has to lie on the floor, the air conditioning is kept on full, he has very few clothes, and he shivers … All his letters and cards have been taken away from him and he's not receiving any. He has no contact at all with the outside world.' Moazzam Begg, a former detainee who spoke with Hicks, recounted his poor mental state:

One of the things he said to me is, 'Please, when you get out from here, please tell people that my sanity is at risk here.' He used to tell me quite often that he felt like just banging his head so hard against the walls that he just ends up killing himself.

Mamdouh Habib told me that 'there's no way you're gonna come out of Camp Five normal'. Habib has sought treatment to deal with the psychological after-effects of the torture he endured. After several meetings with Habib, I was convinced that he still had a long way to go. While he looked down at his scarred right hand, Mamdouh Habib told me something I cannot soon forget. 'I am here', he said, 'but I am still not free'.

APPENDIX I

HUMAN RESOURCE EXPLOITATION
TRAINING MANUAL - 1983

- -

EXCERPT: Section K: Coercive Techniques. Note: In the following pages, letters and digit(s) in left margin are slide numbers. Hand-written changes included in the declassified version are ~~struck through~~ and presented in THIS FONT.

For the full manual, visit www.americantorture.com

- -

L-0

COERCIVE TECHNIQUES

I. THE THEORY OF COERCION

L-1 A. THE PURPOSE OF ALL COERCIVE TECHNIQUES IS
TO INDUCE PSYCHOLOGICAL REGRESSION IN THE
SUBJECT BY BRINGING A SUPERIOR OUTSIDE FORCE
TO BEAR ON HIS WILL TO RESIST. REGRESSION IS
L-2 BASICALLY A LOSS OF AUTONOMY, A REVERSION TO
AN EARLIER BEHAVIORAL LEVEL. AS THE SUBJECT
REGRESSES, HIS LEARNED PERSONALITY TRAITS
FALL AWAY IN REVERSE CHRONOLOGICAL ORDER. HE
BEGINS TO LOSE THE CAPACITY TO CARRY OUT THE
HIGHEST CREATIVE ACTIVITIES, TO DEAL WITH
COMPLEX SITUATIONS, TO COPE WITH STRESSFUL
INTERPERSONAL RELATIONSHIPS, OR TO COPE WITH
REPEATED FRUSTRATIONS. THE USE OF MOST COERCIVE
TECHNIQUES IS IMPROPER AND VIOLATES LAWS.

L-3 B. THERE ARE THREE MAJOR PRINCIPLES INVOLVED
IN THE SUCCESSFUL APPLICATION OF COERCIVE
TECHNIQUES:

L-3   DEBILITY (PHYSICAL WEAKNESS)
        FOR CENTURIES "QUESTIONERS" HAVE EMPLOYED
        VARIOUS METHODS OF INDUCING PHYSICAL
        WEAKNESS: PROLONGED CONSTRAINT; PROLONGED
        EXERTION; EXTREMES OF HEAT, COLD OR
        MOISTURE; AND DEPRIVATION OF FOOD OR
        SLEEP. THESE TECHNIQUES SHOULD NOT BE USED.
        THE ASSUMPTION ~~IS~~ OF THOSE THAT USE THEM
        THAT LOWERING THE SUBJECT'S PHYSIOLOGICAL
        RESISTANCE WILL LOWER HIS PSYCHOLOGICAL
        CAPACITY FOR RESISTANCE: HOWEVER, THERE
        HAS BEEN NO SCIENTIFIC INVESTIGATION OF
        THIS ASSUMPTION.

[K-1]

MANY PSYCHOLOGISTS CONSIDER THE THREAT OF
INDUCING DEBILITY TO BE MORE EFFECTIVE
THAN DEBILITY ITSELF. PROLONGED CONSTRAINT
OR EXERTION, SUSTAINED DEPRIVATION OF
FOOD OR SLEEP, ETC. OFTEN BECOME PATTERNS
TO WHICH A SUBJECT ADJUSTS BY BECOMING
APATHETIC AND WITHDRAWING INTO HIMSELF, IN
SEARCH OF ESCAPE FROM THE DISCOMFORT AND
TENSION. IN THIS CASE DEBILITY WOULD BE
COUNTER PRODUCTIVE.

~~THE QUESTIONER SHOULD BE CAREFUL~~ ANOTHER
COERCIVE TECHNIQUE IS TO MANIPULATE
THE SUBJECT'S ENVIRONMENT TO DISRUPT
PATTERNS, NOT TO CREATE THEM~~.~~ , SUCH AS
ARRANGING MEALS AND SLEEP ~~SHOULD BE
GRANTED~~ SO THEY OCCUR IRREGULARLY, IN
MORE ABUNDANCE OR LESS THAN ADEQUACY, ON
NO DISCERNABLE TIME PATTERN. THIS ~~***~~ IS
DONE TO DISORIENT THE SUBJECT AND ~~**~~ ~~****~~
~~****~~ DESTROY~~ING~~ HIS CAPACITY TO RESIST.
HOWEVER, IF SUCCESSFUL, IT CAUSES SERIOUS
PSYCHOLOGICAL DAMAGE AND THEREFORE IS A
FORM OF TORTURE.

L-4 <u>DEPENDENCY</u>
HE IS HELPLESSLY DEPENDENT UPON THE
"QUESTIONER" FOR THE SATISFACTION OF ALL
BASIC NEEDS.

L-5 <u>DREAD (INTENSE FEAR & ANXIETY)</u>
SUSTAINED LONG ENOUGH, A STRONG FEAR OF
ANYTHING VAGUE OR UNKNOWN INDUCES REGRESSION.
ON THE OTHER HAND, MATERIALIZATION OF THE
FEAR IS LIKELY TO COME AS A RELIEF. THE
SUBJECT FINDS THAT HE CAN HOLD OUT AND HIS
RESISTANCE IS STRENGTHENED.

~~A WORD OF CAUTION.~~ IF THE DEBILITY-
DEPENDENCY-DREAD STATE IS UNDULY PROLONGED,
THE SUBJECT MAY SINK INTO A DEFENSIVE APATHY
FROM WHICH IT IS HARD TO AROUSE HIM. ~~IT IS
ADVISABLE TO HAVE A PSYCHOLOGIST AVAILABLE
WHENEVER REGRESSION IS INDUCED~~. THIS
ILLUSTRATES WHY THIS COERCIVE TECHNIQUE MAY
PRODUCE TORTURE.

L-6

II. OBJECTIONS TO COERCION
   A. THERE IS A PROFOUND MORAL OBJECTION
   TO APPLYING DURESS BEYOND THE POINT OF
   IRREVERSIBLE PSYCHOLOGICAL DAMAGE SUCH AS
   OCCURS DURING BRAINWASHING. BRAINWASHING
   INVOLVES THE CONDITIONING OF A SUBJECT'S
   "STIMULUS-RESPONSE BOND" THROUGH THE
   USE OF THESE SAME TECHNIQUES, BUT THE
   OBJECTIVE OF BRAINWASHING IS DIRECTED
   PRIMARILY TOWARDS THE SUBJECT'S ACCEPTANCE
   AND ADOPTION OF BELIEFS, BEHAVIOR, OR
   DOCTRINE ALIEN TO HIS NATIVE CULTURAL
   ENVIRONMENT FOR PROPAGANDA RATHER THAN
   INTELLIGENCE COLLECTION PROCESS. ~~ASIDE
   FROM THIS EXTREME, WE WILL NOT JUDGE THE
   VALIDITY OF OTHER ETHICAL ARGUMENTS.~~ THIS
   TECHNIQUE IS ILLEGAL AND MAY NOT BE USED.

L-7

   B. MOREOVER SOME PSYCHOLOGISTS FEEL
   THAT THE SUBJECT'S ABILITY TO RECALL AND
   COMMUNICATE INFORMATION ACCURATELY IS
   AS IMPAIRED AS HIS WILL TO RESIST. ~~THIS
   OBJECTION HAS SOME VALIDITY BUT THE USE OF
   COERCIVE TECHNIQUES WILL RARELY CONFUSE A
   RESISTANT SUBJECT SO COMPLETELY THAT HE
   DOES NOT KNOW WHETHER HIS OWN CONFESSION
   IS TRUE OR FALSE. HE DOES NEED MASTERY
   OF ALL HIS MENTAL AND PHYSICAL POWERS TO
   KNOW WHETHER HE IS A SPY OR NOT.~~

ONCE A CONFESSION IS OBTAINED, THE
CLASSIC CAUTIONS APPLY. THE PRESSURES
ARE LIFTED ENOUGH SO THAT THE SUBJECT
CAN PROVIDE INFORMATION AS ACCURATELY AS
POSSIBLE. IN FACT, THE RELIEF GRANTED THE
SUBJECT AT THIS TIME FITS NEATLY INTO
THE "QUESTIONING" PLAN. HE IS TOLD THAT
THE CHANGED TREATMENT IS A REWARD FOR
TRUTHFULLNESS AND EVIDENCE THAT FRIENDLY
HANDLING WILL CONTINUE AS LONG AS HE
COOPERATES.

III. JUSTIFICATION FOR USING COERCIVE
     TECHNIQUES
     THESE TECHNIQUES SHOULD BE RESERVED FOR
     THOSE SUBJECTS WHO HAVE BEEN TRAINED OR
     WHO HAVE DEVELOPED THE ABILITY TO RESIST
     NON-COERCIVE TECHNIQUES.

L-8

   IV. COERCIVE TECHNIQUES
L-8   A. ARREST

        THE MANNER AND TIMING OF ARREST SHOULD
        BE PLANNED TO ACHIEVE SURPRISE AND THE
        MAXIMUM AMOUNT OF MENTAL DISCOMFORT. HE
        SHOULD THEREFORE BE ARRESTED AT A MOMENT
        WHEN HE LEAST EXPECTS IT AND WHEN HIS
        MENTAL AND PHYSICAL RESISTANCE IS AT ITS
        LOWEST, IDEALLY IN THE EARLY HOURS OF
        THE MORNING. WHEN ARRESTED AT THIS TIME,
        MOST SUBJECTS EXPERIENCE INTENSE FEELINGS
        OF SHOCK, INSECURITY, AND PSYCHOLOGICAL
        STRESS AND FOR THE MOST PART HAVE GREAT
        DIFFICULTY ADJUSTING TO THE SITUATION. IT
        IS ALSO IMPORTANT THAT THE ARRESTING PARTY
        BEHAVE IN SUCH A MANNER AS TO IMPRESS THE
        SUBJECT WITH THEIR EFFICIENCY.

                    [K-4]

L-9   B. DETENTION

-cut   A PERSON'S SENSE OF IDENTITY DEPENDS
hair   UPON A CONTINUITY IN HIS SURROUNDINGS,
-issue   HABITS, APPEARANCE, ACTIONS, RELATIONS
baggy   WITH OTHERS, ETC. DETENTION PERMITS THE
clothing   "QUESTIONER" TO CUT THROUGH THESE LINKS
             AND THROW THE SUBJECT BACK UPON HIS OWN
             UNAIDED INTERNAL RESOURCES. DETENTION
             SHOULD BE PLANNED TO ENHANCE THE
             SUBJECT'S FEELINGS OF BEING CUT OFF FROM
             ANYTHING KNOWN AND REASSURING.
             LITTLE IS GAINED IF CONFINEMENT MERELY
             REPLACES ONE ROUTINE WITH ANOTHER. THE
             SUBJECT SHOULD NOT BE PROVIDED WITH ANY
             ROUTINE TO WHICH HE CAN ADAPT. NEITHER
             SHOULD DETENTION BECOME MONOTONOUS TO
             THE POINT WHERE THE SUBJECT BECOMES
             APATHETIC. APATHY IS A VERY EFFECTIVE
             DEFENSE AGAINST "QUESTIONING".
             CONSTANTLY DISRUPTING PATTERNS WILL
             CAUSE HIM TO BECOME DISORIENTED AND
             TO EXPERIENCE FEELINGS OF FEAR AND
             HELPLESSNESS.

             IT IS IMPORTANT TO DETERMINE IF THE
             SUBJECT HAS BEEN DETAINED PREVIOUSLY,
             HOW OFTEN, HOW LONG, UNDER WHAT
             CIRCUMSTANCES, AND WHETHER HE WAS
             SUBJECTED TO "QUESTIONING". FAMILIARITY
             WITH DETENTION OR EVEN WITH ISOLATION
             REDUCES THE EFFECT.

                          [K-5]

L-10 C. DEPRIVATION OF SENSORY STIMULI

SOLITARY CONFINEMENT ACTS ON MOST PERSONS
AS A POWERFUL STRESS. A PERSON CUT OFF FROM
EXTERNAL STIMULI TURNS HIS AWARENESS INWARD
AND PROJECTS HIS UNCONSIOUS OUTWARD. THE
SYMPTOMS MOST COMMONLY PRODUCED BY SOLITARY
CONFINEMENT ARE SUPERSTITION, INTENSE LOVE
OF ANY OTHER LIVING THING, PERCEIVING
INANIMATE OBJECTS AS ALIVE, HALLUCINATIONS,
AND DELUSIONS. DELIBERATELY CAUSING THESE
SYMPTOMS IS A SERIOUS IMPROPRIETY AND ...

~~ALTHOUGH CONDITIONS IDENTICAL TO THOSE OF~~
~~SOLITARY CONFINEMENT FOR THE PURPOSE OF~~
~~"QUESTIONING" HAVE NOT BEEN DUPLICATED~~
~~FOR SCIENTIFIC EXPERIMENTATION, A NUMBER~~
~~OF EXPERIMENTS HAVE BEEN CONDUCTED WITH~~
~~SUBJECTS WHO VOLUNTEERED TO BE PLACED IN~~
~~"SENSORY DEPRIVATION TANKS". THEY WERE~~
~~SUSPENDED IN WATER AND WORE BLACK-OUT~~
~~MASKS, WHICH ENCLOSED THE ENTIRE HEAD AND~~
~~ONLY ALLOWED BREATHING. THEY HEARD ONLY~~
~~THEIR OWN BREATHING AND SOME FAINT SOUNDS~~
~~FROM THE PIPING.~~

...TO USE PROLONGED SOLITARY CONFINEMENT FOR
THE PURPOSE OF EXTRACTING INFORMATION IN
QUESTIONING VIOLATES POLICY.

[K-6]

TO SUMMARIZE THE RESULTS OF THESE
EXPERIMENTS.

1) EXTREME DEPRIVATION OF SENSORY STIMULI
INDUCES UNBEARABLE STRESS AND ANXIETY. AND
IS A FORM OF TORTURE. ITS USE CONSTITUTES A
SERIOUS IMPROPRIETY AND VIOLATES POLICY. THE
MORE COMPLETE THE DEPRIVATION, THE MORE
RAPIDLY AND DEEPLY THE SUBJECT IS AFFECTED.

2) THE STRESS AND ANXIETY BECOME UNBEARABLE
FOR MOST SUBJECTS. THEY HAVE A GROWING
NEED FOR PHYSICAL AND SOCIAL STIMULI.
HOW MUCH THEY ARE ABLE TO STAND DEPENDS
UPON THE PSYCHOLOGICAL CHARACTERISTICS
OF THE INDIVIDUAL. NOW LET ME RELATE
THIS TO THE "QUESTIONING" SITUATION. AS
THE "QUESTIONER" BECOMES LINKED IN THE
SUBJECT'S MIND WITH HUMAN CONTACT AND
MEANINGFUL ACTIVITY, THE ANXIETY LESSENS.
THE "QUESTIONER" CAN TAKE ADVANTAGE OF THIS
RELATIONSHIP BY ASSUMING A BENEVOLENT ROLE.

3) SOME SUBJECTS PROGRESSIVELY LOSE TOUCH
WITH REALITY, FOCUS INWARDLY, AND PRODUCE
DELUSIONS, HALLUCINATIONS, AND OTHER
PATHOLOGICAL EFFECTS. IN GENERAL, THE
MORE WELL-ADJUSTED A SUBJECT IS, THE MORE
HE IS AFFECTED BY DEPRIVATION. NEUROTIC
AND PSYCHOTIC SUBJECTS ARE COMPARATIVELY
UNAFFECTED OR SHOW DECREASES IN ANXIETY.

[K-7]

L-11 D. THREATS AND FEAR

THE THREAT OF COERCION USUALLY WEAKENS OR
DESTROYS RESISTANCE MORE EFFECTIVELY THAN
COERCION ITSELF. FOR EXAMPLE, THE THREAT
TO INFLICT PAIN CAN TRIGGER FEARS MORE
DAMAGING THAN THE IMMEDIATE SENSATION OF
PAIN. IN FACT, MOST PEOPLE UNDERESTIMATE
THEIR CAPACITY TO WITHSTAND PAIN. IN
GENERAL, DIRECT PHYSICAL BRUTALITY CREATES
ONLY RESENTMENT, HOSTILITY, AND FURTHER
DEFIANCE.

THE EFFECTIVENESS OF A THREAT DEPENDS ON
THE PERSONALITY OF THE SUBJECT, WHETHER
HE BELIEVES THE "QUESTIONER" CAN AND WILL
CARRY OUT THE THREAT, AND ON WHAT HE
BELIEVES TO BE THE REASON FOR THE THREAT.
A THREAT SHOULD BE DELIVERED COLDLY, NOT
SHOUTED IN ANGER, OR MADE IN RESPONSE TO
THE SUBJECT'S OWN EXPRESSIONS OF HOSTILITY.
EXPRESSIONS OF ANGER BY THE "QUESTIONER"
ARE OFTEN INTERPRETED BY THE SUBJECT AS
A FEAR OF FAILURE, WHICH STRENGTHENS HIS
RESOLVE TO RESIST.

A THREAT SHOULD GRANT THE SUBJECT TIME
FOR COMPLIANCE AND IS MOST EFFECTIVE WHEN
JOINED WITH A SUGGESTED RATIONALIZATION FOR
COMPLIANCE. IT IS NOT ENOUGH THAT A SUBJECT
BE PLACED UNDER THE TENSION OF FEAR: HE
MUST ALSO DISCERN AN ACCEPTABLE ESCAPE
ROUTE.

[K-8]

THE THREAT OF DEATH HAS BEEN FOUND TO
BE WORSE THAN USELESS. THE PRINCIPLE
REASON IS THAT IT OFTEN INDUCES SHEER
HOPELESSNESS; THE SUBJECT FEELS THAT HE
IS AS LIKELY TO BE CONDEMNED AFTER
COMPLIANCE AS BEFORE. SOME SUBJECTS
RECOGNIZE THAT THE THREAT IS A BLUFF AND
THAT SILENCING THEM FOREVER WOULD DEFEAT
THE "QUESTIONER'S" PURPOSE.

~~IF A SUBJECT REFUSES TO COMPLY ONCE A THREAT
HAS BEEN MADE, IT MUST BE CARRIED OUT. IF
IT IS NOT CARRIED OUT, THEN SUBSEQUENT
THREATS WILL ALSO PROVE INEFFECTIVE.~~ THE
PRINCIPLE DRAWBACK TO USING THREATS OF
PHYSICAL COERCION OR TORTURE IS THAT THE
SUBJECT MAY CALL THE BLUFF. IF HE DOES, AND SINCE
SUCH THREATS CANNOT BE CARRIED OUT, THE USE
OF EMPTY THREATS COULD RESULT IN SUBJECT'S
GAINING RATHER THAN LOSING SELF-CONFIDENCE.

L-12 E. PAIN

EVERYONE IS AWARE THAT PEOPLE REACT VERY
DIFFERENTLY TO PAIN BUT THE REASON IS NOT
BECAUSE OF A DIFFERENCE IN THE INTENSITY
OF THE SENSATION ITSELF. ALL PEOPLE HAVE
APPROXIMATELY THE SAME THRESHOLD AT WHICH
THEY BEGIN TO FEEL PAIN AND THEIR ESTIMATES
OF SEVERITY ARE ROUGHLY THE SAME. THE WIDE
RANGE OF INDIVIDUAL REACTIONS IS BASED
PRIMARILY ON EARLY CONDITIONING TO PAIN.

THE TORTURE SITUATION IS AN EXTERNAL
CONFLICT, A CONTEST BETWEEN THE SUBJECT
AND HIS TORMENTOR. THE PAIN WHICH IS BEING
INFLICTED UPON HIM FROM OUTSIDE HIMSELF MAY
ACTUALLY INTENSIFY HIS WILL TO RESIST. ON
THE OTHER HAND, PAIN WHICH HE FEELS HE IS
INFLICTING UPON HIMSELF IS MORE LIKELY TO
SAP HIS RESISTANCE.

[K-9]

FOR EXAMPLE, IF HE IS REQUIRED TO MAINTAIN
RIGID POSITIONS SUCH AS STANDING AT
ATTENTION OR SITTING ON A STOOL FOR LONG
PERIODS OF TIME, THE IMMEDIATE SOURCE OF
~~PAIN~~ DISCOMFORT IS NOT THE "QUESTIONER"
BUT THE SUBJECT HIMSELF. HIS CONFLICT IS
THEN AN INTERNAL STRUGGLE. AS LONG AS HE
MAINTAINS THIS POSITION, HE IS ATTRIBUTING
TO THE "QUESTIONER" THE ABILITY TO DO
SOMETHING WORSE. BUT THERE IS NEVER A
SHOWDOWN WHERE THE "QUESTIONER" DEMONSTRATES
THIS ABILITY. AFTER A PERIOD OF TIME,
THE SUBJECT ~~IS LIKELY TO~~ MAY EXHAUST
HIS INTERNAL MOTIVATIONAL STRENGTH. THIS
TECHNIQUE MAY ONLY BE USED FOR PERIODS OF TIME
THAT ARE NOT LONG ENOUGH TO INDUCE PAIN OR
PHYSICAL DAMAGE.

INTENSE PAIN IS QUITE LIKELY TO PRODUCE
FALSE CONFESSIONS, FABRICATED TO AVOID
ADDITIONAL PUNISHMENT. THIS RESULTS IN A
TIME CONSUMING DELAY WHILE INVESTIGATION
IS CONDUCTED AND THE ADMISSIONS ARE PROVEN
UNTRUE. DURING THIS RESPITE, THE SUBJECT
CAN PULL HIMSELF TOGETHER AND MAY EVEN
USE THE TIME TO DEVISE A MORE COMPLEX
CONFESSION THAT TAKES STILL LONGER TO
DISPROVE.

SOME SUBJECTS ACTUALLY ENJOY PAIN AND
WITHHOLD INFORMATION THEY MIGHT OTHERWISE
HAVE DIVULGED IN ORDER TO BE PUNISHED.

[K-10]

IF PAIN IS NOT USED UNTIL LATE IN THE
"QUESTIONING" PROCESS AND AFTER OTHER
TACTICS HAVE FAILED, THE SUBJECT IS LIKELY
TO CONCLUDE THAT THE "QUESTIONER" IS
BECOMING DESPARATE. HE WILL FEEL THAT IF HE
CAN HOLD OUT JUST A LITTLE LONGER, HE WILL
WIN THE STRUGGLE AND HIS FREEDOM. ONCE A
SUBJECT HAS SUCCESSFULLY WITHSTOOD PAIN, HE
IS EXTREMELY DIFFICULT TO "QUESTION" USING
MORE SUBDUED METHODS.

L-13 F. HYPNOSIS AND HEIGHTENED SUGGESTIBILITY

THE RELIABILITY OF ANSWERS OBTAINED FROM
A SUBJECT ACTUALLY UNDER THE INFLUENCE OF
HYPNOTISM IS HIGHLY DOUBTFUL. HIS ANSWERS
ARE OFTEN BASED UPON THE SUGGESTIONS OF
THE "QUESTIONER" AND ARE DISTORTED AND
FABRICATED.

HOWEVER, THE SUBJECT'S STRONG DESIRE TO
ESCAPE THE STRESS OF THE SITUATION CAN
CREATE A STATE OF MIND WHICH IS CALLED
HEIGHTENED SUGGESTIBILITY. THE "QUESTIONER"
CAN TAKE ADVANTAGE OF THIS STATE OF MIND
BY CREATING A "HYPNOTIC SITUATION", AS
DISTINGUISHED FROM HYPNOSIS ITSELF. THIS
HYPNOTIC SITUATION CAN BE CREATED BY THE
L-14 "MAGIC ROOM" TECHNIQUE.

[K-11]

FOR EXAMPLE, THE SUBJECT IS GIVEN AN
HYPNOTIC SUGGESTION THAT HIS HAND IS
GROWING WARM. HOWEVER, HIS HAND ACTUALLY
DOES BECOME WARM WITH THE AID OF A
CONCEALED DIATHERMY MACHINE. HE MAY BE
GIVEN A SUGGESTION THAT A CIGARETTE WILL
TASTE BITTER AND HE COULD BE GIVEN A
CIGARETTE PREPARED TO HAVE A SLIGHT BUT
NOTICEABLY BITTER TASTE.

A PSYCHOLOGICALLY IMMATURE SUBJECT, OR
ONE WHO HAS BEEN REGRESSED, COULD ADOPT A
SUGGESTION THAT HE HAS BEEN HYPNOTIZED,
WHICH HAS RENDERED HIM INCAPABLE OF
RESISTANCE. THIS RELIEVES HIM OF THE
FEELINGS OF RESPONSIBILITY FOR HIS ACTIONS
AND ALLOWS HIM TO REVEAL INFORMATION.

L-15 H. NARCOSIS

THERE IS NO DRUG WHICH CAN FORCE EVERY
SUBJECT TO DIVULGE ALL THE INFORMATION
HE HAS, BUT JUST AS IT IS POSSIBLE TO
CREATE A MISTAKEN BELIEF THAT A SUBJECT
HAS BEEN HYPNOTIZED BY USING THE "MAGIC
ROOM" TECHNIQUE, IT IS POSSIBLE TO CREATE A
MISTAKEN BELIEF THAT A SUBJECT HAS BEEN
L-16 DRUGGED BY USING THE "PLACEBO" TECHNIQUE.

[K-12]

STUDIES INDICATE THAT AS HIGH AS 30 TO
50 PERCENT OF INDIVIDUALS ARE PLACEBO
REACTORS. IN THIS TECHNIQUE THE SUBJECT IS
GIVEN A PLACEBO (A HARMLESS SUGAR PILL) AND
LATER IS TOLD HE WAS GIVEN A TRUTH SERUM,
WHICH WILL MAKE HIM WANT TO TALK AND WHICH
WILL ALSO PREVENT HIS LYING. HIS DESIRE TO
FIND AN EXCUSE FOR COMPLIANCE, WHICH IS HIS
ONLY AVENUE OF ESCAPE FROM HIS DEPRESSING
SITUATION, MAY MAKE HIM WANT TO BELIEVE
THAT HE HAS BEEN DRUGGED AND THAT NO ONE
COULD BLAME HIM FOR TELLING HIS STORY NOW.
THIS PROVIDES HIM WITH A RATIONALIZATION
THAT HE NEEDS FOR COOPERATING.

THE FUNCTION OF BOTH THE "PLACEBO"
TECHNIQUE AND THE "MAGIC ROOM" TECHNIQUE
IS TO CAUSE CAPITULATION BY THE SUBJECT,
TO CAUSE HIM TO SHIFT FROM RESISTANCE
TO COOPERATION. ONCE THIS SHIFT HAS
BEEN ACCOMPLISHED, THESE TECHNIQUES
ARE NO LONGER NECESSARY AND SHOULD NOT
BE USED PERSISTENTLY TO FACILITATE THE
"QUESTIONING" THAT FOLLOWS CAPITULATION.

[K-13]

IV. REGRESSION

AS I SAID AT THE BEGINNING OF OUR
DISCUSSION OF CEORCIVE TECHNIQUES, THE
PURPOSE OF ALL COERCIVE TECHNIQUES IS TO
INDUCE REGRESSION. HOW SUCCESSFUL THESE
TECHNIQUES ARE IN INDUCING REGRESSION
DEPENDS UPON AN ACCURATE PSYCHOLOGICAL
ASSESSMENT OF THE SUBJECT AND A PROPER
L-17 MATCHING OF METHOD TO SOURCE. THERE ARE
A FEW NON-COERCIVE TECHNIQUES WHICH CAN
ALSO BE USED TO INDUCE REGRESSION, BUT ~~TO~~
~~A LESSER DEGREE THAN CAN BE OBTAINED WITH~~
~~COERCIVE TECHNIQUES. THE EFFECTIVENESS~~
~~OF THESE TECHNIQUES DEPENDS UPON THE~~
~~"QUESTIONER'S" CONTROL OF THE ENVIRONMENT.~~
~~FOR EXAMPLE.~~ IT IS ILLEGAL AND AGAINST POLICY
TO USE THEM TO PRODUCE REGRESSION. FOLLOWING
IS A LIST OF THESE NON-COERCIVE TECHNIQUES
WHICH REQUIRE GREAT CARE BECAUSE OF THEIR
SUSCEPTIBILITY TO ABUSE:

A. PERSISTANT MANIPULATION OF TIME
B. RETARDING AND ADVANCING CLOCKS
C. SERVING MEALS AT ODD TIMES
D. DISRUPTING SLEEP SCHEDULES
E. DISORIENTATION REGARDING DAY AND NIGHT
F. UNPATTERNED "QUESTIONING" SESSIONS
G. NONSENSICAL QUESTIONING
H. INGNORING HALF-HEARTED ATTEMPTS TO
   COOPERATE
I. REWARDING NON-COOPERATION

IN GENERAL, THWARTING ANY ATTEMPT BY THE
SUBJECT TO RELATE TO HIS NEW ENVIRONMENT
WILL REINFORCE THE EFFECTS OF REGRESSION
AND DRIVE HIM DEEPER AND DEEPER INTO
HIMSELF, UNTIL HE NO LONGER IS ABLE TO
CONTROL HIS RESPONSES IN AN ADULT FASHION.

[K-14]

WHETHER REGRESSION OCCURS SPONTANEOUSLY
UNDER DETENTION OR IS INADVERTENTLY
INDUCED BY THE "QUESTIONER", IT ~~SHOULD NOT~~
~~BE ALLOWED TO CONTINUE BEYOND THE POINT~~
~~NECESSARY TO OBTAIN COMPLIANCE.~~ CALLS FOR
REMEDIAL TREATMENT AS SOON AS IT IS NOTICED. IN
SOME CASES A PSYCHIATRIST SHOULD BE CALLED.
~~PRESENT IF SEVERE TECHNIQUES ARE TO BE~~
~~EMPLOYED, TO ENSURE FULL REVERSAL LATER.~~
~~AS SOON AS POSSIBLE, THE "QUESTIONER"~~
~~SHOULD PROVIDE THE SUBJECT WITH THE~~
~~RATIONALIZATION THAT HE NEEDS FOR GIVING IN~~
~~AND COOPERATING. THIS RATIONALIZATION IS~~
~~LIKELY TO BE ELEMENTARY, AN ADULT VERSION~~
~~OF A CHILDHOOD EXCUSE SUCH AS:~~
~~1. "THEY MADE YOU DO IT."~~
~~2. "ALL THE OTHER BOYS ARE DOING IT."~~
~~3. "YOU'RE REALLY A GOOD BOY AT HEART."~~

[K-15]

Source: National Security Archive

NOTES

The references are arranged by chapter, page number and topic with a portion of a quotation or relevant phrase in **bold**.

IN THEIR OWN WORDS
pp. 1–11 Habib and Hicks
Personal Interview with Habibs Mamdouh and Maha Habib, Sydney, New South Wales, 22 May 2006, 24 May 2006, and 29 May 2006. **Hicks' Personal Letters ... Federal Police Record** Whitmont, ABC, *Four Corners.* **Hicks affidavit** 'The David Hicks Affidavit', 5 August 2004.

pp. 11–13 An Overview
'[Ashcraft's] eyes became blinded by a powerful electric light' *Ashcraft v State of Tennessee* (1944). **'The Constitution of the United States stands as a bar against the conviction'** ibid. **'The United States now holds more than 14 000 prisoners'** Associated Press, 'US Overseas Detention System Numbers'. **'much like the Cold War went on for many years'** Department of Defense, 'Remarks by Secretary Rumsfeld in a "Town Hall" Event with US Troops in Al Asad, Iraq –Headquarters 3rd Marine Air Wing'. **'800 allegations of abuse ... 34 ... murdered'** Associated Press, 'US Overseas Detention System Numbers'. **'Every country has its own way of torturing'** Golden, 'The Battle for Guantánamo'. **'alternative set of procedures'** The White House, 'President Discusses Creation of Military Commissions to Try Suspected Terrorists'.

1. A CLIMATE OF FEAR
pp. 14–15 Cardinal Mindszenty
'I am guilty in principle and in detail' United Press, 'Mindszenty Denies Plot But Affirms Guilt in Principle'. **'called for a general amnesty for all political prisoners'** United Press, 'Cardinal Urges Amnesty'. **'threatened to excommunicate any Catholic'** Associated Press, 'Hungarian Cardinal Fights Seizure of Schools By State'. **'reactionary ... liquidation of clerical reaction'** Associated Press, 'Cardinal Mindszenty Siezed By Red Regime in Hungary'.

'forged or false' United Press, 'Cardinal Retracts Pre-Trial Letter and Denies Duress'. **'May the mock trial ... arouse all Christians'** Special to the *New York Times*, 'Protests Rising in Primate's Case'. **'morally and civilly innocent'** Associated Press, 'Mindszenty is Found Guilty, Court Gives Life Sentence, Flood of Protests Rising'. **'a sickening sham'** Special to the *New York Times*, 'Truman Condemns Arrest of Cardinal Mindszenty'. **'nerve-destroying Actedron'** Associated Press, 'Fear Cardinal Will Be Given Drug By Reds'.

pp. 15–16 Robert Vogeler's account
'confessed to having committed sabotage' Associated Press, 'Hungarian Reds Hurl Spy Charge at Seized Yank'. **'Hungarian government nationalised all ITT holdings'** Dispatch of *The Times*, London, 'Hungarians Seize Foreign Companies in Sweeping Move'. **'he [Vogeler] joined the company in 1943'** Associated Press, 'Vogeler's Recital Stirs Skepticism'. **'I used my business activities only as a cover ... without a show of emotion'** Associated Press, 'Avowal of Guilt Made by Vogeler in Budapest Trial'. **'phrases in his confession he never employed'** Special to the *New York Times*, 'Action on Vogeler Denounced by US'. **'so-called confession nor his self-incriminating testimony'** *Chicago Daily Tribune*, 'State Dept. Raises Questions'. **'diabolical puppet show'** *New York Times*, Editorial, '"Confession" in Hungary'.

pp. 16–17 Possibilities behind mind control/brainwashing
'"black psychiatry", drugs, or physical torture' Lawrence, 'Why Do They Confess—A Communist Enigma'. **'The intent is to change a mind radically'** Edward Hunter, *Brainwashing: From Pavlov to Powers*, Bookmaster, New York, 1960, p. 309, cited in Taylor, *Brainwashing: The Science of Thought Conrol*, p. 3. **'lurid mythology'** Robert Jay Lifton, MD, *Thought Reform and the Psychology of Totalism: A Study of "Brainwashing" in China*, WW Norton, New York, 1961, pp. 3–5, cited in Zwieback, 'The 21 Turncoat GIs: Nonrepatriations and the Political Culture of the Korean War'.

pp. 17–18 William Oatis account/American response
'charged Oatis with "hostile activities"' Associated Press, 'Czechs Holding AP Writer for "Hostile" Acts'. **'phony confessions forced from helpless victims ... a hoax'** Special to the *New York Times*, 'US Calls Trial a Hoax'. **'Surely we have reached a point'** *New York Times*, Editorial, 'Tactics of Terror'. **'acceptable norms of human conduct do not apply'** Jimmy Doolittle, 'The Report on the Covert Activities of the Central Intelligence Agency', 30 September 1954, Appendix A, p. 54, cited in Best and Boerstling, 'IC21: The Intelligence Community in the 21st Century'.

pp. 18–19 US Naval Technical Mission/Dachau experimentation
'Technical Mission swept across Europe ... most intimate secrets' Lee and Shlain, *Acid Dreams*, pp. 5–6. **'valuable information about German V2 rockets'** Frederick Graham, 'Nazi Scientists Aid Army on Research'. **'recruited Dr Kurt Plotner'** McCoy, *A Question of Torture*, p. 21. **The Nuremburg Code** 'Trials of War Criminals before the Nuremberg Military Tribunals under Control Council Law', US Government Printing Office, pp. 181–2.

p. 19 Operation Chatter
'amazing results' cited in 'Church Committee Report', p. 387. **'we had to do it for the good of the country'** cited in John Marks, *The Search for the 'Manchurian Candidate'*, p. 37.

pp. 19–21 CIA history
'procure intelligence both by overt and covert methods' cited in CIA, *Factbook on Intelligence*, pp. 4–5. **'animated by a new fanatic faith'** National Security Council, 'NSC 68: United States Objectives and Programs for National Security'. **'country was in desperate peril ... the first line of defense'** Marks, *The Search for the 'Manchurian Candidate'*, p. 28. **'perform such other functions and duties related to intelligence'** *National Security Act of 1947*, Section 103(d)(5) (50 USC 403-3). **'ordered covert manipulation of the Italian elections'** US State Department, 'History of the National Security Council'. **'describing in lurid detail the sex lives'** Blum, *Killing Hope*, p. 32. **'must be supplemented by covert psychological operations'** National Security Council, 'NSC 4-A: Psychological Operations'. **'organization, functions, names, officials, titles, salaries'** CIA, *Factbook on Intelligence*, pp. 4–5.

p. 21 CIA programs start
'Some unknown force' Marks, *The Search for the 'Manchurian Candidate'*, p. 21. **'Mindszenty Effect'** Special to the *New York Times*, 'Mind-Control Studies Had Origins in Trial of Mindszenty'; Special to the *New York Times*, 'Files Show Tests for Truth Drug Began in OSS'. **'There is ample evidence'** 'Memorandum from the Chief of the Medical Staff', 25 January 1952, cited in the 'Church Committee Report', p. 393.

pp. 21–3 Bluebird
'The program's official objectives were' CIA memorandum to the Select Committee, 'Behavioral Drugs and Testing', 11 November 1975, cited in the 'Church Committee Report', p. 387. **'There were some experiments on pain'** Marks, *The Search for the 'Manchurian Candidate'*, p. 22. **'a thousand times more potent than mescaline'** ibid., p. 58. **'a peculiar sensation'** Rensberger, 'CIA in the Early Nineteen-Fifties Was Among Pioneers in Research on LSD's Effects'. **'It is awfully hard in this day and age'** Testimony of CIA officer, 21 November 1975, p. 33, cited in the 'Church Committee Report', pp. 392–3. **'not too high mentality ... nothing serious or dangerous'** Cockburn and St Clair, *Whiteout*, p. 154. **'expanded the trials to more than 7000 unwitting US soldiers'** ibid. **'putting some in a city water supply'** cited in Marks, *The Search for the 'Manchurian Candidate'*, p. 58. **'testing of materials under accepted scientific procedures'** Inspector General's Report on MKULTRA, 1969, p. 21, cited in the 'Church Committee Report', p. 391. **'individuals of dubious loyalty'** Marks, *The Search for the 'Manchurian Candidate'*, p. 31. **'potential agents, defectors, refugees'** Lee and Shlain, *Acid Dreams*, p. 10. **'ideal research material'** Marks, *The Search for the 'Manchurian Candidate'*, p. 31. **'terminal experiments'** ibid., p. 32.

p. 23 Artichoke
'the application of tested psychiatric and psychological techniques'
McCoy, 'Cruel Science', p. 217. 'controlling an individual to the point'
Marks, *The Search for the 'Manchurian Candidate'*, p. 58. 'to perfect techniques'
Memorandum from the Director of Security to Artichoke representatives,
Subject: 'ARTICHOKE Restatement of Program', cited in the 'Church
Committee Report', p. 393. 'double, triple, and quadruple doses' Lee and
Shlain, *Acid Dreams*, p. 25. 'can be useful in reverse' ibid., p. 12.

pp. 23–7 MKULTRA
'budget of US$300 000' Marks, *The Search for the 'Manchurian Candidate'*, p. 57.
'the development of a chemical material' Memorandum from ADDP items
to DCI Dulles, 4/3/53. tab A., p. 2, cited in the 'Church Report', p. 399. 'US$25
million … 149 projects and thirty-three more subprojects' McCoy,
'Cruel Science', p. 217. '185 non-governmental researchers at eighty
institutions' Horrock, '80 Institutions Used in CIA Mind Studies'; Thomas, 'CIA
Says It Found More Secret Papers on Behavior Control'. 'threats, coercion,
imprisonment, deprivation' Weinstein, *Father, Son and CIA*, p. 139. 'Wolff
was considered a top expert' Marks, *The Search for the 'Manchurian Candidate'*,
p. 148. 'Ford and Rockefeller foundations' McCoy, 'Cruel Science', p. 218.
'Research in the manipulation of human behavior' Inspector General's
Report on MKULTRA, 1963, pp. 1–2, cited in the 'Church Committee Report',
p. 390. 'informers or members of suspect … individuals at all social
levels' Inspector General's Report on MKULTRA, 1963, p. 21, cited in the
'Church Committee Report', p. 391. 'One such victim was Dr Frank Olson'
Hersh, 'Family Plans to Sue CIA Over Suicide in Drug Test'; Ignatieff, 'What
Did the CIA Do to Eric Olson's Father?'. 'well-known New York hoodlum'
Special to the New York Times, 'Files Show Tests for Truth Drug Began in OSS'.
'the sense of humor is accentuated' Lee and Shlain, *Acid Dreams*, p. 4.
'Operation Midnight Climax' Schmeck, 'Bureau of Narcotics Tied To CIA's
Drug Program'; Thomas, 'CIA Sought to Spray Drug on Partygoers'; Segel,
'Medical Mayhem: Operation Midnight Climax'.

p. 27 MKULTRA wrap-up
'more than 25 000 doses of LSD' *The Washington Star*, 'CIA Considered Big
LSD Purchase'. 'nothing to do with covering up' Thomas, 'Key Figure
Testifies in Private on CIA Drug Tests'. 'Precautions must be taken' Inspector
General's Survey of TSD, 1957, p. 217, cited in the 'Church Committee Report',
p. 394.

2. STRESS INOCULATION
pp. 28–9 Chinhae school
'prison camp school' United Press, 'Air Force Trained to Bear Red Jails'. Note:
The Air Force opened a survival school in 1947 at Marks Air Force Base, Alaska.
This program taught pilots how to survive in arctic climates but did not include
stress inoculation training. 'the Air Force's Psychological Warfare Division'
Weinstein, *Father, Son and CIA*, p. 137. 'stress inoculation involves gaining

awareness' Tucker-Ladd, 'Stress-inoculation'. **'the psychosis of prisoner-of-war life'** United Press, 'Air Force Trained to Bear Red Jails'. **'When the students arrive for their six-day training'** ibid.

pp. 29–33 Early accounts of Soviet torture
'[Rubashov] could only remember separate fragments' Koestler, *Darkness at Noon*, pp. 171–2. **'These other questioners saw to it that he was in constant slight pain'** Orwell, *Nineteen Eighty-Four*, pp. 253–4. **'I was ordered to stand facing the wall'** Waggoner, 'How Reds Get Confessions Revealed to US by Victim'. **'stand a man in water up to his waist'** Evans, 'Life in a Soviet Satellite'. **'Robert Vogeler ... was released'** Associated Press, 'Vogeler Freed; 17 Months in Solitary Cell!'. **'initial interrogation lasted seventy-eight hours'** Kennedy, 'Vogeler Describes Torture Used to Make Him Confess in Hungary'. **'Oatis was granted a pardon'** Associated Press, 'Oatis, Freed, Says He Was Not Abused in Jail by Czechs'. **'I was desperate for sleep. So I signed'** Oatis, 'How Reds Forced Oatis to "Confess"'. **'I walked the floor like a caged animal'** Oatis, 'Life in Prison Like "Living Death" to Oatis'. **'without the use of narcotics, hypnosis ... little, if any, threat to National Security'** Lee and Shlain, *Acid Dreams*, p. 17.

p. 33 Camp Mackall
'forced to endure isolation, sleep deprivation and self-inflicted pain' Associated Press, 'Bare Cruelty Courses for US Military'.

p. 33 Red GIs
'twenty-one American POWs held an impromtu press conference' Associated Press, 'Peiping Agrees to Take 21 Red GIs, 326 Others'; Zweiback, 'The 21 Turncoat GIs: Nonrepatriations and the Political Culture of the Korean War'. **'warns us to prepare better defenses against similar brainwashing'** *New York Times*, Editorial, 'Fruits of Brainwashing'. **'70 per cent of the 7190 US POWs had co-operated'** United Press, 'POW Study Finds 70% Helped Reds'.

pp. 33–4 Schwable capture
'shot down over North Korean territory' Associated Press, 'Marine Air Wing Leader Missing in Korean Action'. **'biological contamination belt ... nothing could appear in writing'** Associated Press, 'Reds Ignore US Offer to Swap Ill Korea POWs'. **'in excellent English without the usual mistakes'** Special to the *New York Times*, 'Red Germ Charges Cite 2 US Marines'. **'It's all a damn lie'** Rosenthal, 'Germ War Inquiry Demanded of Reds'. **'mind-annihilating methods'** Special to the *New York Times*, 'Red China Steps Up Germ War Charges'. **'Operation Big Switch'** Jordan, 'Last POWs Freed in Korea Exchange by Allies and Reds'. **'Marine Corps launched an inquiry'** Special to the *New York Times*, 'Marine Colonel Will Face Inquiry Today On "Confession" to Reds on Germ Warfare'. **'cowardly conduct'** Uniform Code of Military Justice, Section 899, Art 99.

pp. 34–5 Schwable inquiry
'morally broken ... a world of fancy' Associated Press, 'Ex-POW Describes Red Brainwashing'. **'It wasn't a method of physical torture ... always**

in solitary confinement' Associated Press, 'Tell Red Torture in Germ War "Confessions"'. **'people can understand physical torture better … held out longer if he had been better prepared'** Young, 'Col. Schwable Tells Torture by Korean Reds'. **'shine lights into his eyes'** United Press, 'Army Challenged on POW Charges'. **'forced to stand at attention … forced to sit'** Associated Press, 'Confess or Die of Cold, Choice Given Colonel'. **'beast in a cage'** Young, 'Couldn't Stand Brainwashing, Gen. Dean Says'. **'menticide … psychological attack'** W. K., '"Menticide" Is Listed as a New Crime'. **'No man alive could withstand'** Associated Press, 'Psychiatrist Aids "Germ" Confessor'. **'directed the … THC truth drug trials'** Lee and Shlain, *Acid Dreams*, p. 3. **'There is no indestructible man'** Young, 'Reds Destroy Mind, Quiz Told'. **'Marine court issued a verdict'** Associated Press, 'Text of Inquiry Findings on Marine Col. Schwable and Comments by Defense Officials'.

p. 35 Schwable wrap-up
'Legion of Merit' Special to the *New York Times*, 'Marines Award Schwable Medal'. **'serious offenses against comrades'** Leviero, 'New Code Orders POWs to Resist in "Brainwashing"'.

pp. 35–6 POW Code of Conduct
'study the techniques of physical and mental persuasion' United Press, 'Officers to Study "Brainwash" Issue'. **'Pentagon issued a definitive Code of Conduct'** Leviero, 'New Code Orders POWs to Resist in "Brainwashing"'. **'stand on the final line to the end'** *Newsweek*, 'What a Man Must Do'.

p. 36 Resistance training spreads
'give specialized training in evasion' United Press, 'Training is Ordered on New POW Code'. **'escape and evasion exercise'** United Press, '"Brainwash" Course Backed by Marines'. **'support a fighting man in the stresses'** Special to the *New York Times*, 'British to Instruct Troops on Capture'.

pp. 36–9 Stead program
'program at Stead Air Force Base' Wyden, 'Ordeal in the Desert: Making Tougher Soldiers to Resist Brainwashing'. **'My own sons are not involved … War is hell'** *Newsweek*, Letters to the Editor. **'temporarily suspended'** Special to the *New York Times*, 'The Air Force Suspends Its "Brainwash" Course'. **'We don't torture … laughing triumphantly'** Norman, 'Air Force Defends Its "Torture" School'.

pp. 39–41 Special Forces torture training
'espionage, assassination, sabotage' Department of the Army, FM 31-21, 'Organization and Conduct of Guerilla Warfare', cited in Metzgar, 'Unconventional Warfare'. **'Anything, Any Time, Any Place, Any How'** Leviero, 'Army's "Toughest" Trained in Wilds'. **'resistance training was held at Camp Mackall'** ibid. **'testimony to the 1967 International War Crimes Tribunal'** Testimony and Questioning of Donald Duncan, International War Crimes Tribunal—The Evidence of Copenhagen. **'we will deny that any such thing is taught or intended'** Donald Duncan, *The New Legions*, Victor Gollancz, London, 1967, pp. 156–9, cited in Blum, *Killing Hope*, p. 128.

3. CODIFYING CRUELTY

pp. 42–4 Sensory deprivation

'the personality can be badly deformed' Hebb, 'The Motivating Effects of Exteroceptive Stimulation', p. 110. 'US$10 000 per year under "Contract X-38"' McCoy, *A Question of Torture*, p. 35. 'looked at the effects of visual deprivation in rats' Klein, 'The Hebb Legacy'. 'possibilities for protection against brainwashing' Hebb, 'The Motivating Effects of Exteroceptive Stimulation', p. 110. 'US$20 per day' Bexton et al., 'Effects of Decreased Variation in the Sensory Environment', p. 71; Heron, 'The Pathology of Boredom', p. 53. 'six weeks … six days' Colligan, 'Brutalizing the Mind: The Science of Torture'. 'fitted with goggles … a procession of squirrels' Heron, 'The Pathology of Boredom', pp. 52–5. 'they were afraid of ghosts' Hebb, 'The Motivating Effects of Exteroceptive Stimulation', p. 111. 'ball of cotton wool floating above my body' Heron, 'The Pathology of Boredom', p. 54. 'snatched immediately to some organization in the States' Weinstein, *Father, Son and CIA*, p. 140.

pp. 44–8 CIA isolation interests

'Hebb's "experiment gets at some of the psychological factors"' McCoy, *A Question of Torture*, pp. 37–8. 'operational tool of potential … interrogation aid' CIA, 'SUBJECT: Project ARTICHOKE', p. 3. 'Baldwin used monkeys' Marks, *The Search for the 'Manchurian Candidate'*, p. 202. 'Baldwin met with Cameron' McCoy, *A Question of Torture*, p. 43. 'The Society for the Investigation of Human Ecology' Rauth and Turner, 'Anatomy of a Public Interest Case Against the CIA', pp. 327–8. 'four steps to a successful conversion' ibid., p. 315. 'no favorable results were obtained' Marks, *The Search for the 'Manchurian Candidate'*, p. 138. 'was directly related to brainwashing' Special to the *New York Times*, 'Private Institutions Used in CIA Effort to Control Behavior'. '"sense of indebtedness" for the nearly US$60 000' ibid., pp. 316, 343. '60 per cent … 23 per cent' ibid., p. 343. 'compensation—Can$100 000 each' CBC News Online, 'Woman Awarded $100 000 for CIA-funded Electroshock'. 'Cameron was irresponsible—criminally stupid' Rauth and Turner, 'Anatomy of a Public Interest Case Against the CIA', p. 336.

pp. 48–50 Russian methods

'When food is presented … docility of a trained animal' CIA, KUBARK (KUSODA), 'Communist Control Techniques', pp. 22–4. 'If he is given an opportunity to talk', ibid., pp. 24, 34. 'forced standing … is a form of physical torture' ibid., p. 36. 'swell to twice their normal … delusions and visual hallucinations' ibid., p. 37. 'stick it out … effective in the breakdown' ibid., pp. 37–8. 'as poignant as a cocked pistol' ibid., p. 59. 'more than 99 per cent' ibid., p. 30.

p. 50 Chinese methods

'require men in total isolation' ibid., p. 78. 'It is a Chinese custom … one of the most fiendish tortures' ibid., p. 79. 'constitute torture and physical 'coercion' ibid., p. 26. **'published a declassified version of their work'** see *AMA Archives of Neurology and Psychiatry*, August 1956, Vol. 76, No. 2.

pp. 50–1 DDD
'have reduced viability, are helplessly dependent' Farber et al., 'Brainwashing, Conditioning, and DDD (Debility, Dependency, and Dread)', p. 273. **'Fear of death, fear of pain, fear of non-repatriation'** ibid. **'As soon as resistance appears … well-nigh intolerable'** ibid., pp. 278, 273.

pp. 51–2 A shift away from drugs
'no such magic brew' Bimmerle, '"Truth" Drugs in Interrogation', p. A17. **'more powerful or more prescient … resist the action of alchohol'** CIA, KUBARK, 'Communist Control Methods', Appendix 1. **'By 1962 and 1963, the general idea'** cited in McCoy, 'Cruel Science', p. 220.

pp. 52–4 Don Compos and DDD
'a pseudonym used by a frequent contributor' Dujmovic, 'Fifty Years of Studies in Intelligence', p. 6. **'like a riding horse, not smashed'** Compos, 'The Interrogation of Suspects Under Arrest', p. 51. **'maltreating the subject … softening-up process'** ibid., p. 52. **'arrest should take the subject by surprise'** ibid., pp. 53–4. **'solitary confinement for a long period'** ibid., p. 55. **'control the psychological factors … futility'** ibid., p. 58. **'place a strain … uncomfortable chair'** ibid., p. 56. **'recording going on … psychological breach'** ibid. **'drastic variation … fifteen hours or shortened'** ibid., pp. 58–9. **'interrogation art … made under duress, during prolonged detention'**, ibid., p. 51.

pp. 54–6 KUBARK manual
'fundamental hypothesis' CIA, KUBARK, *Counterintelligence Interrogation*, p. 41. **'cope with repeated frustrations … his own confession is true or false'** ibid., pp. 83–4. **'bodily harm … medical, chemical, or electrical'** ibid., p. 8. **'four conclusions about isolation'** ibid., p. 90. **'diet, sleep pattern … eight hours had intervened'** ibid., pp. 87, 49–50. **'strong fear of anything … exhaust itself in this internal encounter'** ibid., pp. 90, 94. **'useful to any KUBARK interrogator … no valid experimentation'** ibid., pp. 110–11.

pp. 57–8 Comrade Nosenko
'CIA found an ideal guinea pig … Yuri Nosenko' Thomas, *Journey into Madness*, pp. 394–9. **'nevertheless we were doing our best'** Hearings, House Select Committee on Assassinations, Vol. IV, p. 31, cited in Troy, 'A Look Over My Shoulder (Book Review)'. **'The Farm … "premiere course"'** Bowden, 'The Dark Art of Interrogation', p. 72.

4. The Phoenix Factor
pp. 59–60 Vietnam start
'If Free Vietnam is won' Chomsky, *The Backroom Boys*, p. 15. **'drew up plans for the "pacification"'** Blum, *Killing Hope*, pp. 125–6. **'the suppressive force that can best react'** Lobe, 'US Police Assistance for the Third World', p. 39. **'reaching out into every corner of the country'** Sir Robert Thompson,

Defeating Communist Insurgency, Praeger, New York, 1966, p. 85, cited in Lobe, 'US Police Assistance for the Third World', p. 36.

pp. 60–2 CIA involvement

'CIA was responsible for training the VBI' Valentine, *The Phoenix Program*, p. 32. 'OPS was staffed with CIA officers' Lobe, 'US Police Assistance for the Third World', pp. 57, 60–1. 'US$85 million through the Office of Public Saftey' Lobe, 'US Police Assistance for the Third World', pp 504–14. '80 000 South Vietnamese alone' McCoy, 'Cruel Science', p. 223. 'VBI was the most powerful security force' Valentine, *The Phoenix Program*, p. 32. 'Thieu thanked the free world, "the US most of all"' Langguth, *Hidden Terrors*, p. 135. 'Le Van An defended torture ... "mental or psychological torture"' McCoy, 'Cruel Science', p. 224. 'political and administrative organization ... 63 000 people' CIA, 'Internal Security in South Vietnam—Phoenix', pp. 1, 3. 'abide by the Geneva Conventions' Gebhardt, 'The Road to Abu Ghraib', p. 46. 'violence or threats ... coercion ... murder, torture' *Geneva Convention relative to the Protection of Civilian Persons in Time of War*, Articles 27, 31, and 32 respectively. 'who, at a given moment ... suspected of or engaged ... treated with humanity' ibid., Articles 4 and 5.

pp. 62–4 The book on terror

'developed in tandem, starting in 1964' Valentine, *The Phoenix Program*, p. 63. 'Civilians in the operational area may' FM 33-5, *Psychological Operations*, 1962, p. 115, cited in McClintock, 'Counterterror and Counterorganization', *Instruments of Statecraft*. 'bring danger and death to the Vietcong' Valentine, *The Phoenix Program*, p. 59. 'a unilateral American program' Cooper, 'Operation Phoenix: A Vietnam Fiasco Seen From Within'. 'psychological pressure on the guerrillas' Valentine, *The Phoenix Program*, p. 163. 'deserters, VC turncoats, and bad motherfucker criminals' ibid., p. 61. 'The PRU started off as a counterterror program' ibid., p. 172. 'We wrapped det [detonator] cord' ibid., p. 63. 'retaught with more sophisticated techniques' ibid., p. 84. 'had worked on Russian defectors' ibid.

pp. 64–6 Snow white cell

'electric shock, beat him with clubs, poured water' Pribbenow, 'The Man in the Snow White Cell'. 'totally white, totally bare' Snepp, *Decent Interval*, p. 42. 'trembling in the draft of the air conditioning' ibid., p. 48.

pp. 66–70 PICs

'twenty to sixty solitary ... cold at night in the highlands' Valentine, *The Phoenix Program*, p. 82. 'hired assistants—former cops or Green Berets' ibid., p. 85. 'put in another country, can teach these methods' Testimony and Questioning of Donald Duncan, International War Crimes Tribunal—The Evidence of Copenhagen. 'baptism of fire' Valentine, *The Phoenix Program*, p. 85. '*Khong, danh cho co*' Amnesty International, *Report on Torture*, p. 168. 'all broken and confessed in thirty days' 'Congressional Record', 1 July 1971, p. E6932,

cited in Brown and Luce, *Hostages of War*, p. 10. **'begins with a beating'** Brown
and Luce, *Hostages of War*, p. 29. **'I have seen blind-folded men'** ibid. **'French
first imported the technique'** Rejali, 'Electricity: The Global History of a
Torture Technology'. **'ordered a Vietnamese interrogator to ram needles'**
Langguth, *Hidden Terrors*, p. 225. **'Nguyen Thi Lang was "given electric
shocks"'** Jane Leida G. Barton, 'Women in Prison, Quang Ngai, Vietnam', cited
in Brown and Luce, *Hostages of War*, p. 98. **'Young boy, 17 years old'** Jane
Leida G. Barton, 'Notes on Some Prisoners Treated in the Prison Ward, Quang
Ngai Province Hospital During August 1972', cited in Brown and Luce,
Hostages of War, p. 101. **'testing program in an overseas setting, using
indigenous subjects'** Helms, 'Eyes Only'. **'CIA conducted a host of
terminal electro-shock experiments'** Thomas, *Journey Into Madness*, p. 392.
'CIA team was sent to Bien Hoa Hospital' ibid., p. 400.

pp. 70–2 Sorting out the pieces
'a program of assassination, etc. ... GVN assumed control' CIA,
'Internal Security in South Vietnam—Phoenix', pp. 6, 8. **'rate of 14 000 per
month'** Brown and Luce, *Hostages of War*, p. iii. **'impossible to tell'** cited in
Brown and Luce, *Hostages of War*, p. 7. **'up to 80 per cent'** Brown and Luce,
Hostages of War, p. 15. **'monthly quotas imposed ... incentive effect upon
lower officials'** CIA, 'Internal Security in South Vietnam—Phoenix',
pp. 10–11. **'neutralized 20 587 VCIs'** Blum, *Killing Hope*, p. 131. **'death count
closer to 60 000'** Peterson, 'Vietnam: This Phoenix is a Bird of Death'. **'No,
Congressman. I am not'** Blum, *Killing Hope*, p. 131. **'protect the Vietnamese
people from terrorism'** cited in McCoy, 'Cruel Science', p. 225. **'the use of
electronic gear'** ibid. **'the insertion of the 6-inch dowel'** 22nd Report by
the Committee on Government Operations, 17 October 1972, p. 100, cited in
Brown and Luce, *Hostages of War*, p. 21. **'categorically inhuman ... murder
program'** ibid. **'victims are tortured to discover innocence or guilt'**
Amnesty International, *Report on Torture*, p. 168.

5. IN AMERICA'S BACKYARD
p. 73 Backyard
'structural weaknesses, social cleavages' Dean Rusk, State Department Press
Release, no. 381, 11 June 1962, cited in Lobe, 'US Police Assistance for the Third
World', p. 33. **'including terror. And it must be met'** cited in Blum, *Killing
Hope*, p. 232.

pp. 73–4 Mitrione start
'hard-working, and always eager to please' Walker, ABC Radio National,
'Tortured Questions'. **'corrupted like Mr Kurtz in "Heart of Darkness"'**
ibid. **'US$5.9 million ... 100 000 police officers'** Langguth, *Hidden Terrors*,
p. 140; Lobe, 'US Police Assistance for the Third World', pp. 505, 510. **'right pain
in the right place at the right time'** Riding, 'Cuban "Agent" Says US Police
Aides Urged Torture'.

pp. 74–6 Mitrione in Brazil
'**either talked or were killed**' Langguth, *Hidden Terrors*, p. 139. '**complex art
… just silent blows**' Riding, 'Cuban "Agent" Says US Police Aides Urged
Torture'. '**kneeling on the floor … pre-torture process … cold for a
long time**' Russell Tribunal on Repression in Brazil, Chile and Latin America,
Torture in Brazil, p. 8. '**police in São Paulo also used "the fridge"**' Colligan,
'Brutalizing the Mind'. '**using frayed wires from military field telephones**'
Langguth, *Hidden Terrors*, p. 139. '**a physical and psychological commotion**'
Paulo Shilling, *Brasil: Seis Anos de Dictadura y Torturas,* Quadernos de marcha
No. 37, Montevideo, 1970, cited in Amnesty International, *Report on Torture*, p. 60.
'**Statue of Liberty**' Langguth, *Hidden Terrors,* p. 200. '**the "Vietnam"**' Rejali,
'Of Human Bondage'.

pp. 76–8 Mitrione in Uruguay
'**a new public safety director would be bringing instructions**' Riding,
'Cuban "Agent" Says US Police Aides Urged Torture'. '**academic, almost
clinical atmosphere**' ibid. '**they took beggars, known in Uruguay as
bichicomes**' Manuel Hevia Cosculluella, *Passaporte 11333: Ocho Anos con la CIA*,
Havana, 1978, p. 284, cited, translated in Blum, *Killing Hope*, p. 202. '**People's
Courts … Either everyone dances or no one dances**' ibid., p. 201. '**charge
directly to the gums**' Langguth, *Hidden Terrors*, p. 251. '**force him to stand
facing the wall**' ibid., p. 250. '**poke, prod, or pinch between or on the
buttocks**' 'goose', *The American Heritage Dictionary of the English Language*.
'**Mitrione bragged about that kind of thing**' Walker, 'Tortured Questions'.
'**determine his physical state … a failure by the technician**' Manuel
Hevia Cosculluella, *Passaporte 11333: Ocho Anos con la CIA,* Havana, 1978, cited,
translated in Langguth, 'Torture's Teachers'.

pp. 78–80 Death of Mitrione
'**upon the insistence of the US government**' Blum, *Killing Hope*, p. 203.
'**shot twice in the head**' Fagan, 'Death in Uruguay'. '**this is what Dan was
doing in Uruguay**' Walker, 'Tortured Questions'. '**he was my brother …
dedicate ourselves to that unfinished task**' Tribune Wire Services, '4200
Attend Sinatra-Lewis Show for Slain Official's Kin'. '**most blatant interference
by the United States**' Labrousse, *The Tupamaros*, p. 102. '**advocated
psychological torture … scientific methods of torture**' cited, translated
in Langguth, *Hidden Terrors*, pp. 286–7. '**turned to violent methods … use
violence only as a last resort**' cited, translated in Labrousse, The Tupamaros,
p. 103. '**normal, frequent and habitual occurrence**' Blum, *Killing Hope*,
pp. 201–2. '**more than 5000 while over 40 000 people**' *Repression in Latin
America, a Report of the Russell Tribunal Session in Rome*, Winter, 1975–76, cited in
Chomsky and Herman, *The Washington Connection and Third World Fasicm*,
pp. 272–3. '**ten thousand … one million … shipped more than US$150
million**' Blum, *Killing Hope*, p. 204. '**Torture was commonplace in
twenty-four**' Mathew Gildner, 'Torture and US Foreign Policy', Honors Thesis,
University of Wisconsin, Madison, 2001, p. 2, cited in McCoy, 'Cruel Science',
p. 223.

p. 80 Training goals
'You can help them with information' Priest, 'Army's Project X Had Wider Audience'. **'lessons on intelligence collection, interrogation and detention'** CIA, 'Internal Security in South Vietnam—Phoenix', pp. 29–30.

pp. 80–1 Original Project X
'counterinsurgency techniques learned in Vietnam to Latin American' Department of Defense, 'Subject: USSOUTHCOM CI Training—Supplemental Information'. **'may have found its way into the Project X materials'** Parry, 'Lost History'. **'do not represent US government policy'** Michel, 'Subject: Improper Material in Spanish-Language Intelligence Manuals'. **'abduction, exile, physical beatings and execution'** Priest, 'Army's Project X Had Wider Audience'. **'1968 manual titled *Employee Procurement and Utilization*'** ibid. **'participate in political contests as candidates for government office'** ibid. **'more than 60 000 Latin American officers'** Priest, 'US Instructed Latins on Executions, Torture'. **'halted by [the] Carter Administration'** Department of Defense, 'Subject: USSOUTHCOM CI Training—Supplemental Information'. **'the Reagan administration had broader interests'** Cohn and Thompson, 'A Carefully Crafted Deception'.

pp. 81–3 Making new manuals
'provide all forms of training, equipment, and related assistance' Cohn and Thompson, 'When a Wave of Torture and Murder Staggered a Small US Ally, Truth Was a Casualty'. **'working group decided to use Project X material'** Kennedy, 'Report on the School of the Americas'. **'word-for-word'** ibid. **'lighting, heating, and configuration of the interrogation room'** Department of the Army, FM 34-52, *Intelligence Interrogation*, 1987, Chapter Three: Approach. **'Montgomery was a veteran of the Phoenix program'** Hodge and Cooper, 'Roots of Abu Ghraib in CIA Techniques'. **'stamped "approved" and "unchanged"'** Department of Defense, 'Subject: USSOUTHCOM CI Training—Supplemental Information'.

pp. 83–4 Spanish SOA manuals
'consequences for the employee and his family' Department of Defense, *Manejo de Fuentes*, p. 155; also cited, translated in Haugaard, 'Declassified Army and CIA Manuals Used in Latin America'. **'gag, bind and blindfold suspects'** Haugaard, 'Torture 101 in the School of the Americas (SOA)'. **'induce cooperation'** Department of Defense, *Interrogación*, p. 95. **'demand necessitates that information be made quickly available'** ibid., p. 95. **'crushed emotionally … something very horrible'** ibid. **'trained in subversion of the democratic process'** Haugaard, 'Torture 101 in the School of the Americas (SOA)'. **'can have as its cause political, social, and economic activities'** ibid. **'pseudo-religion … spectre is surrounding the whole world'** Department of Defense, *Guerra Revolucionaria, Guerrilleria e Ideología Comunista*, p. 128; also cited, translated in Haugaard, 'Declassified Army and CIA Manuals Used in Latin America'. **'thousand copies … offensive and objectionable'** Michel, 'Subject: Improper Material in Spanish-Language Intelligence Manuals'.

pp. 84–5 Human resource exploitation
'lectures in the classroom ... practical work with prisoners' CIA, *Human Resource Exploitation Training Manual,* 1983, p. A-3. 'coercive "questioning"' ibid. 'the proper way to use them' ibid., p. A-2. 'the three major principles' ibid., p. K-1. 'induce psychological regression in the subject' ibid. 'immediately blindfolded and handcuffed' ibid., p. F-1. 'isolation, both physical and psychological' ibid., p. F-2. 'any time the subject is moved ... stripped and told to take a shower' ibid., p. F-3. 'all body cavities ... ill-fitting clothing ... total isolation' ibid., p. F-4. 'sense of time ... recovering from shock ... heat, air and light' ibid., p. E-3. 'defensive apathy ... have a psychologist available' ibid., p. K-3.

p. 85 Similarities to SOA manual
'means for establishing a bargaining position ... it must be carried out' ibid., pp. I-8, K-9. 'employee realizes that such threats could be carried out' Department of Defense, *Handling of Sources,* also cited, translated in CNN, 'Army Manuals Appear to Condone Human Rights Abuse'. '1) Turn him over ... 7) Physical violence' CIA, *Human Resource Exploitation Training Manual,* 1983, p. I-8. 'imprison the employee or give him a beating' Department of Defense, *Handling of Sources,* p. 79, also cited, translated in Haugaard, 'Declassified Army and CIA Manuals Used in Latin America', and cited, translated in Myers, 'Be All That You Can Be: Your Future as an Extortionist'. 'experience and imagination of the "questioner"' CIA, *Human Resource Exploitation Training Manual,* p. J-2. 'only limited by the agent's imagination' Department of Defense, *Handling of Sources,* p. 155, also cited, translated in Haugaard, 'Declassified Army and CIA Manuals Used in Latin America'.

pp. 85–7 Standard DDD set-up
'disorient ... destroy his capacity to resist' CIA, Human Resource Exploitation Training Manual, p. K-2. 'stays at his side the entire time' ibid., p. E-3. 'fear of anything vague or unknown ... induces regression' ibid., p. K-2. 'forsaken by his comrades' ibid., p. F-4. 'constant disrupting patterns' ibid., p. K-5. 'If pain is not used until late ... sap his resistance' ibid., pp. K-9, K-10. mere 'psychological techniques' ibid., p. A-2. 'The effects of isolation ... disturbances of many bodily processes' CIA, KUBARK (KUSODA), 'Communist Control Techniques', p. 26.

6. THE HUMAN COST
pp. 88–90 Creation of Battalion 316
'to combat both domestic and regional subversive movements' CIA cable, 'The 316th MI Battalion', 18 February 1995. 'considered Alvarez to be one of the country's top officers' Gill, *The School of the Americas,* pp. 85–9; Hitz and Cinquegrana, 'Report of Investigation: Selected Issues Relating to CIA Activities in Honduras in the 1980s', p. 11. 'a hard man but effective officer' LeMoyne, 'Testifying to Torture'. 'It was [the Americans'] idea' Cohn and Thompson, 'When a Wave of Torture and Murder Staggered a Small US Ally, Truth was a Casualty'. 'not all of them are fair' ibid. 'I was

taken to Texas with twenty-four others' LeMoyne, 'Testifying to Torture', p. 62.
'"human resources exploitation" course' citing Richard Stolz, in Cohn et al., 'Torture was Taught by CIA'. **'The course consisted of three weeks of classroom instruction'** Cohn and Thompson, 'When a Wave of Torture and Murder Staggered a Small US Ally, Truth was a Casualty'. **'If a person did not like cockroaches'** Thompson and Cohn, 'Torturers' Confessions'. **'The first thing we would say'** ibid. **'They always asked to be killed'** Cohn and Thompson, 'When a Wave of Torture and Murder Staggered a Small US Ally, Truth was a Casualty'.

pp. 90–2 Inés Murillo episode
'One victim who survived an encounter' Cohn and Thompson, 'A Survivor Tells Her Story'. **'The Americans knew everything'** Thompson and Cohn, 'Torturers' Confessions'. **'worked to promote the restoration'** Cohn and Thompson, 'A Carefully Crafted Deception'. **'When it comes to subversion, [Alvarez]'** Cohn and Thompson, 'When a Wave of Torture and Murder Staggered a Small US Ally, Truth was a Casualty'. **'begging for them to take some action'** Kennedy, 'Report on the School of the Americas'.

pp. 92–6 Truth and consequences
'Phoenix veteran and adviser' McGehee, 'Operation Phoenix'. **'officials can be "neutralized"'** Kennedy, 'Report on the School of the Americas'. **'You're not in the office any more'** 'Skirmishes Over a Primer', *Time*. **'CIA's first explicit policy statement'** Hitz and Cinquegrana, 'Report of Investigation: Selected Issues Relating to CIA Activities in Honduras in the 1980s', p. 18. **'Whether regression occurs spontaneously'** CIA, *Human Resource Exploitation Training Manual*, p. K-15. **'added at the front of the manual in March 1985'** Cohn et al., 'Torture was Taught by CIA'. **'While we deplore'** CIA, *Human Resource Exploitation Training Manual*, p. A-2. **'why, in 1983, it became necessary'** Cohn et al., 'Torture was Taught by CIA'. **'might appear harsh'** US Senate, Select Committee on Intelligence, Transcript of Proceedings before the Select Committee on Intelligence: Honduran Interrogation Manual Hearing, 16 June 1988 (Box 1 CIA Training Manuals, Folder: Interrogation Manual Hearings, National Security Archives), 33–6, cited in McCoy, 'Cruel Science', p. 235. **'participate directly in nor to encourage'** Kennedy, 'Report on the School of the Americas'. **'most cooperative'** US Senate, Honduran Interrogation Manual Hearing, cited in McCoy, 'Cruel Science', p. 235. **'unable to resolve whether'** Hitz and Cinquegrana, 'Report of Investigation: Selected Issues Relating to CIA Activities in Honduras in the 1980s', p. 4. **'[Redacted] continues to deny'** Hitz and Cinquegrana, 'Report of Investigation: Selected Issues Relating to CIA Activities in Honduras in the 1980s', p. 27. **'in violation of legal, regulatory, or policy prohibitions'** Michel, 'Subject: Improper Material in Spanish-Language Intelligence Manuals'.

pp. 96–8 New Army field manual
'Interrogation is the process' Department of the Army, FM 34-52, *Intelligence Interrogation,* 1992, pp. 1-6. **'Experience indicates'** ibid., pp. 1-8. **'Torture is

defined' ibid. 'Coercion is defined' ibid. 'questions directly related' ibid., pp. 3-14–3-16. 'two tests' ibid., pp. 1-9.

7. ALIVE AND LEGAL

pp. 99–102 Concerning the Code
'Evil Empire' Blumenthal, 'The U-Turn that Saved the Gipper'. 'a sailor suffocated' Williams and Kasindorf, 'The Navy: Torture Camp'. 'Lieutenant Wendell Richard Young … filed suit' ibid. 'speculation and controversy concerning validity' Department of Defense, 'Report of the Defense Review Committee for the Code of Conduct', p. 1. 'from pillar to post' cited in Kalven, 'Limbaugh Repeated NewsMax.com's False Claim'. 'I told lies' Scherer, 'Will Bush and Gonzales Get Away With It?' 'living conditions in [Vietnamese] prison' Weinraub, 'Sailor Says Faith in God and Skipper Helped Him'. 'Some PWs and detainees' Department of Defense, 'Report of the Defense Review Committee for the Code of Conduct', pp. 10–13. 'assignment has a high risk' Department of Defense, AR 350-30, *Code of Conduct, Survival, Evasion, Resistance, and Escape (SERE) Training,* p. 3.

pp. 102–5 SERE techniques
'shifted to Fairchild from Stead' Associated Press, 'Exam at School is 5.5 Days Long'. 'the executive officer's sex toy' ABC, *20/20,* 'Conduct Unbecoming—Sexual Abuse at Air Force Academy', 7 April 1995, cited in Palmer, 'Her Own Private Tailhook'. 'act like he's having sex' ibid., cited in Charles, 'AFA Scandals Confirm Senate Oversight Failure'. 'too pretty and too confident' Palmer, 'Her Own Private Tailhook', pp. 22–4. 'estimated US$3 million' Charles, 'AFA Scandals Confirm Senate Oversight Failure'. 'We were penned in concrete cell blocks' Cole, 'Guantánamo Controversies: The Bible and the Koran'. 'they lose their freedom, all freedom' Savidge, CNN, *CNN Presents.* 'kicked the Bible around' Benjamin, 'Torture Teachers'.

pp. 105–6 SERE effects
'deliver incredible levels of stress' Morgan and Hazlett, 'Assessment of Humans Experiences Uncontrollable Stress'. 'they're basically shooting blanks' Savidge, CNN, *CNN Presents.*

p. 106 SERE questions
'Sometimes you fly really tired' Palmer, 'Her Own Private Tailhook', p. 24. 'SERE camps were "laboratories"' cited in Cole, 'Guantánamo Controversies: The Bible and the Koran'. 'were also allowed to hone their own skills' Bauer, 'My Experience With Abusive Interrogation Tactics'.

pp. 106–9 CAT start
'clearly express United States opposition to torture' Ronald Reagan, *Message from the President of the United States Transmitting the Convention Against Torture and Other Cruel, Inhuman or Degrading Treatment or Punishment,* S Treaty Doc. No. 100-20, at iii (1988), cited in Levin, 'Re: Legal Standards Applicable Under 18 USC §§ 2340–2340A', p. 1. 'electric shocks; suspension; suffocation' Wendland, *Handbook on State Obligations under the UN Convention Against Torture,*

p. 25. **'Kenya, Yemen, Cyprus and Northern Ireland'** Vallely, 'A Systematic Process Learned From Cold War'. **'designed to disorientate and break down the resistance'** Weinraub, 'British in Ulster Accused of Psychological Torture'. **'suffering of the particular intensity and cruelty'** *Ireland v United Kingdom* 5310/71 [1971] ECHR 1 (18 January 1978). **'(1) restraining in very painful positions, (2) hooding'** Committee Against Torture, CAT/C/SR.297ADD.1, Conclusions, para 6-4, cited in Harbury, *Truth, Torture, and the American Way*, p. 122. **'one must preserve basic standards of behavior'** Sontag, 'Israeli Court Bans Most Use of Force in Interrogations'.

pp. 109–11 Retooling the CAT: Reagan
'extremely cruel ... "police brutality" ... specifically intended' Senate Treaty Doc. No. 100-20, pp. 4–5, cited in Bybee, 'Re: Standards of Conduct for Interrogation Under 18 USC §§ 2340–2340A', pp. 16–17. **'A specific intent crime is one in which'** *United States v Blair*, 54 F 3d 639 at 642 (10th Cir 1995) (quotation marks and citations omitted). **'A person entered a bank and took money'** *United States v Lewis*, 628 F 2d 1276 at 1279 (10th Cir 1980). **'increased "precision"'** US State Department, 'Implementation of Specific Articles'. **'extend the widest possible protection'** United Nations, 'Body of Principles for the Protection of All Persons under Any Form of Detention or Imprisonment', Principle 7. **'prohibited by the Fifth, Eighth, and/or Fourteenth Amendments'** Senate Treaty Doc No. 100-20, pp. 15–16, cited in Bybee, 'Re: Standards of Conduct for Interrogation Under 18 USC §§ 2340–2340A', p. 17. **'reservation has far-reaching implications'** Amnesty International, 'A Briefing for the UN Committee against Torture'.

pp. 111–13 Retooling the CAT: Bush
'sends chills ... the needle under the fingernail' *Convention Against Torture*: Hearing Before the Senate Committee On Foreign Relations, 101st Congress, 1990, cited in Bybee, 'Re: Standards of Conduct for Interrogation Under 18 USC §§ 2340–2340A', pp. 19–20. **'problem with the Torture Convention ... unacceptable element'** ibid., cited in Levin, 'Re: Legal Standards Applicable Under 18 USC §§ 2340–2340A', p. 11. **'only four specific variations'** *United Nations Convention Against Torture*, 'United States—Declarations and Reservations', Understanding II.1(a). **'turns the very idea of the prohibition against torture on its head'** Borchelt, *Break Them Down*, p. 79. **'incompatible with the object and purpose'** Committee Against Torture, 'Status of the Convention and Reservations, Declarations and Objections Under the Convention'. **'to mean "if it is more likely than not"'** United Nations, CAT, 'United States—Declarations and Reservations', Understanding II.2. **'places a higher burden of proof on someone'** Amnesty International, 'A Briefing for the UN Committee against Torture'. **'new hidden right is not lurking'** Roth, 'The Charade of US Ratification of International Human Rights Treaties', p. 348. **'withdraw its reservations, interpretations and understandings'** Committee Against Torture, 'Conclusions and Recommendations of the Committee against Torture: United States of America', Paragraph 180.

pp. 113–14 Torture laws in the USA
Torture Victim Protection Act of 1991 28 USC § 1350, Public Law 102–256.
Federal Torture Statute 18 USC §§ 2340–2340A. **'prosecutions have been
hampered'** *Hilao v Estate of Marcos*, 103 F 3d 767 at 798, 790 (9th Cir 1996), and
Eastman Kodak v Kavlin, 978 F Supp 1078 at 1093 (SD Fla 1997).

pp. 114–15 Rendition
'to send terrorism suspects for interrogation and trial in Cairo' Mayer,
'Outsourcing Torture'. **'Egypt is consistantly cited'** US State Department,
'Egypt—Country Report on Human Rights Practices for 1996'. **'electrical
shocks to his genitals' … 'not sure'** Mayer, 'Outsourcing Torture'. **'can use
the fruits'** Priest and Gellman, 'US Decries Abuse but Defends Interrogations'.

pp. 115–16 WCA
War Crimes Act of 1996 18 USC § 2441. **'I just thought that was wrong'**
Scherer, 'Will Bush and Gonzales Get Away With It?' **'Jones and other
advocates'** Smith, 'Detainee Abuse Charges Feared'. **'wilful killing, torture or
inhuman treatment … a) Violence to life'** *Geneva Convention relative to the
Protection of Civilian Persons in Time of War*, Articles 147, 3.

8. The Gloves Come Off, Part I
pp. 117–18 Gearing up
'We are at war … going to kick some ass' Clark, *Against All Enemies*, p. 24.
'We also have to work … the dark side' The White House, 'The Vice
President Appears on Meet the Press with Tim Russert'. **'needed new robust
authority'** Woodward, *Bush at War*, p. 76. **'"targeted killing" missions'**
Gellman, 'CIA Weighs "Targeted Killing" Missions'. **'detain al Qaeda
operatives worldwide … Arab Liaison Services'** Woodward, *Bush at War*,
pp. 76–7. **'authorised the CIA to kill, apprehend, or detain members of
al Qaeda'** Priest, 'CIA Holds Terror Suspects in Secret Prisons'. **'After 9/11
the gloves come off'** House and Senate Intelligence Committee Hearing,
'Testimony of Cofer Black'. **'someone dies, we'll be held responsible'** Priest,
'Wrongful Imprisonment: Anatomy of a CIA Mistake'. **'bin Laden's head
brought to him on ice'** PBS, *Frontline*, 'The Torture Question', Interview with
Michael Scheuer.

pp. 118–21 Al-Libi
'ranked number seventeen' US State Department, 'Comprehensive List of
Terrorists and Groups Identified Under Executive Order 13224'. **'Reid …
Moussaoui … trained at the Khalden camp'** Mayer, 'Outsourcing Torture'.
'netted some of the US government's best pre-9/11 intelligence' Vest,
'Pray and Tell'. **'I think you should go pray … this thing called due
process'** ibid. **'stand as a shining example of what we feel is right'** Mayer,
'Outsourcing Torture'. **'Al-Libi was handed over to the CIA'** Hirsh et al.,
'A Tortured Debate'. **'off he apparently goes to Cairo, in a box'** Vest, 'Pray
and Tell'.

pp. 121 Extraordinary rendition
'really went out of control' Mayer, 'Outsourcing Torture'. **'more than 100 suspects have been rendered'** Priest, 'Italy Knew About Plan to Grab Suspect'. **'if we believe it more likely than not'** Department of Justice, 'Prepared Remarks by Attorney General Alberto R. Gonzales'. **'We don't kick the [expletive] out of them'** Priest and Gellman, 'US Decries Abuse but Defends Interrogations'. **'Habib's account is not unique'** Amnesty International, 'Below the Radar'.

pp. 121–2 Maher Arar
'based on classified information ... I would be deported to Syria' Arar, 'Chronology of Events'. **'administering electrical shocks; pulling out fingernails'** US State Department, 'Syria—Country Reports on Human Rights Practices for 2003'. **'black electrical cable, about two inches thick ... hear the others screaming'** Arar, 'Maher's Statement to the Media'. **'erroneous rendition'** Priest, 'Wrongful Imprisonment: Anatomy of a CIA Mistake'.

pp. 122–3 Black site: Afghanistan
'kept these prisoners in metal shipping containers' Priest, 'CIA Holds Terror Suspects in Secret Prisons'. **'secret prison, known as a "black site"'** ibid. **'hand lists of questions to interrogators'** Priest and Gellman, 'US Decries Abuse but Defends Interrogations'.

p. 123 Getting authorisation
'the agency sought legal guidance' Jehl, 'Report Warned CIA on Tactics In Interrogation'. **'the US intelligence community is palsied by lawyers'** PBS, *Frontline*, 'The Torture Question'.

pp. 123–4 The torture memos, Part I
'highest assurance that no court would subsequently entertain charges' Ashcroft, Letter to President Bush. **'substantially reduces the threat of domestic criminal prosecution'** Gonzales, 'Decision re application of the Geneva Convention on Prisoners of War to the conflict with al Qaeda and the Taliban'. **'renders quaint some of its provisions'** ibid.

pp. 124–5 Geneva and US history
'abide by the humanitarian principles ... particularly common Article Three' Joseph P. Bialke, 'United Nations Peace Operations', *Air Force Law Review*, Vol. 50, Winter 2001, p. 63, n 235, cited in Yoo and Delahunty, 'Application of Treaties and Laws to al Qaeda and Taliban Detainees', p. 26. **'General Tommy Franks ordered troops to follow the Geneva Conventions'** Margulies, *Guantánamo and the Abuse of Presidential Power*, p. 83. **'the United States has never, to our knowledge, suspended'** Yoo and Delahunty, 'Application of Treaties and Laws to al Qaeda and Taliban Detainees', p. 30.

pp. 125–6 Conventions
'nobody in enemy hands can fall outside the law' International Committee of the Red Cross, *Commentary*, ed. Jean S. Pictet, ICRC, Geneva, 1958, p. 51, cited in Margulies, *Guantánamo and the Absuse of Presidential Power*, p. 55. **'technically

not acts of "non international character"' Yoo and Delahunty, 'Application of Treaties and Laws to al Qaeda and Taliban Detainees', p. 11. **'merely a violent political movement ... not a nation state'** ibid., p. 1. **'As the Supreme Court later affirmed'** *Hamdan v Rumsfeld*, 548 US, 126 S Ct 2749, L Ed 2d (2006). **Afghanistan is simply a 'failed state'** Yoo and Delahunty, 'Application of Treaties and Laws to al Qaeda and Taliban Detainees', p. 2. **'enemy aliens'** Philbin and Yoo, 'Possible Habeas Jurisdiction over Aliens Held in Guantánamo Bay, Cuba', p. 1.

pp. 126–7 Actual rights of prisoners
'either a prisoner of war ... [or] a civilian' International Committee of the Red Cross, *Commentary*, ed. Jean S. Pictet, ICRC, Geneva, 1958, p. 51, cited in Margulies, *Guantánamo and the Absuse of Presidential Power*, p. 55. **'combatants must satisfy four specific criteria'** Article 4, *Geneva Convention relative to the Treatment of Prisoners of War*. **'persons shall enjoy the protection of the present Convention'** Article 5, *Geneva Convention relative to the Protection of Civilian Persons in Time of War*. **'nevertheless be treated with humanity'** ibid.

p. 127 Backup justification
'including those concerning the treatment of prisoners' Yoo and Delahunty, 'Application of Treaties and Laws to al Qaeda and Taliban Detainees', p. 11. **'his determination is fully discretionary and will not be reviewed'** Ashcroft, Letter to President Bush. **'power to interpret treaties ... obviate the need for Article 5 tribunals'** Bybee, 'Status of Taliban Forces Under Article 4 of the Third Geneva Convention of 1949'. **'Addington's fingerprints'** Mayer, 'The Hidden Power'. **'if the President wants torture he should get torture'** ibid.

pp. 127–8 Critiques
'did not by its terms limit its application ... preserves US credibility' Powell, 'Draft Decision Memorandum for the President on the Applicability of the Geneva Convention to the Conflict in Afghanistan'. **'base 'its conduct ... on its international legal obligations'** Taft, 'Comments on Your Paper on the Geneva Convention'. **'bound to comply with their obligations under international humanitarian law'** United Nations Security Council, Resolution 1193 (1998), Item 12.

pp. 128–9 Decision
'On 19 January 2001, Donald Rumsfeld officially rescinded' Margulies, *Guantánamo and the Abuse of Presidential Power*, p. 83. **'war against terrorism ushers in a new paradigm'** Bush, 'Humane Treatment of al Qaeda and Taliban Detainees'. **'an ambigous term last used during World War II'** Lardner, 'Nazi Saboteurs Captured! FDR Orders Secret Tribunal—1942 Precedent Invoked By Bush Against al Qaeda'. **'in a manner consistent with the principles of Geneva'** Bush, 'Humane Treatment of al Qaeda and Taliban Detainees'.

pp. 129–30 SERE docs
'you also know how to stress people, in order to get them to talk'
Mayer, 'The Experiment'. **'supporting combat operations against Al Qaeda
and Taliban fighters'** American Psychological Association, '2003 Members'
Biographical Statements'. **'what human behavior in captivity is like'**
Mayer, 'The Experiment'. **'consulted on various interrogation techniques'**
American Psychological Association, '2003 Members' Biographical Statements'.
'elicit a psychological condition known as "learned helplessness"'
Mayer, 'The Experiment'. **'six "enhanced" interrogation techniques
were authorised'** Ross and Esposito, 'CIA's Harsh Interrogation Techniques
Described'. **'A.The Attention Grab … F. Water Boarding'** ibid. **'personally
authorised by George Bush'** Ross, 'History of an Interrogation Technique'.
'OLC wrote several specific memos' Jehl, 'Report Warned CIA on Tactics In
Interrogation'.

pp. 130–1 Using SERE on al-Libi
'al-Libi was back in US custody in Afghanistan' Hemmer, CNN,
Saturday Morning News. **'al-Libi was progressively subjected to the six
SERE techniques'** Ross and Esposito, 'CIA's Harsh Interrogation Techniques
Described'.

p. 131 Zubaydah
'rendered to Thailand to a newly constructed CIA black site' Priest,
'CIA Holds Terror Suspects in Secret Prisons'. **'rapport-building and stroking
aren't the top things on your agenda'** Johnston, 'At Secret Interrogation,
Dispute Flared Over Tactics'. **'including the cold cell and food, sleep and
light deprivation'** Van Natta, 'Questioning Terror Suspects in a Dark and Surreal
World'; Johnston, 'At Secret Interrogation, Dispute Flared Over Tactics'. **'after
the agency interrogators began using more stringent tactics'** Johnston, 'At
Secret Interrogation, Dispute Flared Over Tactics'. **'went to OLC lawyer Yoo
for an opinion on bolder methods'** Hirsh et al., 'A Tortured Debate'.

pp. 131–2 August torture memos
'ICC … can still prosecute states not party to the treaty' Lobe, 'Bush
"Unsigns" War Crimes Treaty'. **'Yoo argued that American interrogators
need not worry'** Yoo, 'Interrogation Methods to be Used During the Current
War on Terrorism'. **'intentional infliction of severe pain or suffering,
whether physical or mental'** Rome Statute of the International Criminal
Court, Part 2, Article 7(2)e. **'even if certain interrogation methods being
contemplated amounted to torture …'** Yoo, 'Interrogation Methods to be
Used During the Current War on Terrorism'.

pp. 132–3 Bybee–Addington
'written with extensive input from David Addington' Mayer, 'The Hidden
Power'. **'a variety of defences "would negate any claim"'** Bybee, 'Standards
of Conduct for Interrogation under 18 USC §§ 2340–2340A', p. 1. **'act
committed by a person under the color of law …'** Federal Torture Statute,
18 USC §§ 2340–2340A. **'A good faith belief need not be a reasonable**

one' Bybee, 'Standards of Conduct for Interrogation under 18 USC §§ 2340–2340A', pp. 4–5. **'he lacks the mental state necessary'** ibid., p. 8. **'serious physical injury such as death or organ failure'** ibid., p. 46.

pp. 133–4 King Bush
'height in the middle of a war … troop movements on the battlefield' ibid., pp. 34–5. **'a question "to be decided by him"'** *Prize Cases*, 67 US 635 at 670 (1862), cited in Bybee, 'Standards of Conduct for Interrogation under 18 USC §§ 2340–2340A', p. 28. **'must stem either from an act of Congress or from the Constitution itself'** *Youngstown Sheet and Tube Co. v Sawyer*, 343 US 579 (1952), cited in Urofsky, *Basic Readings in US Democracy*, Part IV. **'such core war matters as the detention and interrogation'** Bybee, 'Standards of Conduct for Interrogation under 18 USC §§ 2340–2340A', p. 31. **'doing so in order to prevent further attacks on the United States'** ibid., p. 46.

pp. 134–5 Fallout?
'power to commit genocide, to sanction slavery, to promote apartheid' Liptak, 'Legal Scholars Criticize Memos on Torture'. **'policy decisions … are still valid'** Jehl, 'Report Warned CIA on Tactics In Interrogation'.

p. 135 Endgame
'schooled in the harsher interrogation procedures … blasts of music' Johnston, 'At Secret Interrogation, Dispute Flared Over Tactics'. **'selective use of drugs'** Priest and Gellman, 'US Decries Abuse but Defends Interrogations'. **'pain control … "is a very subjective thing"'** ibid.

p. 135 The Promotion
'He just disappeared from the face of the earth' Priest, 'CIA Avoids Scrutiny of Detainee Treatment'.

pp. 135–6 KSM
'On 1 March 2003, the CIA scored their biggest catch' Bowden, 'The Dark Art of Interrogation', p. 51. **'marijuana, heroin, and sodium pentothal'** ibid., p. 52. **'accelerate and exacerbate … breakdown of resistance'** CIA, KUBARK, 'Communist Control Methods', Appendix 1.

9. Guantánamo
pp. 137–8 Welcome to GTMO
'you are now the property of the US Marine Corps' Rasul et al., 'Composite Statement', pp. 23–4, 28. **'conditions as the Secretary of Defense may prescribe'** Bush, 'Military Order of November 13th 2001'. **'allowed statements made under torture'** Patel, 'Yes, Commissions Can Allow In Evidence Obtained Under Torture'. **'the kind of treatment of these individuals that we believe they deserve'** White House, 'Vice President Addresses US Chamber of Commerce'.

p. 138 A place outside the law
'challenge the legality of his status and treatment' Philbin and Yoo, 'Possible Habeas Jurisdiction over Aliens Held in Guantánamo Bay, Cuba', p. 8. **'system that has been developed'** ibid.

pp. 138–9 GTMO history
'**17 miles of a 10-foot high cyclone fence topped by barbed wire**'
Pomfret, *The History of Guantánamo Bay*, Chapter 5. '**for use as coaling or
naval stations only**' Agreement Between the United States and Cuba for the
Lease of Lands for Coaling and Naval stations, 23 February 1903. '**complete
jurisdiction and control … ultimate sovereignty**' ibid. '**agree to a
modification of its present limits**' Treaty Between the United States of
America and Cuba, 29 May 1934. '**The naval base is a dagger plunged into
the Cuban soil**' Pomfret, *The History of Guantánamo Bay*, Chapter 5.

pp. 139–40 GTMO case law
'**1966 Pellicier murder case**' Pomfret, *The History of Guantánamo Bay*,
Chapter 5. '**Jamaican man was brought to the US**' *United States v Lee*, 906
F 2d 117 (4th Cir 1990). '**issued a writ of habeas corpus to a Marine**' *Burtt
v Schick*, 23 MJ 140 (USCMA, 1986), cited in *Rasul v Bush,* 542 US 466 (2004).
'**is subject to the exclusive control and jurisdiction of the United States**'
Haitian Centers Council Inc v McNary, 969 F 2d 1326 (2nd Cir 1992), cited in
Philbin and Yoo, 'Possible Habeas Jurisdiction over Aliens Held in Guantánamo Bay,
Cuba', p. 6. '**could not properly exercise habeas jurisdiction**' Philbin and Yoo,
'Possible Habeas Jurisdiction over Aliens Held in Guantánamo Bay, Cuba', p. 1.

pp. 140–1 What is GTMO?
'**create dependency and trust**' Woolfolk, 'Declaration'. '**psychological
impacts on the delicate subject–interrogator relationship**' Jacoby,
'Declaration'.

pp. 141–2 X-Ray
'**couldn't lean on the wire fence … given very little time to eat**' Rasul
et al., 'Composite Statement', p. 32. '**took a sick pleasure from seeing us
degraded**' ibid., p. 33.

pp. 142–3 Hicks and Habib
'**David Hicks and us three (when we were together) would always talk**'
ibid., p. 54. '**He was a very surprising sight**' ibid., p. 127. '**Habib himself
was in catastrophic shape**' ibid., p. 123.

p. 143 Al-Qahtani, part I
'**Qahtani was detained in the Orlando International Airport**' Zagorin and
Duffy, 'Inside the Interrogation of Detainee 063'. '**FBI agents at Guantánamo
Bay discovered that the fingerprints**' ibid. '**very high-value target
detainee**' Department of Defense, 'Media Availability with Commander, US
Southern Command General James T. Hill'.

pp. 143–4 Who's in GTMO?
'**worst of a very bad lot**' The White House, 'The Vice President Appears on
Fox News Sunday'. '**more than half of the detainees didn't belong there**'
Mayer, 'The Hidden Power'. '**thirty to forty "real" terrorists**' Agence France
Presse, 'Guantánamo May Have 30–40 "Real" Cases: OSCE Inspector'. '**these
guys weren't fighting. They were running**' Mintz, 'Most at Guantanamo to

Be Freed or Sent Home, Officer Says'. **'8 per cent … 60 per cent … 86 per cent'** cited in Lithwick, 'Invisible Men'. **'turned in by Northern Alliance forces for US$1000'** Whitmont, ABC, *Four Corners*. **'piles of US twenty-dollar bills'** Friedman, 'Psychological Operations in Afghanistan', Leaflet AFD29p. **'You can receive millions of dollars'** Friedman, 'Psychological Operations in Afghanistan', Leaflet TF11–RP09.

pp. 144–5 Getting approval
'enormous amount of specific and general insights into 9/11' Zagorin and Duffy, 'Inside the Interrogation of Detainee 063'. **'trained in resistance techniques and was using them'** Department of Defense, 'Media Availability with Commander, US Southern Command General James T. Hill'. **'pressure from military intelligence officials to bend army doctrine'** Alden et al., 'Can Iraq Torture Be Linked to the White House?'

p. 145 Miller time
'no prior detention or interrogation experience' Margulies, Guantánamo and the Abuse of Presidential Power, p. 96. **'"the war is on" … leniency in the rules'** Lewis, 'In New Book Ex-Chaplain at Guantánamo Tells of Abuses'. **'An inherent conflict exists between guarding and protecting'** Gebhardt, 'The Road to Abu Ghraib', p. 50. **'intelligence to dominate how military police treated detainees'** Alden et al., 'Can Iraq Torture Be Linked to the White House?'

pp. 145–6 BSCT
'purpose was to help us break them' Neil, 'Interrogators Cite Doctors' Aid at Guantánamo'. **'we know how to hurt people better than others'** Mayer, 'The Experiment'. **'BSCTs … should have a SERE background'** ibid. **'acute, uncontrollable stress erodes established behavior'** Bloche and Marks, 'Doctors and Interrogators at Guantánamo Bay'. **'"consult on interrogation approach techniques"'** Department of Defense, BSCT Standard Operating Procedures, 11 November 2002. **'inform interrogators about "cultural issues"'** Department of Defense, BSCT Standard Operating Procedures, 28 March 2005, p. 3. **'strategies for increasing positive behavior'** ibid., p. 4 **'strategies for increasing pro-American sentiment'** ibid., p. 3. **'BSCT personnel have full and direct access'** ibid., p. 4.

pp. 146–8 SERE import
'staff at Guantánamo working with behavioral scientists' Department of Defense, 'Media Availability with Commander, US Southern Command General James T. Hill'. **'"Category I" and "Category II" "counter-resistance" techniques'** Phifer, 'Request for Approval of Counter-Resistance Strategies'. **'not intended to cause gratuitous, severe, physical pain'** 'Effectiveness of the Use of Certain Category II Counter-Resistance Strategies', Memo to [Redacted] from [Redacted]. **'approval for four "Category III" techniques'** Phifer, 'Request for Approval of Counter-Resistance Strategies'. **'proposed strategies do not violate applicable federal law'** Beaver, 'Legal Review of Aggressive Interrogation Techniques'. **'"constrained by" the**

Geneva Conventions' ibid. 'enhance our efforts to extract additional
information' Dunlavey, 'Counter-Resistance Strategies'. 'desire to have
as many options as possible at my disposal' Hill, 'Counter-Resistance
Strategies'. 'all Category III techniques may be legally available' Haynes,
'Counter-Resistance Strategies'. 'Blanket authorisation was rescinded'
Mayer, 'The Memo'. 'Why is standing limited to four hours? D.R.' Haynes,
'Counter-Resistance Strategies'.

pp. 148–9 Al-Qahtani, part II
'kept Rumsfeld informed in weekly briefs' Scherer and Benjamin, 'What
Rumsfeld Knew'. 'he became impatient with the FBI interrogations'
Mayer, 'The Experiment'. 'Qahtani was "totally isolated ... a canine
was used"' Harrington, 'Suspected Mistreatment of Detainees', and Zagorin
and Duffy 'Inside the Interrogation of Detainee 063'. 'various JTF GTMO
interrogators compiled it' Zagorin and Duffy 'Inside the Interrogation of
Detainee 063'.

pp. 149–51 Interrogator logbook
'0940: Detainee was given three and one-half bags of IV' Department
of Defense, 'Interrogation Log Detainee 063', p. 6. 'This is Major John
Leso' Bloche and Marks, 'Doctors and Interrogators at Guantánamo Bay'.
'1000: Control puts detainee in swivel chair' Department of Defense,
'Interrogation Log Detainee 063', p. 12. 'plunged into the strange' CIA,
KUBARK, *Counterintelligence Interrogation*, July 1963, p. 86. '1115 ... Began
teaching the detainee lessons such as stay, come, and bark' Department
of Defense, 'Interrogation Log Detainee 063', pp. 47–8. 'performed a puppet
show' ibid., p. 20. 'drink water or wear it' ibid. p. 52. 'kept naked in his
cell and women's underwear' White, 'Abu Ghraib Tactics Were First Used at
Guantánamo'. 'shrine to Osama bin Laden and forced Qhatani to pray to
it' Department of Defense, 'Interrogation Log Detainee 063', p. 47.

pp. 151–2 SERE spreads
'my predecessor, arranged for SERE instructors to teach their
techniques' Department of Defense, 'Summarized Witness Statement of
Lt. Col. [Redacted]'. 'the SERE methods were designed for use in a
battlefield environment' Department of Defense, 'JTF GTMO "SERE"
INTERROGATION SOP DTD 10 DEC 02'. 'establish the SERE model
of interrogation as policy here' 'GTMO Matters', e-mail forwarded from
[Redacted] to Frank Battle.

pp. 152–4 SERE effects
'around the end of 2002. That is when short-shackling started' Rasul,
et al, 'Composite Statement', p. 67. 'I was taken into a room and short
shackled' ibid., p. 81. 'On a couple of occassions [sic]' 'RE GITMO',
[Redacted] e-mail to [Redacted], 2 August 2004. 'I've met with the BISC
(Biscuit) people several times' 'Re: GTMO', [Redacted] e-mail to [Redacted],
31 July [Redacted]. 'Towards the end of December 2002 a new system
was introduced' Rasul et al., 'Composite Statement', pp. 65–6. 'exploit a

detainee's longing for his mother' Slevin and Stephens, 'Detainees' Medical Files Shared'.

pp. 154–5 SERE sex tactics
'We didn't hear anybody talking about being sexually humiliated'
Rasul, et al., 'Composite Statement', p. 68. **'Sex, I believe, came from the BSCTs'** Mayer, 'The Experiment'. **'began to cry like a baby'** Associated Press, 'Translator Corroborates Guantánamo Sex Tactics'. **'The detainee was shackled ... fetal position on the floor and crying in pain'** Harrington, 'Suspected Mistreatment of Detainees', 14 July 2004.

p. 155 SERE flag technique
'Israeli flag draped around him, loud music being played' 'RE GTMO', [Redacted] e-mail to [Redacted], 30 July 2004.

p. 155 SERE holy book desecration
'Koran desecration was also widely reported' Cageprisoners, 'Report into the Systematic and Institutionalized US Desecration of the Qur'an and Other Islamic Rituals'. **'kick the Koran, throw it into the toilet and generally disrespect it'** Rasul et al., 'Composite Statement', p. 34. **'Koran was wrapped inside an Israeli flag and then stomped on'** Mayer, 'The Experiment'. **'guards defiled at least five Muslim holy books'** Associated Press, 'US Confirms Gitmo Soldier Kicked Quran'.

pp. 155–7 FBI v DOD
'have produced no intelligence of a threat neutralization nature' 'Impersonating FBI at GTMO', e-mail from [Redacted] to Bald, Gary, BATTLE, FRANKIE, CUMMINGS, ARTHUR. **'showing a detainee homosexual porn movies'** 'Re: GTMO," [Redacted] e-mail to [Redacted], 31 July [Redacted]. **'use aggressive interrogation tactics ... of questionable effectiveness'** 'GTMO-INTEL', From CIRG, Behavioral Analysis Unit to Raymond S Mey, Marion E Bowman, Hector M Pesquera and Frank Figliuzzi. **'the FBI's continued objection to the use of SERE ... techniques'** 'Detainee Interviews (Abusive Interrogation Issues)', 6 May 2004. **'we met with Generals Dunlevey [sic] & Miller ...'** 'Instructions to GTMO interrogators', e-mail from [redacted] to TJ Harrington, 10 May 2004.

p. 157 Mental toll al-Qahtani
'talking to non-existent people, reporting hearing voices' Harrington, 'Suspected Mistreatment of Detainees'. **'some pretty good stuff'** Department of Defense, 'Media Availability with Commander, US Southern Command General James T. Hill'. **'painfully described how he could not endure the months of isolation'** Zagorin, 'Exclusive: "20th Hijacker" Claims That Torture Made Him Lie'. **'presented with evidence coughed up by others in detention'** Zagorin and Duffy 'Inside the Interrogation of Detainee 063'.

pp. 157–8 Mental toll Tipton Three
'I started to suffer what I believe was a break down' Rasul et al., 'Composite Statement', p. 64. **'I said it wasn't me but [a female**

interrogator] kept pressing' ibid., p. 85. **'you are entirely powerless and have no way of having your voice heard'** ibid., p. 67.

pp. 158–60 Mental toll Habib and Hicks
'every way be under the control of the people who held them there' ibid., p. 123. **'there was no natural light at all there'** ibid. **'not going to let anyone out of there with their minds'** Mamdouh Habib, Sydney, New South Wales, 22 May 2006. **'David Hicks? He's finished'** ibid. **'We thought that he had gone downhill'** ibid., p. 127. **'I believe that al-Qaeda camps provided'** ABC, 'The Case of David Hicks'. **'Dear Dad, I feel as though I'm teetering on the edge of losing my sanity'** ibid. **'I've reached the point where I'm highly confused and lost'** ibid.

10. THE GLOVES COME OFF, PART II
pp. 161–2 Wish list
'one victory in a war on terror that began on September the 11th' The White House, 'President Bush Announces Combat Operations in Iraq Have Ended'. **'Captain William Ponce ... wrote an e-mail to interrogators'** PBS, *Frontline*, 'The Torture Question', e-mail from Cpt. William Ponce; also in 'Subject: Taskers', [Redacted] e-mail to [Redacted], 14 August 2003, Exhibit E, in Department of the Army, Commanders Inquiry (15-6). **'4th Infantry Division ... requested authorisation for techniques'** Alternative Interrogation Techniques (Wish List), 4th Infantry Davision, ICE, Exhibit D, in Department of the Army, Commanders Inquiry (15-6). **'today's enemy understands force'** ACLU, 'Latest Government Documents Show Army Command Approved and Encouraged Abuse of Detainees, ACLU Says'. **'close confinement quarters ... fear of dogs and snakes ... I firmly agree'** White, 'Soldiers' "Wish Lists" of Detainee Tactics Cited'. **'used in part to develop a new list'** ibid.

pp. 162–3 Sanchez's authorisations
'"modelled" on the one implemented at Guantánamo Bay' Sanchez, 'CJTF-7 Interrogation and Counter-Resistance Policy', 14 September 2003. **'sitting, standing ... qualified medical personnel'** ibid. **'not applicable to the interrogation of unlawful combatants'** Sanchez, 'CJTF-7 Interrogation and Counter-Resistance Policy', 10 September 2003. **'this technique in certain circumstances to be inhumane'** Sanchez, 'CJTF-7 Interrogation and Counter-Resistance Policy', 14 September 2003. **'controls all aspects of the interrogation'** Sanchez, 'CJTF-7 Interrogation and Counter-Resistance Policy', 12 October 2003.

pp. 163–4 Confusion and permissibility
'great deal of confusion as to the status of detainees' ACLU, 'Latest Government Documents Show Army Command Approved and Encouraged Abuse of Detainees, ACLU Says'. **'we don't have to follow these Geneva Convention articles'** Human Rights Watch, 'No Blood, No Foul'. **'Death crosses the line, but you know, torture doesn't'** PBS, *Frontline*, 'The Torture Question', Interview with Tony Lagouranis. **'We kept it to broken arms and legs and shit'** Human Rights Watch, 'Leadership Failure', p. 10.

pp. 164–5 Abu Ghraib history

'British-built ... 50 000 men and women' Youssef, 'Abu Ghraib No Longer
Houses Any Prisoners, Iraqi Officials Say'. **'150 prisoners crammed into cells'**
Martin, 'Her Job: Lock up Iraq's Bad Guys'. **'concerned they wouldn't want
to leave'** ibid.

pp. 165–6 MTT at Abu Ghraib

'previously worked with interrogators at Guantánamo and Bagram'
Fay, 'AR 15-6 Investigation of the Abu Ghraib Detention Facility and 205th
Military Intelligence Brigade', pp. 62–4. **'may have contributed to the
abuse'** ibid., p. 63. **'ideas as to how to get these prisoners to talk'** Fay,
'AR 15-6 Investigation of the Abu Ghraib Detention Facility and 205th Military
Intelligence Brigade', Annex B, Appendix 1 (WALTERS 20040621), declassified
as 'Regarding Our Conversation', e-mail from [Redacted] to [Redacted],
21 June 2004, Annex to Fay/Jones/Kern Report. **'My only intent was for
the prisoner to imagine what could happen'** ibid.

pp. 166–7 Red Cross inspection

'completely naked in totally empty concrete cells' International
Committee of the Red Cross, 'Report of the International Committee of
the Red Cross (ICRC)', p. 13. **'prolonged periods in stress positions ...
photographed in this position'** ibid., p. 12. **'effects of these tortures'** ibid.,
p. 13. **'barred inspectors' access to eight "high value" detainees'** Fay,
'AR 15-6 Investigation of the Abu Ghraib Detention Facility and 205th Military
Intelligence Brigade', p. 66.

pp. 167–8 MP–MI relationship

'not yet set conditions for successful operations' Miller, 'Assessment of
DoD Counter-Terrorism Interrogation and Detention Operations in Iraq', p. 6.
'strictly dictated by military intelligence' White and Hingham, 'Sergeant
Says Intelligence Directed Abuse'. **'Everybody is far too subtle and smart
for that ...'** ibid. **'beat a military intelligence detainee to death with
military intelligence there'** Reuters, 'England Sentenced to 3 Years Jail'.
'Laugh and point at his penis' Ambuhl, 'Former Abu Ghraib Guard Speaks
Out'. **'They just told us, hey, you're doing great. Keep it up'** Zahn, Paula,
CNN, *Paula Zahn Now.*

pp. 168–70 Tuguba

'sadistic, blatant, and wanton' Tuguba, 'Article 15-6 Investigation of the 800th
Military Police Brigade', p. 16. **'It violated everything I personally believed
in'** Associated Press, 'Prison Abuse Report "Hard Call"'; 'Army Specialist Joseph
Darby to Receive Special Profile in Courage Award', Press Release. **'They
received me there with screaming'** Sheikh, Sworn Statement. **'punched,
slapped, kicked, forcibly arranged'** Tuguba, 'Article 15-6 Investigation of the
800th Military Police Brigade', p. 17.

p. 170 BSCT sex

'are essential in developing integrated interrogation strategies'
Miller, 'Assessment of DoD Counter-Terrorism Interrogation and Detention

Operations in Iraq', p. 5. **'A physician and a psychiatrist are on hand to monitor'** Article 15-6 Investigation interview with Colonel Thomas M. Pappas, Commander, 205th Military Intelligence Brigade, 9 February 2004, p. 3, cited in Borchelt, *Break Them Down,* pp. 46–7. **'really hate being sexually humiliated'** PBS, *Frontline*, 'The Torture Question', Interview with Tony Lagouranis. **'directing nakedness ... to humiliate and break down detainees'** Fay, 'AR 15-6 Investigation of the Abu Ghraib Detention Facility and 205th Military Intelligence Brigade', p. 69. **'contributed to an escalating "de-humanization"'** ibid., p. 88.

pp. 170–1 BSCT violence
'He didn't know anything about Arabs or Arabic or Islam' PBS, *Frontline*, 'The Torture Question', Interview with Tony Lagouranis. **'In my view, it was to establish control'** White, 'Detainee in Photo With Dog Was "High Value" Suspect'. **'The MP guard and MP Dog Handler opened a cell in which two juveniles'** [Redacted], Sworn Statement, SPC/E-4, B Company.

pp. 171–3 BSCT ethics and influence
'aware of detainee abuse at Abu Ghraib and failed to report it' Fay, 'AR 15-6 Investigation of the Abu Ghraib Detention Facility and 205th Military Intelligence Brigade', p. 136. **'Layton advised guards to stop beating his wounded leg'** cited in Miles, *Oath Betrayed*, p. 121. **'Aldape-Moreno ... saw a "pyramid of naked guys"'** ibid., p. 120. **'they beat them up until they dropped on the floor'** Sharoni, Translation of Statement. **'contravention of medical ethics for health personnel, particularly physicians'** UN *Principles of Medical Ethics Relevant to the Protection of Prisoners Against Torture*, Principle 4. **'by virtue of their medical authority helped sustain it'** Lifton, 'Doctors and Torture'.

pp. 173–4 CIA/special forces at Abu Ghraib
'greater "internee access"' Miller, 'Assessment of DoD Counter-Terrorism Interrogation and Detention Operations in Iraq', p. 3. **'didn't know what they were doing ... [but] we heard a lot of screaming'** Mayer, 'A Deadly Interrogation'. **'blood gushed from his mouth "as if a faucet had been turned on"'** Associated Press, 'Iraqi Died While Hung From Wrists'. **'Mark Swanner, the CIA agent directing his interrogation'** Mayer, 'A Deadly Interrogation'. **'I called them the disappearing ghosts'** Hersh, 'The Gray Zone'. **'led to a loss of accountability, abuse ... unhealthy mystique'** Fay, 'AR 15-6 Investigation of the Abu Ghraib Detention Facility and 205th Military Intelligence Brigade', p. 53. **'Hersh revealed ... Pentagon Special Access Program'** Hersh, 'The Gray Zone'.

pp. 174–6 Nama
'6-26 was formed in mid 2003 from two Special Operations units' Schmitt and Marshall, 'In Secret Unit's "Black Room," a Grim Portrait of US Abuse'. **'The door was black, everything was black'** Human Rights Watch, 'No Blood, No Foul', p. 9. **'Sleep deprivation, environmental controls, hot and cold, water ...'** ibid. **'He was stripped naked, put in the mud and**

sprayed' ibid., p. 11. **'I never saw a sheet that wasn't signed'** ibid., p. 12. **'The interpreter told me to take off my clothes … I passed out …'** [Redacted], Sworn Statement, 5 August 2004, Exhibit 7, in Department of the Army, CID Report of Investigation—Final, pp. 19–22. **'involvment in Special Access Program's (SAP)'** [Redacted], 'Subject: Memorandum for Record', Memorandum for Commander, 8 April 2005, in Department of the Army, CID Report of Investigation—Final, p. 72. **'losing 70 percent … Hell, even if we reopened it'** 0213-04-CID259-80250 (DATF), 11 February 2005, in Department of the Army, CID Report of Investigation—Final, p. 79.

pp. 176–7 SERE flip
'since 1984, Level C SERE training has been mandatory' Hankinson, 'SERE in Transition'. **'a new requirement at SERE'** Mayer, 'The Experiment'. **'We did this when we learned people were flipping it'** ibid.

pp. 177–8 SERE murder
'Previous interrogations were non-threatening … I took the gloves off' White, 'Documents Tell of Brutal Improvisation by GIs'. **'savagely beaten by CIA and special forces … the Scorpions'** ibid.; Kusnetz, 'Preview'. **'First he took him up to the roof of the detention centre'** Danzig, 'Welshofer In His Own Words'. **'convinced that his father thought he died'** Kusnetz, 'Preview'. **'asphyxiation due to smothering and chest compression'** White, 'Documents Tell of Brutal Improvisation by GIs'.

pp. 178–80 SERE defence
'I do not believe that I ever operated outside acceptable methods' Welshofer, 'Rebuttal to General Letter of Reprimand', p. 2. **'In SERE … we frequently used close confinement positions'** ibid. **'Defense [attorney]: You also poured water on the General'** Danzig, 'Welshofer In His Own Words'. **'He explained it was something he learned in SERE'** Danzig, 'The Proceedings So Far: In Their Own Words'. **'Defense: Why did you place your right hand over his mouth'** Danzig, 'Welshofer In His Own Words'. **'Prosecutor: What is wrong with saying Wallah?'** ibid. **'No jail sentence was imposed'** Kusnetz, 'Case Closed?'.

CONCLUSION: THE DUAL STATE
pp. 181–2 New field manual
'The Army has taken pretty dramatic steps' Department of Defense, 'DoD News Briefing with Deputy Assistant Secretary Stimson and Lt. Gen. Kimmons from the Pentagon'. **'All prisoners and detainees, regardless of status, will be treated humanely'** Department of the Army, FM 2-22.3, *Human Intelligence Collector Operations*, pp. 5-21. **'forcing an individual to perform or simulate sexual acts … "Waterboarding"'** ibid. **'MPs will not take any actions to set conditions for interrogations'** ibid., pp. 5-16. **'unlawful enemy combatants "engage in acts against the United States"'** ibid., pp. 6-8.

pp. 182–3 Separation

'Separation does not constitute sensory deprivation' ibid., pp. M-8. 'detainee getting four hours of continuous sleep every 24 hours' ibid., pp. M-10.

pp. 183–4 Rapport-building

'Building rapport is an integral part of the approach phase' ibid., pp. 8–4. 'careful that he does not threaten or coerce a source' ibid., pp. 8–10. 'a ruse "to build rapport"' ibid., pp. 8–4. 'Use of torture is not only illegal but also it is a poor technique' ibid., pp. 5-21. 'No good intelligence is going to come from abusive practices' Department of Defense, 'DoD News Briefing with Deputy Assistant Secretary Stimson and Lt. Gen. Kimmons from the Pentagon'.

pp. 184–5 Revelations

'have been held and questioned outside the United States, in a separate program' The White House, 'President Discusses Creation of Military Commissions to Try Suspected Terrorists'. 'burden of this program will not rest only on the shoulders of the CIA' Priest, 'Officials Relieved Secret Is Shared'. 'bought special insurance policies that would cover any civil judgments' Smith, 'Worried CIA Officers Buy Legal Insurance'. 'CIA interrogation techniques ... became "problematic"' Fox News, *FOX News Sunday With Chris Wallace.*

pp. 185–6 The 'problem' with Common Article 3

'vague and undefined' The White House, 'President Discusses Creation of Military Commissions to Try Suspected Terrorists'. 'risk of prosecution under the War Crimes Act—simply for doing their jobs' ibid. 'You can't ask a young professional ... to violate law' The White House, 'Press Conference of the President'. 'CIA used an alternative set of procedures ... safe, and lawful, and necessary' The White House, 'President Discusses Creation of Military Commissions to Try Suspected Terrorists'. 'face justice' ibid.

p. 186 Behind the MCA

'prolonged sleep deprivation and forced standing or other stress positions' Smith, 'Behind the Debate, Controversial CIA Techniques'. 'match the techniques used by the agency in the past ...' ibid. 'preserves the most single—most potent tool ... to get their secrets' The White House, 'President Thanks Senate for Agreement on Pending War on Terror Legislation', 21 September 2006.

pp. 186–8 The MCA and its discontents

'strips the writ of habeas corpus' *Military Commissions Act of 2006*, Sec 7(a)(e)(1). 'detention, transfer, treatment, trial, or conditions of confinement' ibid., Sec 7(a)(2). 'secret evidence' ibid., § 949d, Sessions (f)(2)(A)(i). 'coerced evidence' ibid., § 949a, Rules (2)(C). 'purposefully and materially supported hostilities against the United States' ibid., § 948a(1)(i). 'President or the Secretary of Defense' ibid., § 948a(1)(ii). 'no person—not even a US citizen—can invoke the rights guaranteed by Geneva' ibid., Sec 5(a).

'Only the president ... can determine what is and what is not a breach'
ibid., Sec 6(a)(3)(A). '"cruel or inhuman" ... must produce "serious"
physical or mental pain' ibid., Sec 6(b)(1)(B). '(a) inflict "bodily injury"; and
(b) involves either "substantial risk ..."' ibid. 'four predicate acts listed in
the federal torture statute' ibid. 'non-transitory mental harm (which need
not be prolonged)' ibid. 'makes all these changes retroactive back to 1997'
ibid., Sec 6(b)(2).

pp. 188–9 Sealing the deal
'If there's public discussion of techniques' Klein, 'Congress in Dark on
Terror Program'. 'none of them know which ones would be permissible'
ibid. 'nor should I know' ibid. 'prefered to "coddle" terrorists rather
than interrogate them' Nagourney, 'Dispute on Intelligence Report Disrupts
Republicans' Game Plan'.

pp. 189–90 The dual state
'unlimited arbitrariness and violence unchecked by any legal
guarantees' Ernst Fraenkel, *The Dual State: A Contribution to the Theory of
Dictatorship*, 1941, cited in Preuss, Lawrence, 'The Dual State', Book Review,
American Journal of International Law, Vol. 35, No. 3, July 1941, pp. 584–5.
'Each of us has our task to do' Barnes, 'CIA Can Still Get Tough on Detainees'.
'61 per cent of Americans polled believed torture could be justified'
Associated Press, 'AP Poll: Most Say Torture OK in Rare Cases'. '63 per cent
said they supported secret detention and interrogation' *Mother Jones MoJo
Blog*, 'Poll Numbers on Torture'.

pp. 190–1 Torture is self-defeating
'The US is doing what the British did in the nineteen-seventies' Mayer,
'Outsourcing Torture'. 'now he's a bad guy because of the way we treated
him' Human Rights Watch, 'Leadership Failure', p. 10. 'moral Chernobyl'
Hitchens, 'A Moral Chernobyl'. 'after Abu Ghraib, the number dropped to
9 per cent' Zakaria, 'Pssst ... Nobody Loves A Torturer'. 'We've been paying
for that for a long period of time' The White House, 'President Bush and
Prime Minister Tony Blair of the United Kingdom Participate in Joint Press
Availability'. 'Burton L. Gerber, a former Moscow CIA station chief ...
has spoken out' Vest, 'CIA Veterans Condemn Torture'. 'We, as Americans,
must not let our methods betray our goals' Pribbenow, 'The Man in the
Snow White Cell'. 'Do you fight the enemy in the gutter' Vest, 'CIA Veterans
Condemn Torture'. 'it nonetheless has the upper hand' Hockstader, 'Israel's
Court Bars Abuse of Suspects'.

pp. 191–2 Torture is unnecessary
'The world changed on 9/11. Some people get that and some people
don't' McNeill, 'Davis, Hurst Clash in Congressional Debate'. 'torture
warrant' CNN, CNN-ACCESS, 'Dershowitz: Torture Can Be Justified'. 'flaw
in this fanciful scenario is its pretzel-like, ex post facto logic' McCoy,
A Question of Torture, p. 192. 'So it's not like Sipowicz from the TV show'
Department of Defense, 'DoD News Briefing with Deputy Assistant Secretary
Stimson and Lt. Gen. Kimmons from the Pentagon'.

pp. 192–4 Torture does not yield reliable information
'This was a vital piece of the puzzle' The White House, 'President Discusses Creation of Military Commissions to Try Suspected Terrorists'. **'Zubaydah identified KSM under FBI rapport-building techniques'** Johnston, 'At Secret Interrogation, Dispute Flared Over Tactics'. **'collected US$25 million after leading the CIA directly to KSM'** Ron Suskind, *The One Percent Doctrine* (2006), cited in Eggen and Linzer, 'Secret World of Detainees Grows More Public'. **'CIA already knew KSM's alias as early as August 2001'** Eggen and Linzer, 'Secret World of Detainees Grows More Public'. **'plots to kill innocent Americans'** The White House, 'President Discusses Creation of Military Commissions to Try Suspected Terrorists'. **'cut down the Brooklyn Bridge—with a blow torch'** Thomas, '"24" Versus the Real World'. **'morass of stonewalling, half-truths and moral posturing'** ibid. **'Iraq has trained Al Qaeda members in bomb making and poisons and gases'** Pincus, 'Report Cast Doubt on Iraq-Al Qaeda Connection'. **'According to Powell, a "senior al Qaeda terrorist"'** CNN, *War In Iraq*, 'Transcript of Powell's UN Presentation: Part 9: Ties to al Qaeda'. **'it is more likely this individual is intentionally misleading the debriefers'** Jehl, 'Report Warned Bush Team About Intelligence Suspicions'. **'subsequently recounted a different story'** Isikoff, 'Iraq and al Qaeda'.

pp. 194–5 Torture is corruptive
'the use of dogs, stress positions, sleep management, [and] sensory deprivation' Emily Bazelon, 'From Bagram to Abu Ghraib'. **'removing clothing, isolating people for long periods of time, using stress positions'** Fay, 'AR 15-6 Investigation of the Abu Ghraib Detention Facility and 205th Military Intelligence Brigade', p. 29. **'We keep the PUCs awake for the first twenty-four hours that they are here'** SGT [Redacted], Subject: Interview of Orgun-E Military Intelligence Detention Facility Interrogator.

pp. 195–6 SERE techniques constitute torture
'"torture" or even "abuse," as some Administration critics dishonestly charge' *Wall Street Journal*, Editorial, 'An Antiterror Victory'. **'constitute torture as defined in Article 1'.** Committee Against Torture, CAT/C/SR.297ADD.1, Conclusions, para. 6-4, cited in Harbury, *Truth, Torture, and the American Way*, p. 122. **'methods of torture'** US State Department, 'Jordan—Country Reports on Human Rights Practices for 2005'. **'The effects of isolation ... disturbances of many bodily processes'** CIA, KUBARK (KUSODA), 'Communist Control Techniques', p. 26. **'a favorite militia torture ... confessions by torture'** Evans, 'Life in a Soviet Satellite'.

pp. 196–9 SERE techniques profoundly disrupt the body and mind
'methods and duration of interrogation' International Committee of the Red Cross, 'Report of the International Committee of the Red Cross (ICRC)', p. 13. **'talking to non-existent people ... reporting hearing voices'** Harrington, 'Suspected Mistreatment of Detainees'. **'swell to twice their normal ... delusions and visual hallucinations'** CIA, KUBARK (KUSODA), 'Communist Control Techniques', p. 37. **'kept awake for

twenty-nine nights' Associated Press, 'Torture is Told by Mindszenty'. **'In the head of the interrogated prisoner a haze begins to form'** cited in Malinowski, 'Call Cruelty What It Is'. **'more painful and cause more severe and long-lasting damage'** Borchelt, *Break Them Down,* p. 48. **'Often a distinction is made between physical and mental torture'** Peter Kooijmans, UN Special Rapporteur on Torture, quoted in Report of the Special Rapporteur on Torture and Other Cruel, Inhuman or Degrading Treatment or Punishment, UN GAOR, 59th Session, Agenda Item 107(a), 2004; para 45, UN Doc. A/59/324, cited in Borchelt, *Break Them Down,* p. 49. **'October 2006, Vice President Dick Cheney confirmed'** Landay, 'Cheney Confirms that Detainees were subjected to Water-boarding'. **'Waterboarding is a torture. Period'** Kurtz, 'Readers Intimately Familiar with US Military Protocols for Training Service Members to Survive Capture'. **'traumatized for years'** Mayer, 'Outsourcing Torture'. **'One of the reasons why I haven't spoken about my personal experience'** Walker, 'Tortured Questions'. **'very, very depressed'** Associated Press, 'Guantánamo Inmate Tells of Worsening Conditions'. **'my sanity is at risk here'** Whitmont, ABC, *Four Corners.*

BIBLIOGRAPHY

URLs provided when available.

ARTICLES

Agence France Presse, 'Guantánamo May Have 30–40 "Real" Cases: OSCE Inspector', 1 July 2006. <http://uk.news.yahoo.com/01072006/323/guantanamo-30-40-real-cases-osce-inspector.html>

Alden, Edward, Peter Spiegel and Demetri Sevastopulo, 'Can Iraq Torture Be Linked to the White House?' *Financial Times*, 16 June 2004. <http://search.ft.com/searchArticle?id=040616008429>

Ambuhl, Megan, 'Former Abu Ghraib Guard Speaks Out', *Washington Post*, 23 January 2006. <http://www.washingtonpost.com/wp-dyn/content/discussion/2006/01/23/DI2006012300493_pf.html>

American Psychological Association, '2003 Members' Biographical Statements', Presidential Task Force on Psychological Ethics and National Security, Society for the Study of Peace, Conflict, and Violence, Peace Psychology Division 48. <http://www.webster.edu/peacepsychology/tfpens.html>

Arar, Maher, 'Chronology of Events: September 26 2002 to October 5 2003', *MaherArar.ca*. <http://www.maherarar.ca/mahers%20story.php>

—— 'Maher's Statement to the Media', *MaherArar.ca*, 4 November 2003. <http://www.maherarar.ca/mahers%20story.php>

Associated Press, 'AP Poll: Most Say Torture OK in Rare Cases', *ABC News*, 6 December 2005. <http://abcnews.go.com/US/wireStory?id=1378454>

—— 'Avowal of Guilt Made by Vogeler in Budapest Trial', *New York Times*, 19 February 1950, p. 1.

—— 'Bare Cruelty Courses for US Military', *Chicago Daily Tribune*, 8 September 1955, p. 1.

—— 'Cardinal Mindszenty Siezed By Red Regime in Hungary', *New York Times*, 28 December 1948, p. 1.

—— 'Confess or Die of Cold, Choice Given Colonel', *Chicago Daily Tribune*, 8 September 1953, p. 5.

—— 'Czechs Holding AP Writer for "Hostile" Acts', *Chicago Daily Tribune*, 27 April 1951, p. B19.

—— 'Exam at School is 5.5 Days Long', *New York Times*, 9 May 1967, p. 9.

—— 'Ex-POW Describes Red Brainwashing', *New York Times*, 26 February 1954, p. 2.

—— 'Fear Cardinal Will Be Given Drug By Reds', *Chicago Daily Tribune*, 23 January 1949, p. 12.

—— 'Guantánamo Inmate Tells of Worsening Conditions', *Guardian*, 7 July 2006. <http://www.guardian.co.uk/guantanamo/story/0,,1814907,00.html>

—— 'Hungarian Cardinal Fights Seizure of Schools By State', *Chicago Daily Tribune*, 16 May 1948, p. 47.

—— 'Hungarian Reds Hurl Spy Charge at Seized Yank', *Chicago Daily Tribune*, 23 November 1949, p. 3.

—— 'Iraqi Died While Hung From Wrists', *Common Dreams News Center*, 17 February 2005. <http://www.commondreams.org/headlines05/0217-09.htm>

—— 'Marine Air Wing Leader Missing in Korean Action', *New York Times*, 13 July 1952, p. 2.

—— 'Mindszenty is Found Guilty; Court Gives Life Sentence; Flood of Protests Rising', *New York Times*, 8 February 1949, p. 1

—— 'Oatis, Freed, Says He Was Not Abused in Jail by Czechs', *New York Times*, 17 May 1953, p. 1.

—— 'Peiping Agrees to Take 21 Red GIs, 326 Others', *Chicago Daily Tribune*, 27 January 1954, p. 8.

—— 'Prison Abuse Report "Hard Call"', *Washington Times*, 7 August 2004. <http://washingtontimes.com/national/20040806-101703-5440r.htm>

—— 'Psychiatrist Aids "Germ" Confessor', *New York Times*, 10 March 1954, p. 3.

—— 'Reds Ignore US Offer to Swap Ill Korea POWs', *Chicago Daily Tribune*, 23 February 1953, p. 7.

—— 'Tell Red Torture in Germ War "Confessions"', *Chicago Daily Tribune*, 24 September 1953, p. 1.

—— 'Text of Inquiry Findings on Marine Col. Schwable and Comments by Defense Officials', *New York Times*, 28 April 1954, p. 16.

—— 'Torture is Told by Mindszenty', *New York Times*, 6 December 1956, p. 5.

—— 'Translator Corroborates Guantánamo Sex Tactics', *The Age*, 28 January 2005. <http://www.theage.com.au/news/War-on-Terror/Translator-corroborates-Guantanamo-sex-tactics/2005/01/28/1106850088186.html>

—— 'US Confirms Gitmo Soldier Kicked Quran', *San Francisco Chronicle*, 4 June 2005. <http://www.sfgate.com/cgi-bin/article.cgi?f=/n/a/2005/06/03/national/w163533D64.DTL>

——'US Overseas Detention System Numbers', *Washington Post*, 17 September 2006. <http://www.washingtonpost.com/wp-dyn/content/article/2006/09/17/AR2006091700271_pf.html>

—— 'Vogeler Freed; 17 Months in Solitary Cell!', *Chicago Daily Tribune*, 29 April 1951, p. 1.

—— 'Vogeler's Recital Stirs Skepticism', *New York Times*, 19 Feb 1950, p. 41.

Barnes, Julian E., 'CIA Can Still Get Tough on Detainees', *Los Angeles Times*, 8 September 2006. <http://www.latimes.com/news/nationworld/nation/la-na-methods8sep08,1,1920452.story?coll=la-headlines-nation>

Bauer, Peter, 'My Experience With Abusive Interrogation Tactics', *Thinkprogress. com*, 1 December 2005. <http://thinkprogress.org/2005/12/01/torture-doesnt-work>

Bazelon, Emily, 'From Bagram to Abu Ghraib', *Mother Jones*, March/April 2005. <http://www.motherjones.com/news/feature/2005/03/03_2005_Bazelon.html>

Benjamin, Mark, 'Torture Teachers', *Salon.com*, 29 June 2006. <http://www.salon.com/news/feature/2006/06/29/torture/print.html>

Bexton, W. H., W. Heron and T. H. Scott, 'Effects of Decreased Variation in the Sensory Environment', *Canadian Journal of Psychology*, Vol. 8, no. 2, 1954, pp. 70–6.

Bimmerle, George, '"Truth" Drugs in Interrogation', *Studies in Intelligence*, Vol. 5, No. 2, 1961, pp. A1–A19. <https://www.cia.gov/csi/kent_csi/author-combine.htm>

Bloche, M. Gregg, and Jonathan H. Marks, 'Doctors and Interrogators at Guantánamo Bay', *New England Journal of Medicine*, Vol. 353, No. 1, 7 July 2005. <http://content.nejm.org/cgi/content/full/353/1/6>

Blumenthal, Sidney, 'The U-Turn that Saved the Gipper', *Guardian*, 10 June 2004. <http://www.guardian.co.uk/usa/story/0,,1235360,00.html>

Bowden, Mark, 'The Dark Art of Interrogation', *The Atlantic Monthly*, Vol. 292, no. 3, October 2003, pp. 51–76.

CBC News, 'Woman Awarded $100 000 for CIA-funded Electroshock', 10 June 2004. <http://www.cbc.ca/story/canada/national/2004/06/10/shock_award040610.html>

Charles, Roger, 'AFA Scandals Confirm Senate Oversight Failure', *STTF.org/ Defense Watch*, 10 March 2004. <http://www.navyseals.com/community/articles/article.cfm?id=2844>

Chicago Daily Tribune, 'State Dept. Raises Questions', 19 February 1950, p. 12.

CNN, 'Army Manuals Appear to Condone Human Rights Abuse', *CNN.com*, 21 September 1996. <http://www.cnn.com/US/9609/21/pentagon.manuals/index.html>

Cohn, Gary, and Ginger Thompson, 'A Carefully Crafted Deception', *Baltimore Sun*, 18 June 1995. <http://www.baltimoresun.com/news/local/bal-negroponte4,0,2326054.story??track=sto-relcon>

—— 'A Survivor Tells Her Story', *Baltimore Sun*, 15 June 1995. <http://www.baltimoresun.com/news/local/bal-negroponte3a,0,3966794.story??track=sto-relcon>

—— 'When a Wave of Torture and Murder Staggered a Small US Ally, Truth was a Casualty', *Baltimore Sun*, 11 June 1995. <http://www.baltimoresun.com/news/local/bal-negroponte1a,0,3704648.story>

Cohn, Gary, Ginger Thompson and Mark Matthews, 'Torture was Taught by CIA', *Baltimore Sun*, 27 January 1997. <http://www.hartford-hwp.com/archives/40/055.html>

Cole, Juan, 'Guantánamo Controversies: The Bible and the Koran', *Informed Comment*, 16 May 2005. <http://www.juancole.com/2005/05/guantanamo-controversies-bible-and.html>

Colligan, Douglas, 'Brutalizing the Mind: The Science of Torture', *Chicago Tribune*, 12 September 1976, p. A1, Special Perspectives Section.

Compos, Don, 'The Interrogation of Suspects Under Arrest', *Studies in Intelligence*, Vol. 2, No. 3, 1958, pp. 51–61. <https://www.cia.gov/csi/kent_csi/author-combine.htm>

Cooper, Wayne L., 'Operation Phoenix: A Vietnam Fiasco Seen From Within', *Washington Post*, 8 June 1972, p. B1, B4. <http://www.vietnam.ttu.edu/star/images/212/2122405068.pdf>

Dispatch of *The Times*, London, 'Hungarians Seize Foreign Companies in Sweeping Move', *New York Times*, 30 December 1949, p. 1.

Dujmovic, Nicholas, 'Fifty Years of *Studies in Intelligence*', *Studies in Intelligence*, Vol. 49, No. 4, 2005, pp. 1–13. <https://www.cia.gov/csi/studies/vol49no4/studies49_04.pdf>

Eggen, Dan, and Dafna Linzer, 'Secret World of Detainees Grows More Public', *Washington Post*, 7 September 2006. <http://www.washingtonpost.com/wp-dyn/content/article/2006/09/06/AR2006090602142.html>

Evans, Joseph E., 'Life in a Soviet Satellite', *Wall Street Journal*, 24 February 1948, p. 6.

Fagan, Richard R., 'Death in Uruguay', Book Review, *New York Times*, 25 June 1978, p. BR4.

Farber, I. E., Harry F. Harlow and Louis Jolyon West, 'Brainwashing, Conditioning, and DDD (Debility, Dependency, and Dread)', *Sociometry*, Vol. 20, No.4, December 1957, pp. 271–85.

Friedman, Herbert A., 'Psychological Operations in Afghanistan', *Psywarrior.com*. <http://www.psywarrior.com/Herbafghan02.html>

Gebhardt, James F., 'The Road to Abu Ghraib: US Army Detainee Doctrine and Experience', *Military Review*, Jan/Feb 2005, pp. 44–50.

Gellman, Barton, 'CIA Weighs "Targeted Killing" Missions', *Washington Post*, 28 October 2001, p. A01. <http://www.washingtonpost.com/ac2/wp-dyn/A63203-2001Oct27?language=printer>

Golden, Tim, 'The Battle for Guantánamo', *New York Times Magazine*, 17 September 2006. <http://travel2.nytimes.com/2006/09/17/magazine/17guantanamo.html>

Graham, Frederick, 'Nazi Scientists Aid Army on Research, *New York Times*, 4 December 1946, p. 35.

Hankinson, Major Brian, 'SERE in Transition: Meeting the Needs of the Global War on Terrorism', *Special Operations Technology*, Vol. 4, Iss. 3, 12 April 2006. <http://www.special-operations-technology.com/article.cfm?DocID=1395>

Haugaard, Lisa, 'Declassified Army and CIA Manuals Used in Latin America: An Analysis of their Content', *Latin America Working Group*, 18 February 1997. <http://www.lawg.org/misc/Publications-manuals.htm>

——— 'Torture 101 in the School of the Americas (SOA)', *Third World Traveler*, 1996. <http://www.thirdworldtraveler.com/Terrorism/torture101_SOA.html>

Hebb, Donald O., 'The Motivating Effects of Exteroceptive Stimulation', *The American Psychologist*, Vol. 3, No. 3, March 1958, pp. 109–13.

Heron, Woodburn, 'The Pathology of Boredom', *Scientific American*, Vol. 196, No. 1, January 1957, pp. 52–6.

Hersh, Seymour M., 'Family Plans to Sue CIA Over Suicide in Drug Test', *New York Times*, 10 July 1975, p. 1.

—— 'The Gray Zone', *New Yorker*, 24 May 2004. <http://www.newyorker.com/fact/content/?040524fa_fact>

Hirsh, Michael, John Barry and Daniel Klaidman, 'A Tortured Debate', *Newsweek*, 21 June 2004. <http://www.msnbc.msn.com/id/5197853/site/newsweek>

Hitchens, Christopher, 'A Moral Chernobyl', *Slate*, 14 June 2004. <http://www.slate.com/id/2102373/>

Hockstader, Lee, 'Israel's Court Bars Abuse of Suspects', *Washington Post*, 7 September 1999. <http://www.library.cornell.edu/colldev/mideast/isabusc.htm>

Hodge, James, and Linda Cooper, 'Roots of Abu Ghraib in CIA Techniques: 50 Years of Refining, Teaching Torture Found in Interrogation Manuals', *National Catholic Reporter*, 5 November 2004. <http://findarticles.com/p/articles/mi_m1141/is_3_41/ai_n9522565>

Horrock, Nicholas M., '80 Institutions Used in CIA Mind Studies', *New York Times*, 4 August 1977, p. 17.

Ignatieff, Michael, 'What Did the CIA Do to Eric Olson's Father?', *New York Times Magazine*, 1 April 2001, pp. 56–61.

Isikoff, Michael, 'Iraq and al Qaeda', *Newsweek*, 5 July 2005. <http://www.msnbc.msn.com/id/5305085/site/newsweek/>

Jehl, Douglas, 'Report Warned Bush Team About Intelligence Suspicions', *New York Times*, 6 November 2005. <http://www.nytimes.com/2005/11/06/politics/06intel.html?ex=1288933200&en=5a216116a0310ce1&ei=5090&partner=rssuserland&emc=rss>

—— 'Report Warned CIA on Tactics In Interrogation', *New York Times*, 9 November 2005. <http://www.nytimes.com/2005/11/09/politics/09detain.html?ei=5088&en=6fae30b441fa6bb4&ex=1289192400&pagewanted=all>

John F. Kennedy Presidential Library and Museum, Press Release, 'Army Specialist Joseph Darby to Receive Special Profile in Courage Award', 10 March 2005. <http://www.cs.umb.edu/~rwhealan/jfk/pr_pica2005_winners_announce.html>

Johnston, David, 'At Secret Interrogation, Dispute Flared Over Tactics', *New York Times*, 10 September 2006. <http://www.nytimes.com/2006/09/10/washington/10detain.html?_r=1&oref=slogin&pagewanted=print>

Jordan, William J., 'Last POWs Freed in Korea Exchange by Allies and Reds', *New York Times*, 6 September 1953, p. 1.

Kalven, Josh, 'Limbaugh Repeated NewsMax.com's False Claim', *Mediamatters.org*, 9 December 2005. <http://mediamatters.org/items/200512090006?offset=20&show=1>

Kennedy, Paul P., 'Vogeler Describes Torture Used to Make Him Confess in Hungary', *New York Times*, 9 June 1951, p. 6.

Klein, Raymond M., 'The Hebb Legacy', *Canadian Journal of Experimental Psychology*, Vol. 53, No.1, March 1999. <http://www.cpa.ca/Psynopsis/special_eng.html>

Klein, Rick, 'Congress in Dark on Terror Program', *Boston Globe*, 23 September 2006. <http://www.boston.com/news/nation/washington/articles/2006/09/23/congress_in_dark_on_terror_program/>

Kurtz, David, 'Readers Intimately Familiar with US Military Protocols for Training Service Members to Survive Capture', *Talking Points Memo*, 18 November 2006. <http://www.talkingpointsmemo.com/archives/011198.php>

Landay, Jonathan S., 'Cheney Confirms that Detainees were Subjected to Water-boarding', McClatchy Newspapers, 25 October 2006. <http://www.realcities.com/mld/krwashington/15847918.htm>

Langguth, A. J., 'Torture's Teachers', Op-Ed, *New York Times*, 11 June 1979, p.A19.

Lardner, George Jr, 'Nazi Saboteurs Captured! FDR Orders Secret Tribunal: 1942 Precedent Invoked By Bush Against al Qaeda', *Washington Post*, 13 January 2002, p.W12. <http://www.law.uchicago.edu/tribunals/wp_011302.html>

Lawrence, W. H., 'Why Do They Confess—A Communist Enigma', *New York Times Magazine*, 8 May 1949, pp. 7, 26–31.

LeMoyne, James, 'Testifying to Torture', *New York Times Magazine*, 5 June 1988, pp. 44–7, 62–6.

Leviero, Anthony, 'Army's "Toughest" Trained in Wilds', *New York Times*, 31 August 1955, p. 9.

——'New Code Orders POWs to Resist in "Brainwashing'," *New York Times*, 18 August 1955, p. 1.

Lewis, Neil A., 'In New Book Ex-Chaplain at Guantánamo Tells of Abuses', *New York Times*, 3 October 2005. <http://www.truthout.org/docs_2005/100305Q.shtml>

—— 'Interrogators Cite Doctors Aid at Guantánamo', *New York Times*, 24 June 2005. <http://www.nytimes.com/2005/06/24/politics/24gitmo.html?ei=5088&en=b1960558c2ad9fa4&ex=1277265600&partner=rssnyt&emc=rss&pagewanted=print>

Lifton, Robert Jay, MD, 'Doctors and Torture', *New England Journal of Medicine*, Vol. 351, No. 5, pp. 415-16. <http://content.nejm.org/cgi/content/full/351/5/415>

Liptak, Adam, 'Legal Scholars Criticize Memos on Torture', *New York Times*, 25 June 2004. <http://www.nytimes.com/2004/06/25/politics/25LEGA.html?ex=1403582400&en=4da4f479d103fe72&ei=5007&partner=USERLAND>

Lithwick, Dahlia, 'Invisible Men: The Not-People We're Not Holding At Guantánamo Bay', *Slate.com*, 16 February 2006. <http://www.slate.com/id/2136422/>

Lobe, Jim, 'Bush "Unsigns" War Crimes Treaty', *Alternet*, 6 May 2002. <http://www.alternet.org/story/13055>

Malinowski, Tom, 'Call Cruelty What It Is', *Washington Post*, 18 September 2006. <http://www.washingtonpost.com/wp-dyn/content/article/2006/09/17/AR2006091700516.html>

Martin, Susan Taylor, 'Her Job: Lock up Iraq's Bad Guys', *St Petersburg Times*, 14 December 2003. <http://www.sptimes.com/2003/12/14/Worldandnation/Her_job__Lock_up_Iraq.shtml>

Mayer, Jane, 'A Deadly Interrogation', *New Yorker*, 14 November 2005. <http://www.newyorker.com/fact/content/articles/051114fa_fact>

—— 'The Experiment', *New Yorker*, 11 July 2005. <http://www.newyorker.com/fact/content/articles/050711fa_fact4>

—— 'The Hidden Power', *New Yorker*, 3 July 2006. <http://www.newyorker.com/fact/content/articles/060703fa_fact1>

—— 'The Memo', *New Yorker*, 27 February 2006. <http://www.newyorker.com/fact/content/articles/060227fa_fact>

—— 'Outsourcing Torture', *New Yorker*, 14 February 2005. <http://www.newyorker.com/fact/content/articles/050214fa_fact6>

McCoy, Alfred W., 'Cruel Science: CIA Torture & US Foreign Policy', *New England Journal of Public Policy*, Winter 2005, Vol. 19, No. 2.

McGehee, Ralph, 'Operation Phoenix', *CIABASE*, 30 January 1997. <http://www.xs4all.nl/~peace/pubeng/inter/arcnw1.html>

McNeill, Brian, 'Davis, Hurst Clash in Congressional Debate', *Connection Newspapers*, 22 September 2006. <http://www.connectionnewspapers.com/article.asp?article=71439&paper=0&cat=109>

Metzgar, Major Greg E., 'Unconventional Warfare: Definitions from 1950 to the Present', *Special Warfare*, Winter 2001. <http://www.findarticles.com/p/articles/mi_m0HZY/is_1_14/ai_78397582>

Mintz, John, 'Most at Guantánamo to Be Freed or Sent Home, Officer Says', *Washington Post*, 6 October 2004. <http://www.washingtonpost.com/ac2/wp-dyn/A9626-2004Oct5?language=printer>

Morgan, C. A., III and Gary Hazlett, 'Assesment of Humans Experiences Uncontrollable Stress: The SERE Course', *Special Warfare*, Summer 2000, Vol. 13, No. 3, pp. 6–12.

Mother Jones MoJo Blog, 'Poll Numbers on Torture', 6 December 2005. <http://www.motherjones.com/mojoblog/archives/2005/12/04-week/>

Myers, Steven Lee, 'Be All That You Can Be: Your Future as an Extortionist', *New York Times*, 6 October 1996. <http://www.soaw.org/new/newswire_detail.php?id=1121>

Nagourney, Adam, 'Dispute on Intelligence Report Disrupts Republicans' Game Plan', *New York Times*, 28 September 2006. <http://www.nytimes.com/2006/09/28/us/politics/28capital.html>

New York Times, Editorial, '"Confession" in Hungary', 19 February 1950, p. E8.

—— Editorial, 'Fruits of Brainwashing', 28 January 1954, p. 26.

—— Editorial, 'Tactics of Terror', 5 July 1951, p. 24.

Newsweek, Letters to the Editor, 10 October 1955, pp. 14–18.

—— 'What a Man Must Do', 29 August 1955, p. 18.

Norman, Lloyd, 'Air Force Defends Its "Torture" School', *Chicago Daily Tribune*,
     9 September 1955, p. 14.
Oatis, William, 'How Reds Forced Oatis to "Confess,"' *Chicago Daily Tribune*,
     17 September 1953, p. 1.
——— 'Life in Prison Like "Living Death" to Oatis', *Chicago Daily Tribune*,
     18 September 1953, p. 3.
Palmer, Laura, 'Her Own Private Tailhook', *New York Times Magazine*, 28 May
     1995 pp. 22–5.
Parry, Robert, 'Lost History: Project X, Drugs and Death Squads', *Consortium
     Magazine*, 31 March 1997. <http://www.consortiumnews.com/archive/
     lost19.html>
Patel, Priti, 'Yes, Commissions Can Allow In Evidence Obtained Under Torture',
     American Constitution Society Blog, 2 March 2006. <http://www.acsblog.org/
     guest-bloggers-2643-yes-commissions-can-allow-in-evidence-obtained-
     under-torture.html>
Peterson, Iver, 'Vietnam: This Phoenix is a Bird of Death', *New York Times*, 25 July
     1971, p. E2.
Pincus, Walter, 'Report Cast Doubt on Iraq-Al Qaeda Connection', *Washington
     Post*, 22 June 2003. <http://www.washingtonpost.com/ac2/wp-dyn/
     A19822-2003Jun21?language=printer>
Pomfret, John, *The History of Guantánamo Bay*, Vol. II: 1964–1982. <http://www.
     nsgtmo.navy.mil/history/gtmohistoryvol2index.htm>
Preuss, Lawrence, 'The Dual State', Book Review, *American Journal of International
     Law*, Vol. 35, No. 3, July 1941, pp. 584–5.
Pribbenow, Merle L., 'The Man in the Snow White Cell', *Studies in Intelligence*,
     Vol. 48, No. 1, 2004. <https://www.cia.gov/csi/studies/vol48no1/
     article06.html>
Priest, Dana, 'Army's Project X Had Wider Audience', *Washington Post*, 6 March
     1997. <http://www.soaw.org/new/newswire_detail.php?id=996>
——— 'CIA Avoids Scrutiny of Detainee Treatment', *Washington Post*, 3 March
     2005, p. A01. <http://www.washingtonpost.com/wp-dyn/articles/
     A2576-2005Mar2.html>
——— 'CIA Holds Terror Suspects in Secret Prisons', *Washington Post*, 2 November
     2005. <http://www.washingtonpost.com/wp-dyn/content/article/2005/
     11/01/AR2005110101644.html>
——— 'Italy Knew About Plan to Grab Suspect', *Washington Post*, 30 June
     2005, p. A01. <http://www.washingtonpost.com/wp-dyn/content/
     article/2005/06/29/AR2005062902971_pf.html>
——— 'Officials Relieved Secret Is Shared', *Washington Post*, 7 September 2006.
     <http://www.washingtonpost.com/wp-dyn/content/article/2006/09/06/
     AR2006090602055.html>
——— 'US Instructed Latins on Executions, Torture', *Washington Post*, 21 September
     1996. <http://www.soaw.org/new/newswire_detail.php?id=851>
——— 'Wrongful Imprisonment: Anatomy of a CIA Mistake', *Washington Post*,
     4 December 2005, p. A01. <http://www.washingtonpost.com/wp-dyn/
     content/article/2005/12/03/AR2005120301476.html>

Priest, Dana, and Barton Gellman, 'US Decries Abuse but Defends Interrogations', *Washington Post*, 26 December 2002, p. A01. <http://www.washingtonpost. com/ac2/wp-dyn/A37943-2002Dec25?language=printer>

Rauth, Joseph L., Jr and James C. Turner, 'Anatomy of a Public Interest Case Against the CIA', *Hamline Journal of Public Law and Policy*, Vol. 11, 1990, pp. 307–63. <http://www.turnerhome.org/jct/Anatomy.pdf>

Rejali, Darius, 'Electric Torture: A Global History of a Torture Technology', *Connect: art.politics.theory.practice*, June 2001, pp. 101–9. <http://humanrights. uchicago.edu/documents/Torture%20Conference/Rejali.htm>

—— 'Of Human Bondage', *Salon.com*, 18 June 2004. <http://archive.salon.com/ opinion/feature/2004/06/18/torture_methods/>

Rensberger, Boyce, 'CIA in the Early Nineteen-Fifties Was Among Pioneers in Research on LSD's Effects', *New York Times*, 12 July 1975, p. 11.

Riding, Alan, 'Cuban "Agent" Says US Police Aides Urged Torture', *New York Times*, 5 August 1978, p. 3.

Rosenthal, A. M., 'Germ War Inquiry Demanded of Reds', *New York Times*, 28 March 1953, p. 3.

Ross, Brian, 'History of an Interrogation Technique: Water Boarding', *ABC News*, 29 November 2005. <http://abcnews.go.com/WNT/Investigation/ story?id=1356870>

Ross, Brian, and Richard Esposito, 'CIA's Harsh Interrogation Techniques Described', *ABC News*, 18 November 2005. <http://abcnews.go.com/ WNT/Investigation/story?id=1322866>

Roth, Kenneth, 'The Charade of US Ratification of International Human Rights Treaties', *Chicago Journal of International Law*, Vol. 1, No. 2, Fall 2000, pp. 347–53.

Rueters, 'England Sentenced to 3 Years Jail', *OneNews World*, 28 September 2005. <http://tvnz.co.nz/view/page/423466/614709>

Scherer, Michael, 'Will Bush and Gonzales Get Away With It?' *Salon.com*, 2 August 2006. <http://www.salon.com/news/feature/2006/08/02/cronin/print. html>

Scherer, Michael, and Mark Benjamin, 'What Rumsfeld Knew', *Salon.com*, 14 April 2006. <http://www.salon.com/news/feature/2006/04/14/ rummy/>

Schmeck, Harold M., 'Bureau of Narcotics Tied To CIA's Drug Program', *New York Times*, 8 November 1975, p. 12

Schmitt, Eric, and Carolyn Marshall, 'In Secret Unit's "Black Room," a Grim Portrait of US Abuse', *New York Times*, 19 March 2006. <http://www. nytimes.com/2006/03/19/international/middleeast/19abuse.html?ei=5088 &en=e8755a4b031b64a1&ex=1300424400&partner=rssnyt&pagewanted= print>

Segel, Lawrence, 'Medical Mayhem: Operation Midnight Climax', *Medical Post*, Vol. 38, Iss. 22, 17 September 2002.

Slevin, Peter, and Joe Stephens, 'Detainees' Medical Files Shared', *Washington Post*, 10 June 2004. <http://www.washingtonpost.com/wp-dyn/articles/ A29649-2004Jun9.html>

Smith, R. Jeffrey, 'Behind the Debate, Controversial CIA Techniques', *Washington Post*, 28 July 2006. <http://www.washingtonpost.com/wp-dyn/content/article/2006/09/15/AR2006091501252.html>

—— 'Detainee Abuse Charges Feared', *Washington Post*, 28 July 2006. <http://www.washingtonpost.com/wp-dyn/content/article/2006/07/27/AR2006072701908_pf.html>

—— 'Worried CIA Officers Buy Legal Insurance', *Washington Post*, 11 September 2006. <http://www.washingtonpost.com/wp-dyn/content/article/2006/09/10/AR2006091001286.html>

Sontag, Deborah, 'Israeli Court Bans Most Use of Force in Interrogations', *New York Times*, 7 September 1999, p. A1.

Special to the *New York Times*, 'Action on Vogeler Denounced by US', *New York Times*, 22 February 1950, p. 6.

—— 'British to Instruct Troops on Capture', *New York Times*, 16 February 1956, p. 2.

—— 'Files Show Tests for Truth Drug Began in O.S.S.', *New York Times*, 5 September 1977, p. 33.

—— 'Marine Colonel Will Face Inquiry Today On "Confession" to Reds on Germ Warfare', *New York Times*, 16 February 1954, p. 2.

—— 'Marines Award Schwable Medal', *New York Times*, 8 July 1954, p. 8.

—— 'Mind-Control Studies Had Origins in Trial of Mindszenty', *New York Times*, 2 August 1977, p. 16.

—— 'Private Institutions Used in CIA Effort to Control Behavior', *New York Times*, 2 August 1977, p. 1.

—— 'Protests Rising in Primate's Case', *New York Times*, 8 February 1949, p. 2.

—— 'Red China Steps Up Germ War Charges', *New York Times*, 25 February 1953, p. 3.

—— 'Red Germ Charges Cite 2 US Marines', *New York Times*, 23 February 1953, p. 3.

—— 'The Air Force Suspends Its "Brainwash" Course', *New York Times*, 14 December 1955, p. 42.

—— 'Truman Condemns Arrest of Cardinal Mindszenty', *New York Times*, 31 December 1948, p. 6.

—— 'US Calls Trial a Hoax', *New York Times*, 4 July 1951, p. 8.

Testimony and Questioning of Donald Duncan, International War Crimes Tribunal—The Evidence of Copenhagen, 1967. <http://www.vietnamese-american.org/b10.html>

The Washington Star, 'CIA Considered Big LSD Purchase', *New York Times*, 5 August 1976, p. 9.

Thomas, Evan, '"24" Versus the Real World', *Newsweek*, 22 September 2006. <http://www.msnbc.msn.com/id/14924664/site/newsweek/>

Thomas, Jo, 'CIA Says It Found More Secret Papers on Behavior Control', *New York Times*, 3 September 1977, p. 1.

—— 'CIA Sought to Spray Drug on Partygoers', *New York Times*, 21 September 1977, p. 11.

—— 'Key Figure Testifies in Private on CIA Drug Tests', *New York Times*, 22 September 1977, p. 1.

Thompson, Ginger, and Gary Cohn, 'Torturers' Confessions', *Baltimore Sun*, 13 June 1995. <http://www.baltimoresun.com/news/local/bal-negroponte2,0,2194980.story??track=sto-relcon>

Time, 'Skirmishes Over a Primer', 26 November 1984. <http://www.time.com/time/magazine/article/0,9171,926989,00.html>

Tribune Wire Services, '4200 Attend Sinatra-Lewis Show for Slain Official's Kin', *Chicago Tribune*, 30 August 1970, p. C18.

Troy, Thomas M. Jr, 'A Look Over My Shoulder', Book Review, *Studies in Intelligence*, Vol. 48, No. 1, 2004. <https://www.cia.gov/csi/studies/vol48no1/article08.html>

Tucker-Ladd, Clayton, 'Stress-inoculation: Self-instructions and Coping Imagery', *Psychological Self-Help*, Self-Help Foundation, Illinois, 2005. <http://www.psychologicalselfhelp.org/Chapter12/chap12_49.html>

United Press, 'Air Force Trained to Bear Red Jails', *New York Times*, 26 September 1954, p. 25.

—— 'Army Challenged on POW Charges', *New York Times*, 24 January 1954, p. 1.

—— '"Brainwash" Course Backed by Marines', *New York Times*, 15 September 1955, p. 17.

—— 'Cardinal Retracts Pre-Trial Letter and Denies Duress', *New York Times*, 5 February 1949, p. 1.

—— 'Cardinal Urges Amnesty', *New York Times*, 2 August 1946, p. 2.

—— 'Mindszenty Denies Plot But Affirms Guilt in Principle', *New York Times*, 4 February 1949, p. 1.

—— 'Officers to Study "Brainwash" Issue', *New York Times*, 23 August 1954, p. 5.

—— 'POW Study Finds 70% Helped Reds', *New York Times*, 21 June 1956, p. 47.

—— 'Training is Ordered on New POW Code', *New York Times*, 20 August 1955, p. 21.

Vallely, Paul, 'A Systematic Process Learned From Cold War', *Independent*, 14 May 2004. <http://news.independent.co.uk/world/americas/article60331.ece>

Van Natta, Don Jr, 'Questioning Terror Suspects in a Dark and Surreal World', *New York Times*, 9 March 2003. <http://www.globalpolicy.org/wtc/liberties/2003/0309questioning.htm>

Vest, Jason, 'CIA Veterans Condemn Torture', *National Journal*, 19 November 2005. <http://nationaljournal.com/about/njweekly/stories/2005/1119nj1.htm>

—— 'Pray and Tell', *American Prospect*, 3 July 2005. <http://www.prospect.org/web/page.ww?section=root&name=ViewPrint&articleId=9876>

Waggoner, Walter H., 'How Reds Get Confessions Revealed to US by Victim', *New York Times*, 5 March 1950, p. 1.

Wall Street Journal, Editorial, 'An Antiterror Victory', 23 September 2006. <http://www.opinionjournal.com/editorial/feature.html?id=110008986>

Weinraub, Bernard, 'Sailor Says Faith in God and Skipper Helped Him', *New York Times*, 1 March 1969, p. 9.

—— 'British in Ulster Accused of Psychological Torture', *New York Times*, 13 March 1972, p. A2.

White, Josh, 'Abu Ghraib Tactics Were First Used at Guantánamo', *Washington Post*, 14 July 2005. <http://www.washingtonpost.com/wp-dyn/content/article/2005/07/13/AR2005071302380_pf.html>

—— 'Detainee in Photo With Dog Was "High Value" Suspect', *Washington Post*, 13 March 2006. <http://www.washingtonpost.com/wp-dyn/content/article/2006/03/12/AR2006031200962.html>

—— 'Documents Tell of Brutal Improvisation by GIs', *Washington Post*, 3 August 2005. <http://www.washingtonpost.com/wp-dyn/content/article/2005/08/02/AR2005080201941.html>

—— 'New Rules of Interrogation Forbid Use of Harsh Tactics', *Washington Post*, 7 September 2006. <http://www.washingtonpost.com/wp-dyn/content/article/2006/09/06/AR2006090601947.html>

—— 'Soldiers' "Wish Lists" of Detainee Tactics Cited', *Washington Post*, 19 April 2005. <http://www.washingtonpost.com/wp-dyn/articles/A64409-2005Apr18.html>

White, Josh, and Scott Hingham, 'Sergeant Says Intelligence Directed Abuse', *Washington Post*, 20 May 2004. <http://www.washingtonpost.com/wp-dyn/articles/A41035-2004May19.html>

Williams, Dennis A., and Martin Kasindorf, 'The Navy: Torture Camp', *Newsweek*, 22 March 1976.

W. K., '"Menticide" Is Listed as a New Crime', *New York Times*, 11 March 1951, p. 14.

Wyden, Peter, 'Ordeal in the Desert: Making Tougher Soldiers to Resist Brainwashing', *Newsweek*, 12 September 1955, pp. 33–5.

Young, Robert, 'Col. Schwable Tells Torture by Korean Reds', *Chicago Daily Tribune*, 12 March 1954, p. 10.

—— 'Couldn't Stand Brainwashing, Gen. Dean Says', *Chicago Daily Tribune*, 9 March 1954, p. 5.

—— 'Reds Destroy Mind, Quiz Told', *Chicago Daily Tribune*, 5 March 1954, p. B9.

Youssef, Nancy A., 'Abu Ghraib No Longer Houses Any Prisoners, Iraqi Officials Say', McClatchy Newspapers, 26 August 2006. <http://www.mercurynews.com/mld/mercurynews/news/world/15370737.htm>

Zagorin, Adam, 'Exclusive: "20th Hijacker" Claims That Torture Made Him Lie', *Time*, 3 March 2006. <http://www.time.com/time/nation/printout/0,8816,1169322,00.html>

Zagorin, Adam, and Michael Duffy, 'Inside the Interrogation of Detainee 063', *Time*, 20 June 2005. <http://www.time.com/time/magazine/article/0,9171,1071284,00.html?internalid=AM2>

Zakaria, Fareed, 'Pssst … Nobody Loves A Torturer', *Newsweek*, 14 November 2005. <http://www.msnbc.msn.com/id/9939154/site/newsweek/>

Zweiback, Adam J., 'The 21 Turncoat GIs: Nonrepatriations and the Political Culture of the Korean War', *The Historian*, Winter 1988. <http://www.aiipowmia.com/koreacw/zweiback21.html>.

BOOKS

The American Heritage Dictionary of the English Language, Fourth Edition, Houghton Mifflin Company, 2004. <http://www.answers.com>

Blum, William, *Killing Hope: US Military and CIA Interventions Since World War II*, Common Courage, Monroe, Maine, 2004.

Brown, Holmes, and Don Luce, *Hostages of War: Saigon's Political Prisoners*, Indochina Mobile Education Project, Washington, DC, 1973.

Chomsky, Noam, *The Backroom Boys*, Fontana, London, 1973.

Chomsky, Noam, and Edward Herman, *The Washington Connection and Third World Fascism: The Political Economy of Human Rights*, South End Press, Boston, 1979.

Clark, Richard A., *Against All Enemies: Inside America's War on Terror*, Free Press, New York, 2004.

Cockburn, Alexander, and Jeffrey St Clair, *Whiteout: The CIA, Drugs, and the Press*, Verso, New York, 1999.

Gill, Lesley, *The School of the Americas: Military Training and Political Violence in the Americas*, Duke University Press, Durham and London, 2004.

Harbury, Jennifer K., *Truth, Torture, and the American Way: The History and Consequences of US Involvment in Torture*, Beacon Press, Boston, 2005.

Koestler, Arthur, *Darkness at Noon*, trans. Daphne Hardy, Time Inc., New York, (1940) 1962.

Labrousse, Alain, *The Tupamaros: Urban Guerillas in Uruguay*, trans. Dinah Livingstone, Penguin, Harmondsworth, 1973.

Langguth, A. J., *Hidden Terrors*, Pantheon, New York, 1978.

Lee, Martin A., and Bruce Shlain, *Acid Dreams: The Complete Social History of LSD: The CIA, the Sixties, and Beyond*, Grove Press, New York, 1992.

Margulies, Joseph, *Guantánamo and the Absuse of Presidential Power*, Simon & Schuster, New York, 2006.

Marks, John, *The Search for the 'Manchurian Candidate': The CIA and Mind Control*, Allen Lane, London, 1979.

McClintock, Michael, *Instruments of Statecraft: US Guerilla Warfare, Counterinsurgency, and Counterterrorism, 1940–1990*, Pantheon, New York, 1992. Also published online: <http://www.statecraft.org/index.html>

McCoy, Alfred W., *A Question of Torture: CIA Interrogation, from the Cold War to the War on Terror*, Metropolitan Books, New York, 2006.

Miles, Steven H., *Oath Betrayed: Torture, Medical Complicity, and the War on Terror*, Random House, New York, 2006.

Orwell, George, *Nineteen Eighty-Four*, Penguin, London, (1949) 1990.

Russell Tribunal on Repression in Brazil, Chile and Latin America, *Torture in Brazil: Testimony Given to the Rome Session of the Russell Tribunal*, Bertrand Russell Peace Foundation, Nottingham, 1976.

Snepp, Frank, *Decent Interval: The American Debacle in Vietnam and the Fall of Saigon*, Allen Lane, London, 1980.

Taylor, Kathleen, *Brainwashing: The Science of Thought Control*, Oxford Univesity Press, Oxford, 2004.

Thomas, Gordon, *Journey into Madness*, Corgi, London, 1989.

Urofsky, Melvin I. (ed.), *Basic Readings in U.S. Democracy*, United States
    Information Agency, Washington, DC, 1994. Also published online: <http://
    usinfo.state.gov/usa/infousa/facts/democrac/demo.htm>
Valentine, Douglas, *The Phoenix Program*, Authors Guild Backinprint.com Edition,
    iUniverse.com, Lincoln, Nebraska, 2000.
Weinstein, Harvey, *Father, Son and CIA,* Formac Publishing, Halifax, 1990.
Woodward, Bob, *Bush at War*, Simon & Schuster, London, 2002.

CASE LAW

Al Odah, Khaled A. F. v USA, 02-5251a (2003). <http://laws.lp.findlaw.com/dc/
    025251a.html>
Ashcraft v State of Tennessee, 322 US 143 (1944). <http://caselaw.lp.findlaw.com/
    cgi-bin/getcase.pl?court=us&vol=322&invol=143>
Burtt v Schick, 23 MJ 140 (USCMA, 1986).
Eastman Kodak v Kavlin, 978 F Supp 1078 (SD Fla 1997).
Hamdan v Rumsfeld, 548 US, 126 S Ct 2749, L Ed 2d (2006).
Haitian Centers Council Inc v McNary, 969 F 2d 1326 (2nd Cir 1992).
Hilao v Estate of Marcos, 103 F 3d 767 (9th Cir 1996).
Ireland v United Kingdom, 5310/71 [1971] ECHR 1 (18 January 1978).
Prize Cases, 67 US 635 (1862).
Rasul v Bush, 542 US 466 (2004).
United States v Blair, 54 F.3d at 642 (10th Cir. 1995).
United States v Lee, 906 F 2d 117 (4th Cir 1990).
United States v Lewis, 628 F 2d 1276 at 1279 (10th Cir 1980).
Youngstown Sheet and Tube Co. v Sawyer, 343 US 579 (1952).

DISSERTATION

Lobe, Thomas David, 'US Police Assistance for the Third World', University of
    Michigan, doctoral dissertation, 1975.

LAWS AND TREATIES

*Agreement Between the United States and Cuba for the Lease of Lands for Coaling and
    Naval stations*, 23 February 1903. <http://www.yale.edu/lawweb/avalon/
    diplomacy/cuba/cuba002.htm>
Federal Torture Statute, 18 USC §§ 2340–2340A. <http://www4.law.cornell.
    edu/uscode/html/uscode18/usc_sup_01_18_10_I_20_113C.html>
Geneva Convention relative to the Protection of Civilian Persons in Time of War,
    Adopted on 12 August 1949. <http://www.unhchr.ch/html/menu3/b/92.
    htm>
Military Commissions Act of 2006, § 3930. <http://frwebgate.access.gpo.gov/
    cgi-bin/getdoc.cgi?dbname=109_cong_bills&docid=f:s3930enr.txt.pdf>
National Security Act of 1947, Section 103(d)(5) (50 USC § 403-3). <http://www.
    milnet.com/1947-act.htm#s102>
Torture Victim Protection Act of 1991, 28 USC §1350, Public Law 102–256, 106 Stat.
    73. 12 March 1992. <http://www.law.cornell.edu/uscode/html/uscode28/
    usc_sec_28_00001350----000-notes.html>

Treaty Between the United States of America and Cuba, 29 May 1934. <http://www.yale.edu/lawweb/avalon/diplomacy/cuba/cuba001.htm>

Uniform Code of Military Justice, 10 USC § 47. <http://www.au.af.mil/au/awc/awcgate/ucmj.htm>

War Crimes Act of 1996, 18 USC § 2441. <http://www4.law.cornell.edu/uscode/html/uscode18/usc_sec_18_00002441----000-.html>

MANUALS

CIA, KUBARK, *Counterintelligence Interrogation*, July 1963. <http://www.gwu.edu/~nsarchiv/NSAEBB/NSAEBB122/#kubark>

CIA, *Human Resource Exploitation Training Manual*, 1983. <http://www.gwu.edu/~nsarchiv/NSAEBB/NSAEBB122/#hre>

Department of the Army, FM 2-22.3, *Human Intelligence Collector Operations*, Government Printing Office, Washington, DC, 6 September 2006. <http://www.army.mil/references/FM2-22.3.pdf>

—— FM 34-52, *Intelligence Interrogation*, Government Printing Office, Washington, DC, 8 May 1987. <http://www.globalsecurity.org/intell/library/policy/army/fm/fm34-52/>

—— FM 34-52, *Intelligence Interrogation*, Government Printing Office, Washington, DC, 28 September 1992. <http://www.loc.gov/rr/frd/Military_Law/pdf/intel_interrrogation_sept-1992.pdf#search=%22FM%2034-52%2C%20Intelligence%20Interrogation%22>

—— FM 31-21, *Organization and Conduct of Guerilla Warfare*, Government Printing Office, Washington, DC, October 1951.

Department of Defense, AR 350-30, *Code of Conduct, Survival Evasion, Resistance, and Escape (SERE) Training*, Government Printing Office, Washington, DC, 10 December 1985.

—— *Guerra Revolucionaria, Guerrilleria e Ideología Comunista—Manual De Estudio*, 1987. <http://www.soaw.org/new/article.php?id=98>

—— *Interrogación—Manual De Estudio*, 1987. <http://www.soaw.org/new/article.php?id=98>

—— *Manejo de Fuentes—Manual De Estudio*, 1987. <http://www.soaw.org/new/article.php?id=98>

NGO REPORTS

ACLU, 'Latest Government Documents Show Army Command Approved and Encouraged Abuse of Detainees, ACLU Says', Press Release, 19 April 2005. <http://www.aclu.org/safefree/general/17520prs20050419.html>

Amnesty International, 'A Briefing for the UN Committee against Torture', AI Index: AMR51/056/2000, 4 May 2000. <http://web.amnesty.org/library/Index/ENGAMR510562000>

—— 'Below the Radar: Secret Flights to Torture and "Disappearance"', AI Index: AMR 51/051/2006, London, 5 April 2006. <http://web.amnesty.org/library/index/ENGAMR510512006>

—— *Report on Torture*, Duckworth, London, 1975.

Borchelt, Gretchen, *Break Them Down: Systematic Use of Psychological Torture by US Forces*, Physicians for Human Rights, Cambridge, Mass., May 2005. <www. phrusa.org/research/torture/pdf/psych_torture.pdf>

Cageprisoners, 'Report into the Systematic and Institutionalized US Desecration of the Qur'an and Other Islamic Rituals: Testimonies from Former Guantánamo Bay Detainees', 26 May 2005. <http://www.cageprisoners. com/downloads/USQuranDesecration.pdf>

Danzig, David, 'The Proceedings So Far: In Their Own Words', Torture on Trial—HRF Observes Court Martial of Army Officer Accused in Death of Iraqi Major General, Human Rights First, 19 January 2006. <http://www. humanrightsfirst.org/us_law/etn/trial/welshofer-011906d.asp>

—— 'Welshofer In His Own Words', Torture on Trial—HRF Observes Court Martial of Army Officer Accused in Death of Iraqi Major General, Human Rights First, 20 January 2006. <http://www.humanrightsfirst.org/us_law/ etn/trial/welshofer-012006d.asp>

Human Rights Watch, 'Leadership Failure: Firsthand Accounts of Torture of Iraqi Detainees by the US Army's 82nd Airborne Division', Vol. 17, No. 3(G), September 2005. <http://hrw.org/reports/2005/us0905/>

—— '"No Blood, No Foul" Soldiers' Accounts of Detainee Abuse in Iraq', Vol. 18, No. 3(G), July 2006. <http://hrw.org/reports/2006/us0706/ index.htm>

International Committee of the Red Cross, 'Report of the International Committee of the Red Cross (ICRC) on the Treatment by the Coalition Forces of Prisoners of War and Other Protected Persons by the Geneva Conventions in Iraq During Arrest, Internment, and Interrogation', February 2004. <http://www.globalsecurity.org/military/library/ report/2004/icrc_report_iraq_feb2004.pdf>

Kusnetz, Marc, 'Case Closed?' Torture on Trial—HRF Observes Court Martial of Army Officer Accused in Death of Iraqi Major General, Human Rights First, 24 January 2006. <http://www.humanrightsfirst.org/us_law/etn/ trial/welshofer-012406m.asp>

—— 'Preview', Torture on Trial—HRF Observes Court Martial of Army Officer Accused in Death of Iraqi Major General, Human Rights First, 13 January 2006. <http://www.humanrightsfirst.org/us_law/etn/trial/welshofer- 011306.asp>

Rasul, Shafiq, Asif Iqbal and Rhuhel Ahmed, 'Composite Statement: Detention in Afghanistan and Guantánamo Bay', Center for Constitutional Rights, New York, 26 July 2004. <http://www.ccr-ny.org/v2/legal/september_11th/ docs/Guantanamo_composite_statement_FINAL.pdf>

Wendland, Lene, *Handbook on State Obligations under the UN Convention Against Torture*, Association for the Prevention of Torture, Geneva, Switzerland, 2002. <http://www.isn.ch/pubs/ph/details.cfm?lng=en&id=16024>

TELEVISION AND RADIO

CNN, *CNN-ACCESS*, 'Dershowitz: Torture Can Be Justified', 4 March 2003. <http://edition.cnn.com/2003/LAW/03/03/cnna.Dershowitz/>

CNN, *War In Iraq*, 'Transcript of Powell's UN Presentation: Part 9: Ties to al Qaeda', 6 February 2003. <http://www.cnn.com/2003/US/02/05/sprj.irq. powell.transcript.09/index.html>

Fox News, *FOX News Sunday With Chris Wallace*, 'John Negroponte on FNS', 17 September 2006. <http://www.foxnews.com/story/0,2933,214203,00. html>

Hemmer, Bill, CNN, *Saturday Morning News*, 'Ibn Al-Shaykh al-Libi is in US Custody', 5 January 2002. <http://cnnstudentnews.cnn.com/ TRANSCRIPTS/0201/05/smn.06.html>

PBS, *Frontline*, 'The Torture Question', Interview with Michael Scheuer, 21 July 2005. <http://www.pbs.org/wgbh/pages/frontline/torture/interviews/ scheuer.html>

PBS, *Frontline*, 'The Torture Question', Interview with Tony Lagouranis, 25 September 2005. <http://www.pbs.org/wgbh/pages/frontline/torture/ interviews/lagouranis.html>

PBS, *Frontline*, 'The Torture Question', e-mail from Cpt William Ponce, 14 August 2003. <http://www.pbs.org/wgbh/pages/frontline/torture/ paper/ponce.html>

Savidge, Martin, CNN, *CNN Presents*, 'Captured: Inside the Army's Secret School', 10 August 2002. <http://transcripts.cnn.com/TRANSCRIPTS/0208/10/ cp.00.html>

Walker, Ian, ABC Radio National, *Background Briefing*, 'Tortured Questions', 26 May 1996. <http://www.abc.net.au/rn/talks/bbing/stories/s10766.htm>

Whitmont, Debbie, ABC, *Four Corners*, 'The Case of David Hicks', 31 October 2005. <http://www.abc.net.au/4corners/content/2005/s1494795.htm>

Zahn, Paula, CNN, *Paula Zahn Now*, 'Private 1st Class Lynndie England in Court', 3 August 2004. <http://transcripts.cnn.com/TRANSCRIPTS/0408/03/ pzn.00.html>

UNITED NATIONS DOCUMENTS

United Nations Committee Against Torture, 'Conclusions and Recommendations of the Committee against Torture: United States of America', Consideration of Reports Submitted by State Parties Under Article 19 of the Convention, A/55/44, 15 May 2000. <http://www1.umn.edu/humanrts/usdocs/ torturecomments.html>

United Nations Committee Against Torture, 'Status of the Convention and Reservations, Declarations and Objections Under the Convention', 22 January 1998. <http://www.unhchr.ch/tbs/doc.nsf/(Symbol)/ fa6561b18d8a4767802565c30038c86a?Opendocument>

United Nations, 'Body of Principles for the Protection of All Persons under Any Form of Detention or Imprisonment', adopted by General Assembly resolution 43/173 of 9 December 1988. <http://www.unhchr.ch/html/ menu3/b/h_comp36.htm>

United Nations, *Convention against Torture and Other Cruel, Inhuman or Degrading Treatment or Punishment* (CAT), adopted and opened for signature, ratification and accession by General Assembly resolution 39/46 of 10 December 1984.

United Nations, *Convention against Torture and Other Cruel, Inhuman or Degrading Treatment or Punishment* (CAT), 'United States—Declarations and Reservations'. <http://www.unhchr.ch/html/menu2/6/cat/treaties/convention-reserv.htm>

United Nations, *Principles of Medical Ethics Relevant to the Protection of Prisoners Against Torture*, Resolution 37/194 (Principles of Medical Ethics), adopted by the United Nations General Assembly on 18 December 1982. <http://www.cioms.ch/1983_texts_of_guidelines.htm>

United Nations, *Rome Statute of the International Criminal Court*, UN Document A/CONF.183/9. <http://www.un.org/law/icc/statute/romefra.htm>

United Nations Security Council, Resolution 1193 (1998), adopted by the Security Council at its 3921st meeting on 28 August 1998. <http://www.un.org/Docs/scres/1998/scres98.htm>

US GOVERNMENT DOCUMENTS

Ashcroft, John, Letter to President Bush, 1 February 2002. <http://news.findlaw.com/wp/docs/torture/jash20102ltr.html>

Beaver, Diane E., 'Legal Review of Aggressive Interrogation Techniques', Memorandum for Commander, Joint Task Force 170, 11 October 2002. <http://www.washingtonpost.com/wp-srv/nation/documents/dodmemos.pdf>

Best, Richard A. Jr, and Herbert Andrew Boerstling, 'IC21: The Intelligence Community in the 21st Century', Staff Study, Permanent Select Committee on Intelligence, House of Representatives, 104th Congress, Appendix C, 28 February 1996. <http://www.au.af.mil/au/awc/awcgate/congress/ic21/ic21018.html>

Bush, George W., 'Humane Treatment of al Qaeda and Taliban Detainees', 7 February 2002. <http://www.slate.com/features/whatistorture/pdfs/020207.pdf>

—— 'Military Order of November 13th 2001, Detention, Treatment, and Trial of Certain Non-Citizens in the War Against Terrorism.' <http://www.whitehouse.gov/news/releases/2001/11/20011113-27.html>

Bybee, Jay S., 'Standards of Conduct for Interrogation under 18 USC §§ 2340–2340A', Memorandum for Alberto R. Gonzales, 1 August 2002. <http://www.slate.com/features/whatistorture/pdfs/020801.pdf>

—— 'Status of Taliban Forces Under Article 4 of the Third Geneva Convention of 1949', Memorandum for Alberto R. Gonzales, 7 February 2002. <http://news.findlaw.com/wp/docs/torture/bybee20702mem.html>

'Church Committee Report', aka XVII. Testing and Use of Chemical and Biological Agents by the Intelligence Community, US Senate, 94th Congress, 2d Session, Foreign and Military Intelligence, Book I: Final Report of the Select Committee to Study Governmental Operations with Respect to Intelligence Activities, US Government Printing Office, Washington, DC, 1976. <http://www.aarclibrary.org/publib/church/reports/book1/pdf/ChurchB1_17_Chemicals.pdf>

CIA, *Factbook on Intelligence*, December 1992. <http://www.fas.org/irp/cia/
  ciahist.htm>
CIA cable, 'The 316th MI Battalion', 18 February 1995. <http://www.gwu.
  edu/~nsarchiv/latin_america/honduras/cia_ig_report/01-01.htm>
CIA, 'Internal Security in South Vietnam—Phoenix', 12 December 1970.
  <http://www.thememoryhole.org/phoenix/internal-security.htm>
CIA, KUBARK, 'Communist Control Methods', Appendix 1: The Use of
  Scientific Design and Guidance Drugs in Communist Interrogation and
  Indoctrination Procedures', Secret, Undated.
CIA, KUBARK (KUSODA), 'Communist Control Techniques: An Analysis of
  the Methods Used by Communist State Police in the Arrest, Interrogation,
  and Indoctrination of Persons Regarded as "Enemies of the State"', Secret,
  2 April 1956.
CIA, 'SUBJECT: Project ARTICHOKE', Memorandum for the Record,
  31 January 1975, p. 3. <http://www.gwu.edu/~nsarchiv/NSAEBB/
  NSAEBB54/st02.pdf>
Department of the Army, CID Report of Investigation—Final, Supplimental/
  SSI-0213-2004-CID-259-80250-5C2B/5Y2E. [ACLU Document#:
  DOD044418–DOD044496]. <http://www.aclu.org/projects/foiasearch/
  pdf/DOD044418.pdf>
Department of the Army, Commanders Inquiry (15-6), 8 October 2003. [ACLU
  Document# DOD002818-DOD002871] <http://www.aclu.org/projects/
  foiasearch/pdf/DOD002818.pdf>
Department of Defense, 'BSCT Standard Operating Procedures', Memorandum
  for the Record, 11 November 2002. [ACLU Document#: DODDON-
  000776]. <http://www.aclu.org/projects/foiasearch/pdf/
  DODDON000760.pdf>
—— 'BSCT Standard Operating Procedures', 28 March 2005. [ACLU
  Document#: DODDON-000760 – DODDON-000766]. <http://www.
  aclu.org/projects/foiasearch/pdf/DODDON000760.pdf>
—— 'Interrogation Log Detainee 063', SECRET ORCON. <http://jcgi.
  pathfinder.com/time/2006/log/log.pdf>
—— 'DoD News Briefing with Deputy Assistant Secretary Stimson and Lt. Gen.
  Kimmons from the Pentagon', 6 September 2006. <http://www.fas.org/
  irp/news/2006/09/dod090606.html>
—— 'JTF GTMO "SERE" INTERROGATION SOP DTD 10 DEC 02',
  Memorandum from Special Agent in Charge of Criminal Investigation
  Task Force (Deployed) Guanatanamo Bay Cuba to JTF-GTMOS/J2,
  17 December 2002. [ACLU Document# DOD045202–DOD045204].
  <http://www.aclu.org/projects/foiasearch/pdf/DOD045202.pdf>
—— 'Media Availability with Commander, US Southern Command General
  James T. Hill', 3 June 2004. <http://www.defenselink.mil/transcripts/2004/
  tr20040603-0810.html>
—— 'Remarks by Secretary Rumsfeld in a "Town Hall" Event with US Troops
  in Al Asad, Iraq—Headquarters 3rd Marine Air Wing', 10 October 2004.
  <http://www.defenselink.mil/transcripts/2004/tr20041010-secdef1421.html>

—— 'Subject: USSOUTHCOM CI Training—Supplemental Information', Memorandum for the Record, 31 July 1991. <http://www.gwu.edu/~nsarchiv/NSAEBB/NSAEBB122/910801%20USSOUTHCOM%20CI%20Training%20(U).pdf>

—— 'Summarized Witness Statement of Lt. Col. [Redacted]', 22 March 2005, AR 15-6 GTMO Investigation, Exhibit 28 of 76. <http://www.dod.mil/pubs/foi/detainees/SchmidtFurlowEnclosures.pdf>

—— 'Report of the Defense Review Committee for the Code of Conduct', 1976. <http://www.dod.mil/pubs/foi/reading_room/13.pdf>

Department of Justice, 'Prepared Remarks by Attorney General Alberto R. Gonzales at the International Institute for Strategic Studies', London, 7 March 2006. <http://www.usdoj.gov/ag/speeches/2006/ag_speech_060307.html>

'Detainee Interviews (Abusive Interrogation Issues)', 6 May 2004. [ACLU Document#: DETAINEES-3683B] <http://www.aclu.org/projects/foiasearch/pdf/DOJFBI003178.pdf>

Dunlavey, Michael B., 'Counter-Resistance Strategies', Memorandum for Commander, US Southern Command, 11 October 2002. <http://www.washingtonpost.com/wp-srv/nation/documents/dodmemos.pdf>

'Effectiveness of the Use of Certain Category II Counter-Resistance Strategies', Memo to [Redacted] from [Redacted], AR 15-6 GTMO Investigation, Exhibit 66 of 76. <http://www.dod.mil/pubs/foi/detainees/SchmidtFurlowEnclosures.pdf>

Fay, M. G. George R., 'AR 15-6 Investigation of the Abu Ghraib Detention Facility and 205th Military Intelligence Brigade', 2004. <http://fl1.findlaw.com/news.findlaw.com/hdocs/docs/dod/fay82504rpt.pdf>

Gonzales, Alberto R., 'Decision re application of the Geneva Convention on Prisoners of War to the conflict with al Qaeda and the Taliban', Memorandum for the President, 25 January 2002. <http://www.slate.com/features/whatistorture/pdfs/020125.pdf>

'GTMO-INTEL', From CIRG, Behavioral Analysis Unit to Raymond S. Mey, Marion E. Bowman, Hector M. Pesquera and Frank Figliuzzi, 30 May 2003. [ACLU Document#: DETAINEES-1261 – DETAINEES-1267] <http://action.aclu.org/torturefoia/released/022306/1261.pdf>

'GTMO matters', e-mail forwarded from [Redacted] to Frank Battle, 17 December 2002. [ACLU Document#: DOJFBI003522] <http://www.aclu.org/projects/foiasearch/pdf/DOJFBI003522.pdf>

Harrington, T. J., 'Suspected Mistreatment of Detainees', Letter to General Ryder, 14 July 2004. [ACLU Document#: DETAINEES-3823–DETAINEES-3825] <http://www.aclu.org/torturefoia/released/FBI_4622_4624.pdf>

Haynes, William J., 'Counter-Resistance Strategies', Action Memo for Secretary of Defense, 27 November 2002. <http://www.washingtonpost.com/wp-srv/nation/documents/dodmemos.pdf>

Helms, Richard, 'Eyes Only', 17 December 1963. <http://www.levity.com/aciddreams/docs/eyesonly.html>

Hill, James T., 'Counter-Resistance Strategies', Memorandum for Chairman of the Joint Chiefs of Staff, 25 October 2002. <http://www.washingtonpost.com/wp-srv/nation/documents/dodmemos.pdf>

Hitz, Frederick P., and A.R. Cinquegrana, 'Report of Investigation: Selected Issues Relating to CIA Activities in Honduras in the 1980s' (96-0125-IG), CIA, 27 August 1997. <http://www.gwu.edu/~nsarchiv/latin_america/honduras/cia_ig_report/03-01.htm>

'Impersonating FBI at GTMO', e-mail from [Redacted] to Bald, Gary, BATTLE, FRANKIE, CUMMINGS, ARTHUR, 5 December 2003. [Document ID#: DOJFBI002442] <http://www.aclu.org/projects/foiasearch/pdf/DOJFBI002442.pdf>

'Instructions to GTMO interrogators', e-mail from [Redacted] to T. J. Harrington, 10 May 2004. [ACLU Document#: DOJFBI003085-DOJFBI003087] <http://www.aclu.org/projects/foiasearch/pdf/DOJFBI003085.pdf>

Jacoby, Lowell E., 'Declaration', 9 January 2003. <http://www.justicescholars.org/pegc/archive/Padilla_vs_Rumsfeld/Jacoby_declaration_20030109.pdf#search=%22Lowell%20E%20Jacoby%22>

Kennedy, Joseph P., 'Report on the School of the Americas', Kennedy Report to Congress, 6 March 1997. <http://www.fas.org/irp/congress/1997_rpt/soarpt.htm>

Levin, Daniel, 'Re: Legal Standards Applicable Under 18 USC §§ 2340–2340A', Memorandum for James B. Comey, Deputy Attorney General, 30 December 2004. <www.usdoj.gov/olc/dagmemo.pdf>

Michel, Werner E., 'Subject: Improper Material in Spanish-Language Intelligence Manuals', Memorandum for the Secretary of Defense, 10 March 1992. <http://www.gwu.edu/~nsarchiv/NSAEBB/NSAEBB122/#dod1992>

Miller, M. G. Geoffrey, 'Assessment of DoD Counter-Terrorism Interrogation and Detention Operations in Iraq', 13 September 2003. <www.publicintegrity.org/docs/AbuGhraib/Abu3.pdf>

National Security Council, 'NSC 4-A: Psychological Operations', National Security Council Directive, 9 December 1947. <http://www.fas.org/irp/offdocs/nsc-hst/nsc-4.htm>.

National Security Council, 'NSC 68: United States Objectives and Programs for National Security: A Report to the President Pursuant to the President's Directive of January 31, 1950', National Security Council Directive, 14 April 1950. <http://www.fas.org/irp/offdocs/nsc-hst/nsc-68.htm>.

Phifer, Jerald, 'Request for Approval of Counter-Resistance Strategies', Memorandum for Commander, Joint Task Force 170, 11 October 2002. <http://www.washingtonpost.com/wp-srv/nation/documents/dodmemos.pdf>

Philbin, Patrick F., and John C. Yoo, 'Possible Habeas Jurisdiction over Aliens Held in Guantánamo Bay, Cuba', Memorandum for William J. Haynes II, 28 December 2001. <http://www.msnbc.msn.com/id/5022681/site/newsweek/>

Powell, Colin, 'Draft Decision Memorandum for the President on the
Applicability of the Geneva Convention to the Conflict in Afghanistan',
26 January 2002. <http://www.slate.com/features/whatistorture/
pdfs/020126.pdf>

[Redacted], Sworn Statement, SPC/E-4, B Company, 2d Military Intelligence
Battalion, 66th Military Intelligence Group, 24 May 2004, Annex to Fay/
Jones/Kern Report. [ACLU Document#: DOD000745–DOD000746]
<http://www.aclu.org/torturefoia/released/030905/DOD738_779.pdf>

'Regarding Our Conversation', e-mail from [Redacted] to [Redacted],
21 June 2004, Annex to Fay/Jones/Kern Report. [ACLU Document#:
DOD000582]. <http://www.aclu.org/projects/foiasearch/pdf/
DOD000582.pdf>

'Re: GTMO', [Redacted] e-mail to [Redacted], 31 July [Redacted]. [ACLU
Document#: DETAINEES-2600]. <http://action.aclu.org/torturefoia/
released/022306/2600.pdf>

'RE GTMO', [Redacted] e-mail to [Redacted], 30 July 2004. [ACLU
Document#: DETAINEES-1414] <http://www.aclu.org/torturefoia/
released/FBI.121504.4737_4738.pdf>

'RE GTMO', [Redacted] e-mail to [Redacted], 2 August 2004. [ACLU
Document#: DETAINEES-1760] <http://www.aclu.org/torturefoia/
released/FBI.121504.5053.pdf>

Sanchez, Ricardo S., 'CJTF-7 Interrogation and Counter-Resistance Policy',
Memorandum for C2, C3, Commander, 10 September 2003. <http://www.
humanrightsfirst.info/pdf/06124-etn-sep-10-sanchez-memo.pdf>

—— 'CJTF-7 Interrogation and Counter-Resistance Policy', Memorandum for
Commander US Central Command, 14 September 2003. <http://www.
aclu.org/FilesPDFs/september%20sanchez%20memo.pdf>

—— 'CJTF-7 Interrogation and Counter-Resistance Policy', Memorandum for
C2, C3, Commander, 12 October 2003. <http://www.aclu.org/FilesPDFs/
october%20sanchez%20memo.pdf>

Sharoni, Shalan Said al-, Translation of Statement, 17 January 2004, Exhibit 5,
Annex to Tuguba Report. <http://www.washingtonpost.com/wp-srv/
world/iraq/abughraib/swornstatements042104.html>

Sheikh, Ameen Sa'eed al-, Sworn Statement, 16 January 2004, Exhibit 38, Annex
to Tuguba Report. <http://www.washingtonpost.com/wp-srv/world/iraq/
abughraib/swornstatements042104.html>

SGT [Redacted], Subject: Interview of Orgun-E Military Intelligence Detention
Facility Interrogator, Memorandum for the Record, 13 February 2004.
[ACLU Document# DOD045268–DOD045269] <http://www.aclu.org/
projects/foiasearch/pdf/DOD045268.pdf>

Taft, William H. IV, 'Comments on Your Paper on the Geneva Convention',
2 February 2002. <http://www.slate.com/features/whatistorture/
pdfs/020202.pdf>

'Testimony of Cofer Black', House and Senate Intelligence Committee Hearing,
26 September 2002. <http://www.fas.org/irp/congress/2002_hr/
092602black.html>

The White House, 'President Bush and Prime Minister Tony Blair of the United Kingdom Participate in Joint Press Availability', 25 May 2006. <http://www.whitehouse.gov/news/releases/2006/05/20060525-12.html>
—— 'President Bush Announces Combat Operations in Iraq Have Ended', 1 May 2003. <http://www.whitehouse.gov/news/releases/2003/05/20030501-15.html>
—— 'President Discusses Creation of Military Commissions to Try Suspected Terrorists', 6 September 2006. <http://www.whitehouse.gov/news/releases/2006/09/20060906-3.html>
—— 'President Thanks Senate for Agreement on Pending War on Terror Legislation', 21 September 2006. <http://www.whitehouse.gov/news/releases/2006/09/20060921-3.html>
—— 'Press Conference of the President', 15 September 2006. <http://www.whitehouse.gov/news/releases/2006/09/20060915-2.html>
—— 'Vice President Addresses US Chamber of Commerce', Washington, DC, 14 November 2001. <http://www.whitehouse.gov/news/releases/2001/11/20011114-6.html>
—— 'The Vice President Appears on Fox News Sunday', 27 January 2002. <http://www.whitehouse.gov/vicepresident/news-speeches/speeches/vp20020127-1.html>
—— 'The Vice President Appears on Meet the Press with Tim Russert', Camp David, Md., 16 September 2001. <http://www.whitehouse.gov/vicepresident/news-speeches/speeches/vp20010916.html>
'Trials of War Criminals before the Nuremberg Military Tribunals under Control Council Law No. 10', Vol. 2, US Government Printing Office, Washington, DC, 1949. <http://www.hhs.gov/ohrp/references/nurcode.htm>
Taguba, Antonio M., 'Article 15-6 Investigation of the 800th Military Police Brigade', March 2003. <www.npr.org/iraq/2004/prison_abuse_report.pdf>
US State Department, 'Comprehensive List of Terrorists and Groups Identified Under Executive Order 13224', Original Annex, 23 September 2001. <http://www.state.gov/s/ct/rls/fs/2001/6531.htm>
—— 'Egypt–Country Report on Human Rights Practices for 1996', 30 January 1997. <http://www.state.gov/www/global/human_rights/1996_hrp_report/egypt.html>
—— 'History of the National Security Council: 1947–1997', Office of the Historian, Bureau of Public Affairs, August 1997. <http://www.fas.org/irp/offdocs/NSChistory.htm>.
—— 'Implementation of Specific Articles', Initial Report of the United States of America to the UN Committee Against Torture, 15 October 1999. <http://lawofwar.org/U.S._exceptions_regarding_Torture_Convention.htm>
—— 'Second Periodic Report of the United States of America to the Committee Against Torture', 6 May 2005. <http://www.state.gov/documents/organization/62175.pdf>
—— 'Jordan—Country Reports on Human Rights Practices for 2005', 8 March 2006. <http://www.state.gov/g/drl/rls/hrrpt/2005/61691.htm>

—— 'Syria—Country Reports on Human Rights Practices for 2003', 25 February 2004. <http://www.state.gov/g/drl/rls/hrrpt/2003/27938.htm>

Welshofer, Lewis E., 'Rebuttal to General Letter of Reprimand', Memorandum for Commander, 82nd ABD DIV, 11 February 2004. <http://www.lchr.org/pdf/mem-dic021104.pdf>

Woolfolk, Donald D., 'Declaration', 13 June 2002. <http://news.findlaw.com/hdocs/docs/hamdi/hamdi61302wlflkdec.pdf#search=%22Donald%20D%20Woolfolk%22>

Yoo, John C., 'Interrogation Methods to be Used During the Current War on Terrorism', Memorandum for Alberto R. Gonzales, 1 August 2002. <http://news.findlaw.com/wp/docs/doj/bybee80102ltr.html>

Yoo, John, and Robert J. Delahunty, 'Application of Treaties and Laws to al Qaeda and Taliban Detainees', Memorandum for William J. Haynes II, 9 January 2002. <http://www.msnbc.msn.com/id/5197853/site/newsweek>

INDEX

*Human Resource Exploitation Training
    Manual* 12, 84–6, 88, 90, 93–4, 95, 142,
    200–15
Human Rights Watch 112
humiliation 12, 24, 30, 38, 48, 50, 74, 77,
    84, 86, 105, 106, 109, 112, 116, 123,
    129, 133, 153, 167, 170, 187, 192; *see
    also* debility, dependency, and dread
    (DDD); religion tactics; sex tactics
Hungary 14–16, 31, 40
Hunter, Edward 17, 29
Husband, Thomas 80
Hussein, Saddam 164, 174, 177, 193
Huu, Luu Van 61
hypnosis 15, 18, 21, 23, 24, 32, 211–12
hypothermia 12, 32, 34, 40, 48, 58, 59, 67,
    75, 89, 91, 100, 103, 105, 108, 114, 130,
    131, 135, 136, 147, 152, 153, 163, 170,
    174–5, 176, 182, 185, 188, 191, 195,
    201; *see also* water techniques;
    'waterboarding'

'international terrorists' 137–8; *see also*
    'unlawful enemy combatant'
INDUMIL (*Industrias Militares*) 91–2, 95
Inspector General Report 25, 27, 93
International Committee of the Red Cross
    (ICRC) 125, 126, 166–7, 196
International Criminal Court (ICC)
    131–2; *see also* Office of Legal Counsel
    (OLC)
International Police Academy (IPA) 61, 76,
    79, 88
International Telephone and Telegraph
    Company (ITT) 15, 31
International Voluntary Services (IVS) 68
International War Crimes Tribunal (1967)
    40; *see also* Duncan, Donald
Interrogación (Interrogation manual) 83
interrogation *see* coercion; rapport-building;
    torture
interrogation logbook 149–51; *see also*
    Qahtani, Mohammad al-
Iqbal, Asif 141–2, 155, 157–8
Iran 88
Iraq 1, 12, 13, 106, 136, 161–7, 172–3, 177,
    181, 190, 193–4; *see also* Abu Ghraib
    (Iraq); Camp Nama (Iraq)
Ireland v United Kingdom (1978) 108

Islam 2, 4, 5, 114, 142, 154–5, 160, 169,
    170
isolation 6, 9, 10, 29, 30, 31, 32, 33, 37, 40,
    42–7, 50, 51, 55, 56, 57, 62, 84, 86, 107,
    111, 112, 115, 129, 133, 147, 157, 158,
    159, 160, 162, 182, 195, 205; *see also*
    sensory deprivation
isolation box 37, 42, 99; *see also* isolation;
    sensory deprivation
Israel 107–8, 121, 155, 156, 191, 197
Italy 1, 20, 100
Ivan the Terrible 49

Jackson Heights (New York) 15
Jacoby, Lowell E. 140
Jamadi, Manadel al- 173
Jerome, Clayton C. 34
jihad 9, 160
Joint Task Force Guantánamo (JTF
    GTMO) 140, 143, 145–52, 155–7;
    see also Guantánamo Bay (Cuba)
Jones, Walter B. 115
Jordan 1, 118, 121, 174, 195
Jornal do Brasil 79
Journey Into Madness (1989) 70

Kabul (Afghanistan) 122, 137
Kahane, Meir 2
Kandahar (Afghanistan) 5, 8–9
Karachi (Pakistan) 7
Karpinski, Janis L. 165, 173
Keller, Dr Allen 198
Kennedy, John F. 57, 121, 169
Kennedy, Joseph P. 82, 95
KGB (Commmittee for State Security)
    48–50, 57, 83, 142, 192
Khalden (Afghanistan) 118–19
Kherchtou, L'Houssaine 119–20
Kimmons, John 181, 184
Kirkpatrick, John 92
Koestler, Arthur 29–30, 47
Kooijmans, Peter 197
Koran 9, 155, 163; *see also* religion
    tactics
Korea *see* North Korea; South Korea
Korean War 59, 99, 101, 124
Kosovo 4
Kosovo Liberation Army (KLA) 4
Kremlin 99

ACKNOWLEDGEMENTS

This book would not have been possible without the kind support of Dr Ken Macnab, Stuart Rees and Dr Wendy Lambourne of the Centre for Peace and Conflict Studies at the University of Sydney. Their encouragement proved invaluable along the long road to publication. I'd also like to express my sincere gratitude to Luke Fletcher and Harold Braswell for their time with the drafts, and to Christopher Hodson for early help with the case law. Thank you Jeremy Wortsman for directing me to the right places. Thank you Nick Walker and Foong Ling Kong for seeing the potential in the work. Finally, I am indebted to my parents Bernard and Sandra, sisters Michelle and Sharon, and Jessica Sumaryo for their love and patience.